The Church of England and the Home Front 1914–1918

Civilians, Soldiers and Religion in Wartime Colchester

Robert Beaken

with a Foreword by Terry Waite CBE

THE BOYDELL PRESS

First published 2015
The Boydell Press, Woodbridge

ISBN 978 1 78327 051 4

The Boydell Press is an imprint of Boydell & Brewer Ltd
PO Box 9, Woodbridge, Suffolk IP12 3DF, UK
and of Boydell & Brewer Inc.
668 Mount Hope Ave, Rochester, NY 14620–2731, USA
website: www.boydellandbrewer.com

A catalogue record for this book is available
from the British Library

The publisher has no responsibility for the continued existence or accuracy of
URLs for external or third-party internet websites referred to in this book, and
does not guarantee that any content on such websites is, or will remain, accurate
or appropriate

This publication is printed on acid-free paper

Printed and bound in Great Britain by
TJ International Ltd, Padstow, Cornwall

The Church of England and the Home Front
1914–1918

'The Place of Meeting' by Thomas Noyes-Lewis

To ACDB, LAB, CSB and LKB

The author and the Boydell Press gratefully acknowledge the generous support afforded to the publication of this book by:

The Anglo-Catholic History Society

Essex Heritage Trust

The Scouloudi Foundation in association with the Institute of Historical Research

Isobel Thornley's Bequest to the University of London

Contents

Illustrations

Figures

Tables

The author is grateful to the Rev. Canon Philip Ursell for supplying the
frontispiece; to Mr John Byfield for supplying photos 4, 8, 12, 13, 21, 22, 23,
25, 28 and 29; to Mrs Sarah Bradley for supplying photos 7, 9, 10, 16 and
20; and to Mr A.J. Maxse for supplying photo 18. Photos 14, 24 and 25
are reproduced from the collection of local material compiled by A.M.
Jarmin during his mayoralty of Colchester, 1917–18, Local Studies, Colchester Central Library; and photos 15, 19, 26 and 27 from E.A. Hunt, ed.,
Colchester War Memorial Souvenir.

Foreword by Terry Waite CBE

The late Robert Runcie, one-time archbishop of Canterbury and, incidentally, a distinguished holder of the Military Cross, frequently proclaimed that 'nothing was real unless it was local'. Mischievously, his private staff requested that he define what he meant by 'real', even though they knew full well what he really meant.

In a world where history is too often relegated to a lowly place in the school curriculum, another distinguished scholar, Dr Robert Beaken, has done a distinct service to Colchester in recording the impact of the First World War on that ancient garrison town. He has written a focused and detailed local history which he has placed in its wider context, and his careful research has revealed some fascinating statistics. Who would have thought that the Borough of Colchester Social Club for the Troops, well supported by the Church of St Mary-at-the-Walls, would have distributed eleven tons of cake to hungry troops during the war years? That is indeed a lot of cake!

However, Dr Beaken does not confine his research to statistics. Throughout the centuries, Christians of every persuasion have been divided in their attitude to warfare, and the Church of England, as located in and around Colchester, was no exception. The episcopate urged the clergy to remain in their parishes, in order to give pastoral care to the many hundreds of people who were bereaved or who were suffering from other forms of distress as a result of the war. Understandably, such were the social pressures, and their individual convictions, that not all priests felt able to obey this injunction. Most clergy did, and this book illustrates how the Anglican parishes of Colchester served their community in diverse ways during harsh and difficult years of 1914–18. As might be expected, there are many references to the army, and the interaction between the civilian population and the troops, both positive and negative, is well documented.

There has been much controversy across the years in respect of the Church's attitude to warfare, and in particular concerning the thorny question of the blessing of weapons of war. The author quotes research conducted by the director of the Army Chaplaincy Museum, who has been unable to uncover any such incidents, apart from the naming of an aircraft by an obscure princess in 1918. The myth continues, but, says the author, there are no documents to support this claim.

Reading this book, one is reminded what enormous changes have taken place in both Church and society during in the last one hundred years. Then, there was little doubt that the Church of England was in fact the Church for *all* the people of the country, regardless of their religious or political persuasion. Organisations such as the Church of England Men's Society or the Church Lads Brigade flourished, as did their female equivalents. The Church of England was a force to be reckoned with in the Colchester of the early twentieth century, and, without question, it played a substantial role in bringing comfort to those in distress, and in enabling wartime society to hold together.

Dr Beaken clearly shows the impact that the global conflict of 1914–18 had on a local community, and the response of the Church of England. It was real and meaningful, and Dr Runcie would have fully approved.

Terry Waite CBE

Hartest
Suffolk

Author's Acknowledgements

For eight years, it was my privilege to serve as the vicar of a parish in Colchester. Upon taking up my new post, I quickly became aware of the presence of the army in the town: my parish contained the army rifle range, and our services were sometimes irritatingly punctuated by the sound of gunfire; I regularly passed the impressive array of Victorian barracks and military buildings on the southern edge of Colchester, with armed sentries at the gates and names echoing Britain's imperial past; my congregation contained serving soldiers, former soldiers and the families of soldiers; and, in a curious echo of the world of 1914, I soon found myself elected a member of the Colchester Garrison Officers' Club, where there had once been a dramatic scene in August 1914 at the outbreak of the First World War.

As I grew to know Colchester and visited the other parish churches, I noticed that they all contained First World War memorials, ranging from simple brass tablets in my own church to an elaborate Warriors' Chapel in St Mary-at-the-Walls. One end of the High Street, near Colchester Castle, is dominated by what is arguably one of the most impressive and beautiful war memorials – if a war memorial can be said to be a thing of beauty – in England. There were also memorials to the 1914–18 war in the churches of other denominations, as well as in Colchester town hall, the police station, the post office, the borough cemetery, the cavalry barracks, the Royal Grammar School, Colchester Scouts St George's Club, the Co-op restaurant, the Eastern Counties Hospital, the Goat and Boot public house, the Ancient Order of Foresters court room, the Oddfellows Hall, in an insurance office and in a printing works.[1]

---

[1] There is a very impressive index of all memorials of the First World War in Essex in an appendix of Paul Rusiecki's *The Impact of Catastrophe: The People of Essex and the First World War (1914–1920)* (Essex Record Office, Chelmsford, 2008) pp. 401–41

The First World War had evidently had a very considerable impact on Colchester, an important and historic garrison town. I began to wonder what had been the history of Colchester's seventeen Anglican parish churches, twenty-six priests and suffragan bishop during 1914–18, what had been their relationship with the army, and how this related to the wider picture. This book is the result of that train of thought.

As I began to delve into the wartime history of Colchester, it became apparent to me that, fortuitously, the town was a very good one to research, not least because there was an excellent archive with a cache of material relating to the First World War, some of which had been untouched for years. Colchester in 1914–18 was a microcosm of both English society and the Church of England, in all their diversity: at once big enough to contain all this variety, and yet, geographically, not so large that one's imagination struggled to take it all in, in the way that it might have done when confronted with a large city such as London.

The presence of the army, additionally, meant that trends and experiences which were noticeable elsewhere in England in 1914–18 – for example, the impact of wide-scale bereavement, the growth of prayers for the dead, or the wartime exhaustion of the clergy – were sharply felt in Colchester.

This book could not have been written without the help of many people, to whom I should like to record my most grateful thanks and appreciation.

I thank Her Majesty Queen Elizabeth II for graciously granting me permission to use material from the diaries and papers of King George V in the Royal Archives at Windsor Castle.

My especial thanks go to Mr Terry Waite for reading my text, contributing a foreword and encouraging me in this project.

I am particularly indebted to the late Mr Christopher Whitcombe, son of the Right Rev. Dr Robert Whitcombe, bishop of Colchester, 1909–22, who made available to me his family papers and photographs and answered my many questions. My special thanks must go to Mr Andrew Phillips of the Essex Archaeological Society for all his help and encouragement. I am also most grateful to Mrs Jane Bedford and Mr Paul Coverley of the Essex Record Office, and to Mr Richard Shackle and Dr David Muscat of the Local Studies Department of Colchester Library.

I should also like to thank many other people who have kindly helped me with my research, answered my questions, given me lines of inquiry or otherwise been of assistance: The late Rev. Victor Allard; the Rev. Dr Allan Barton; the late Lieutenant-Colonel Sir John Baynes; Miss Mary Beattie; the Rev. Stuart Bell; Mr David Blake, curator of the Museum of Army Chaplaincy; Ms Rachel Boulding; Mrs Sarah Bradley; Mr Mike Brown; Mrs Jenny Buckley; Professor Arthur Burns; the Rev. Dr Perry Butler; Mr John Byfield; the Right Rev. and Right Hon. Dr Richard Chartres; Miss Pamela Clark, senior archivist, the Royal Archives; Chief Inspector Alan Cook, Essex Police; the Right Rev. Stephen Cottrell; Ms Jessica Cuthbert-Smith; the Rev. Paul Davis; Major (retd) Margaret Easey of the Royal Army Chaplains' Department; Mr Tom Foakes, curator of the Museum of the Most Venerable Order of the Hospital of St John of Jerusalem; Mr Christopher Gowing; Mr Jim Graham; the Very Rev. Dr John Hall; the late Rev. Canon Gordon Hewitt; the Right Rev. Edward Holland; Mr Ian Hook, keeper of the Essex Regiment Museum; Colonel Joe Hordern; Mr Marcus Humphreys; the Right Hon. Lord Hurd of Westwell; Dr Heather Jones; Professor Peter Jones; the late Sir John Keegan; Mr A.J. Maxse; Lord Neidpath; Mr Simon Noyes-Lewis; Professor J.S. Oxford; Mr Robert Penkett; the Ven. T.W. Pritchard; the Right Rev. Dr Geoffrey Rowell; Mrs Vera Ruddock of the Office for National Statistics; Dr Paul Rusiecki; Mr James and Mrs Gabrielle Service; Mrs Janet Smith; Dr Mark Smith; Dr Michael Snape; Dr Laurel Spooner; the late Ven. Ernie Stroud; Dr Alan Tadiello; the Rev. Canon Barry Thompson; Mr David Tippett; the Rev. Canon Philip Ursell; the Right Rev. Martin Wallace; Mr Jeremy and Dr Gudrun Warren; the late Rev. Gordon Watkins; the late Earl of Wemyss and March; Dr Robert Whitcombe; the Rev. Canon Alan Wilkinson; the Rev. Canon Robin Wilson; Dr Tim Winder.

I should also like to thank the staff of the following institutions: Balliol College, Oxford; Chelmsford Cathedral Library; the Church of England Record Centre; the Church Union; Colchester Borough Council; Colchester and District Clerical Society; Colchester Garrison Officers' Club; Colchester Library, Local Studies Department; Colchester and Ipswich Museums; Essex Archaeological Society; the University of Essex, Albert Sloman Library; Essex Records Office; Hertfordshire County Council Archives; the Imperial War Museums, Departments of Documents and Printed Books; Lambeth Palace Library; the Ministry of Defence; The National Archives; the National Army Museum,

Department of Archives; Pusey House, Oxford; the Red Cross; the Royal Archives, Windsor Castle; the Royal British Legion.

The publishers and I are grateful to all the institutions and individuals listed for permission to reproduce the materials in which they hold copyright. Every effort has been made to trace the copyright holders; apologies are offered for any omission, and the publishers will be pleased to add any necessary acknowledgement in subsequent editions.

Lastly, I should like to record my indebtedness to three survivors from the Colchester of 1914–18: Jack Ashton, Alice Hicks and Dolly Thimblethorpe, who kindly allowed me to interview them before their deaths, and shared their recollections, photographs and good humour with me.

Robert Beaken

Great Bardfield
Essex

1

The First World War – One Hundred Years On

For the generation that lived, fought and endured between 1914 and 1918, the First World War was frequently understood as nothing less than the 'Great War for Civilization'.[1] Not for nothing does Lutyen's Cenotaph in Whitehall (erected 1920) bear the inscription 'Our Glorious Dead'. A very different view of the First World War, as a tragic and cruel waste of young human life (which, of course, it would be impossible to deny), began to arise half a generation later in the late 1920s and 1930s. This was fed by the growth of pacifism and appeasement as the world drifted towards an almost unthinkable Second World War. To take one example, General (later Field Marshal) Sir Douglas Haig, Commander-in-Chief of the British Armies in France between 1915 and 1918, whose reputation was very high as 'the man who won the war' between the Armistice in 1918 and his death in 1928, was later portrayed by some as 'Butcher Haig', a bogeyman upon whom was focused the blame for what was perceived as the needless loss of hundreds of thousands of young lives on the Western Front.[2] The fact that Great Britain found itself at war

---

[1]   These words appear on the reverse of the Inter-Allied Victory Medal. They were also sometimes inscribed on war memorials

[2]   When Haig died in 1928, 100,000 people filed past his coffin in Edinburgh. Seventy years later, a national newspaper mounted a campaign for his statue in Whitehall to be destroyed. G. Corrigan, *Mud, Blood and Poppycock* (Cassell, London, 2003), p. 13.

Haig's statue in Edinburgh Castle was moved in 2009 from its prominent position on the esplanade to a less impressive position in Hospital Square, on the grounds that it was obscured for part of the year by seating erected on the esplanade for the Edinburgh Tattoo and was a hazard, *Scotsman*, 17 June 2009. Haig's statue does not appear to have been deemed a problem during the preceding fifty years of the Tattoo;. eight other military monuments and statues were left in situ on the Castle esplanade.

Three years earlier, in 2006, the Royal British Legion in Scotland had renamed the Earl Haig Fund as 'Poppyscotland'. Kevin Gray, of the national board of trustees of Legion Scotland, explained in 2014 that the reason 'was because Earl Haig had

Germany again a quarter of a century later added to this view of the First World War as a tragic waste, and as a job only half done, which needed doing again properly.

As the First World War has passed out of living memory, so a more nuanced and balanced understanding has slowly begun to be formulated by historians and writers. Douglas Haig, to continue the example, has started to be reappraised. Although he had his faults, and may be reasonably criticised for some of his decisions, Haig has begun to re-emerge as a better, more gifted and caring commander-in-chief than has long been thought. To take one instance of this change in attitude, the Royal British Legion, which in 1994 had replaced the words 'Haig Fund' with 'Poppy Appeal' on the black centre of its poppies,[3] in 2009 named its new London headquarters 'Haig House'.

Similarly, modern research has shown that if Kaiser Wilhelm II's German empire was not as wicked as Hitler's Third Reich, it was still a militaristic, expansionist and constitutionally unbalanced regime, whose soldiers were responsible for inflicting atrocities upon thousands of civilians in Belgium and France during the war.[4]

One area that has received scant treatment in many of the studies of life in Britain during the First World War is religion. Put simply, if Christianity is not a significant factor in the lives or mental outlook of many modern writers about the First World War, they can sometimes all too easily assume that Christianity was likewise not a meaningful factor in the lives or mental outlook of their subjects a century ago; or it may be that they fail to understand fully the significance of some of the references to Christianity they encounter in their research.

This is emblematic of another contemporary problem: a tendency to picture the men and women of 1914–18 as being just like early twenty-first-century men and women, and to read back into their lives the way in which *we* think and react. In truth, the generation that lived through, and participated in, the First World War were all Victorians, with outlooks and understandings formed during the nineteenth century. For such people,

become somewhat of a toxic brand due to his involvement at the Somme' www.legionscotland.org.uk/news-events/frequently-asked-questions

[3]   Mr Bill Kay, general manager of the Poppy factory, Richmond, to the author, 8 December 2014

[4]   J. Horne and A. Kramer, *German Atrocities 1914: A History of Denial* (Yale University Press, New Haven, CT, and London, 2001), pp. 13–86

Christianity was an important element in their culture, world-view and, in many instances, personal lives. In order to understand life in Britain during the First World War, one must take account of the role played by Christianity, which in England predominantly means the role played by the parishes of the Church of England, the Established Church.

In this book I have sought to recreate the wartime life of Colchester, an important garrison town in north-east Essex, and to understand the part played by its parish churches and their ministry between 1914 and 1918 to soldiers and civilians. The book will begin with a description of Colchester, its parishes and clergy in August 1914, followed by an overview of the impact of the war on the town. We shall then examine the wartime roles and experiences of clergy and laity, and observe how pre-war patterns of ministry and worship were successfully adapted to meet changed needs and conditions. We will look at the National Mission of Repentance and Hope in 1916 and see how Anglicans of all churchmanships collaborated in a not unsuccessful attempt to bring the comfort and challenge of the Gospel to the townsfolk during the war. We shall see how the conflict both narrowed and broadened outlooks, and the book concludes with a study of the development of the rituals of remembrance.

One idea that has been widely repeated by writers and historians, largely without question, is the notion that the Church of England had a 'bad' First World War. This book will challenge that conception, and will demonstrate that the Church of England had a mixed, and on the whole, a better war, at a parochial level, than has long been believed.

2

Colchester

Colchester is situated on the river Colne in Essex, fifty-two miles north-east of London and six miles south of Suffolk, and claims to be Britain's oldest recorded town. By the time of the Roman invasion of England in AD 43, Colchester was an important centre for trade between East Anglia and the continent, and under Roman rule it grew and flourished as a *colonia* or major colony and the first capital of Roman Britain. The Romans developed the port at Sheepen, and good communications ensured that Colchester became an important strategic and economic centre. Colchester remains very conscious of its Roman past: the town is still encircled by the walls constructed by the Roman military engineers, the broad High Street follows the outline of the old Roman arena, and the castle is built on the ruins of the temple of Claudius, later destroyed by Queen Boadicea.

By 1914, the population of Colchester was 43,452.[1] Some of the townsfolk still lived within the Roman walls, but during the nineteenth century the town had expanded beyond them. Upper middle-class housing for the town's professional families had been built along the Lexden Road to the west. Much of Colchester's working-class population lived to the east at the Hythe, in overcrowded and poor conditions – some little better than slums – near to the factories and workshops that had developed in that quarter because of its proximity to the docks and the railway. To the south-east, lower middle-class terraced houses and villas had been built at New Town, whilst to the south-west sprawled the barracks. North of the Roman walls, 'respectable' working-class housing had been developed near to the North Railway Station in the St Paul's district. The town had two other railway stations: St Botolph's Station at the bottom of the Mersea Road, and the Hythe Station by the river.

---

[1] 1911 Census, revised 1912, quoted in *Benham's Almanack and Directory for Colchester, 1914,* p. 4

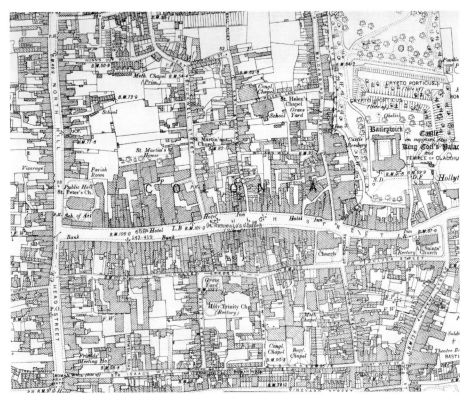

1 Map of Colchester High Street and town centre

In 1914, Colchester remained an important agricultural centre for north Essex and south Suffolk, with regular markets and auctions of livestock. Flour milling and brewing were important local industries. During the last quarter of the nineteenth century, however, the town experienced a belated, but nevertheless important, industrialisation. Three firms came to predominate: Catchpool, Stannard and Stanford, who manufactured farm machinery; A.G. Mumford's, who made marine pumps, compound engines and nautical equipment for the Royal Navy, the merchant navy and the Russian and Italian navies; and James Paxman's Standard Iron-works, which exported electrical equipment for the South African mines, refrigerating equipment for ships in the South American meat trade and carbon-dioxide compressors for the Royal Navy and the Japanese navy.[2]

2 A. Brown, *Colchester, 1815–1914* (Essex Record Office, Chelmsford, 1980), pp. 26ff

2 Colchester High Street and town hall in the early twentieth century

Colchester Garrison

A major influence upon Colchester's life and economy in 1914 was the presence of the garrison. Colchester has been a military centre since Roman times and has housed a garrison intermittently ever since. Towards the end of the Crimean War, the army constructed a large temporary camp to the south of the town between the Mersea and Military Roads.[3] After the Crimean War, the government decided to establish a permanent garrison in Colchester, and barracks were built to replace tents and billets. In 1864, the garrison was increased by the completion of the cavalry barracks on the Abbey Fields, and in 1866 Colchester became the headquarters of

[3]   J. Stone, 'Colchester', *Garrison: Ten British Military Towns*, ed. P. Dietz (Brassey's, London, 1986), pp. 3–22, p. 14

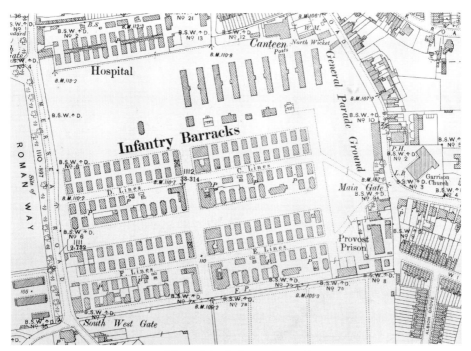

3 Map of the Infantry Barracks

the army's Eastern District. The garrison brought economic renewal to Colchester, and by 1869 it was estimated to be worth £80,000 per annum to the town.[4] This was particularly important after the 1870s when East Anglia began to be affected by a long period of agricultural depression.

The presence of a permanent garrison, however, had its drawbacks. Drunkenness and brawling between soldiers and townsfolk in Colchester became a problem, as did prostitution.[5] Many public houses were fronts for brothels, and in 1870 Sir Henry Storks, the Liberal parliamentary candidate, was defeated in a particularly vicious by-election because of his support for the Contagious Diseases Act, which sought to limit venereal disease in garrison towns by means of compulsory medical examination and treatment, when necessary, of prostitutes brought before magistrates by the police.[6]

---

[4] Stone, 'Colchester', p. 16
[5] Brown, *Colchester*, p. 36. In 1914 Colchester had 181 public houses or one for every 206 of the population. By comparison, the figure for Cardiff was one public house for every 618 of the population
[6] Stone, 'Colchester', p. 15. Brown, *Colchester*, pp. 167ff

Following the Crimean War and the Indian Mutiny, there were sustained attempts – largely, but not entirely, by evangelical Anglicans and Nonconformists – to 'Christianise' army officers and troops by means of the distribution of Bibles, Christian literature and tracts, the establishment of soldiers' institutes and reading rooms, the holding of Bible classes and religious meetings, and so forth. At the same time, the army itself sought to offer its troops improved religious and pastoral care by reorganising and expanding the work of its Chaplains' Department.[7]

As the nineteenth century drew to a close, the friction between the army and the townsfolk of Colchester gradually evaporated; drunkenness and prostitution did not entirely disappear, but they became less noticeable, and the townsfolk started to feel rather proud of their garrison. The first troops to leave England for the Boer War in 1899 departed by train from Colchester and were waved off by an enormous crowd. A newspaper reporter wrote after the relief of Mafeking in 1900, 'Colchester's celebration of Mafeking will never be forgotten in the Borough.'[8] Between 1898 and 1906 the War Office bought more land for Goojerat, Kirklee and McMunn barracks, Reed Hall Camp, and the Ordnance depot.

The garrison played an important part in Colchester's social life. On Sundays many of the townsfolk would stroll over to watch the troops marching behind their band to the Garrison Church or to listen to the band playing after the service. The town's leading citizens were frequently invited to dinners and balls organised by the officers' messes, military bands played at social events and regimental teams participated in cricket matches and other sporting activities. Many officers and soldiers married into local families and settled in Colchester after retirement.

At the outbreak of war in August 1914, Colchester housed part of the Regular 4th Division, including the 11th Infantry Brigade, whose fighting units comprised the 1st Battalion, the Somersetshire Light Infantry (Prince Albert's), the 1st Battalion, the Hampshire Regiment and the 1st Battalion, the Rifle Brigade (Prince Consort's Own). The brigade commander was Temporary Brigadier General Sir Aylmer Hunter-Weston, a much-decorated veteran of Egypt and South Africa. Colchester also housed the XIV Brigade, the Royal Field Artillery, comprising the 39th,

[7]   O. Anderson, 'The Growth of Christian Militarism in Mid-Victorian Britain', *English Historical Review* 86 (January 1971), 46–72

[8]   Stone, 'Colchester', p. 17

4 1st Battalion, Gordon Highlanders, parading on the Abbey Fields,
Colchester, *c.*1911

68th and 88th Batteries, and the 20th Hussars, part of the 5th Cavalry
Brigade. The 9th Company of the Army Veterinary Corps was located
in Colchester, as was a section of the 6th Company, the Army Ordnance
Corps. The town also housed a large military hospital. The last figures
available for the garrison before the war are from 1912, when the garrison
consisted of 4,161 officers and men and 691 female dependants.[9]

Social Class

Dick Porter, a prominent Colchester solicitor who grew up in a prosperous family in the town in the early years of the twentieth century,
described Colchester's hierarchical society before and during the First
World War thus: 'The shopkeepers ran the Council, the clergy spoke to
everyone, the professionals kept themselves aloof, and you needed permission to speak to the Brigade of Guards.' The latter was a reference
to the army officers and their families who lived in houses owned by
the army in The Avenue, Ireton Road, Irvine Road and Victoria Road.[10]
Jack Ashton, a young working-class man in 1914, recalled Colchester as

[9]   *Benham's Directory*, 1914, p. 4
[10] Mr Andrew Phillips, letter to the author, 19 January 1999. Mr Phillips interviewed
      Dick Porter prior to his death in 1998

being a highly stratified and class-conscious town.[11] The local newspapers gave the impression that life in the town was dominated by a small social elite of perhaps some 2,000 mostly upper middle-class and professional people, such as aldermen, borough officials, army officers, industrialists, clergy, doctors and lawyers. Two noticeable features of Colchester's social elite were: (1) that its members were predominantly upper middle class, rather than upper class; and (2) that they were not necessarily indigenous, many having settled in Colchester once they had made their money or otherwise established themselves in other parts of the country or British Empire. Most had been educated at public schools or independent grammar schools. The men and women of Colchester's social elite usually knew each other, frequently socialised together and often intermarried. Churchwardens and other significant Anglican laypeople, such as the 'officers' of Church organisations, were usually drawn from the social elite.

At the other end of the spectrum there existed an underclass of around 2,000 people who lived in poverty and in appalling housing conditions, mostly in the Hythe district of Colchester.

In between were to be found the bulk of Colchester's population: a small middle class and a much larger working class, leading lives of more or less frugal respectability. Unless they commuted by train to Chelmsford or London, they probably worked in Colchester and sent their children to its Church or council schools. They led more comfortable lives than their parents and grandparents but were always afraid of illness and poverty. The ultimate disgrace was to end up in the town's workhouse.

Politics

For much of the late nineteenth century, Colchester elected Liberal town councils and members of Parliament, but the first decade of the twentieth century saw a revival of the Conservative vote. In 1910 a Conservative MP was elected, Laming Worthington-Evans, and shortly afterwards the Conservatives took control of Colchester borough council. This was not as significant as might be imagined: Liberal and Conservative councillors were all drawn from Colchester's elite and there was often a

---

[11]   Mr Jack Ashton, interview, 10 February 1998

Gules, two staves raguly and couped argent, one in pale, surmounted by another in fess between two ducal coronets in chief Or the bottom part of the shaft enfiled with a ducal coronet of the last

5 The arms of the borough of Colchester in 1914

degree of cooperation between them, even on occasion to the extent of one party not putting up a candidate in certain wards during borough elections to ensure that the other party's candidate was returned, and the Labour candidate was kept out. Following the outbreak of war in 1914, Worthington-Evans obtained a commission in a cavalry regiment and spent a short time on the staff of General Plumer before returning to politics and a seat in the cabinet as minister for war.[12]

The Diocese of Chelmsford and its Bishops

Christianity is thought to have come to Colchester with the Roman legions. A bishop from Colchester is believed to have been present at the Synod of Arles in AD 314, and the remains of a small basilica dating from AD 320–40 may be seen besides the Colchester police station. For nine centuries, Essex was part of the diocese of London, but by the mid-nineteenth century the diocese had become too large and unwieldy.

[12]   E.A. Hunt, ed., *Colchester War Memorial Souvenir* (Essex Telegraph, Colchester, 1923), p. 57

In 1845 an Act of Parliament transferred Essex and Hertfordshire to the diocese of Rochester in Kent. This was not a successful arrangement, and in 1877 the new diocese of St Albans was created to cover both Essex and Hertfordshire. The suffragan bishopric of Colchester was revived in 1882, and a further suffragan bishopric of Barking was created in 1901 to try to cope with the growing population of Essex, which then included those parts of east London situated to the east of the river Lea. The Right Rev. Edgar Jacob, who was appointed bishop of St Albans in 1903, soon came to realise that his diocese was too large and populous to be manageable, and that the only workable solution was to create a separate diocese for Essex and 'London-over-the-borders'. It was agreed in principle in 1906 to establish a new diocese, but it was eight years before this was finally achieved. In the meantime, there was much wrangling to try to obtain funding for the new diocese, and six Essex towns competed to become the new cathedral city. Colchester borough council spent ratepayers' money on a campaign to persuade the Church authorities that the new diocese should be centred on Colchester, and they even went so far as to commission architects' proposals to turn St James's Church in East Hill into the cathedral and to build an adjacent close to house the cathedral clergy. In the end, the less historic county town of Chelmsford was selected, principally on the grounds that it was in the centre of Essex and nearer London.

The new diocese of Chelmsford was created by an order-in-council on 23 January 1914. It contained 463 benefices and 1,355,156 people and embraced a vast and diverse area. In the west were the populous suburbs of east London, in the south were the docks and the industrial area around Tilbury, whilst on the east coast were the holiday resorts of Walton-on-the-Naze, Frinton, Clacton and Southend. The centre and north of the diocese was predominantly agricultural.[13]

The first bishop of Chelmsford was John Edwin Watts-Ditchfield, who was offered the bishopric by the prime minister, H.H. Asquith, on 27 January 1914, only four days after the creation of the diocese. Watts-Ditchfield was born in 1861, the son of a Nonconformist Warrington cotton worker who had gone on to become the headmaster of a board school in Patricroft, Manchester. The young Watts-Ditchfield was

---

[13]   E.N. Gowing, *John Edwin Watts-Ditchfield, First Bishop of Chelmsford* (Hodder and Stoughton, London, 1926), p. 132

Or, on a saltire gules a sword in bend sinister argent, the hilt in base gold surmounted in bend dexter by a pastoral staff of the field

6 The arms of the diocese of Chelmsford in 1914

brought up as a Wesleyan Methodist. He underwent a conversion experience aged fourteen during a mission in 1875, and at the age of sixteen became a Wesleyan lay preacher. After a spell as a teacher in Manchester, Watts-Ditchfield began to train for the Wesleyan ministry at Headingly College, Leeds, but when he completed his studies in 1888, he was told there was no vacancy for him in the Wesleyan circuits. He next applied to become a Wesleyan missionary in South Africa, but was once again turned down. One wonders what it was in his personality that worried the Wesleyan authorities.

Having failed to secure ordination as a Wesleyan Methodist, Watts-Ditchfield turned his gaze towards the Church of England. He decided to become an Anglican and was confirmed in Manchester Cathedral in 1888. In January 1889 he arrived in London with just a few shillings in his pocket and secured a job as secretary to the Rev. J. Pullein Thompson, vicar of St Stephen's, North Bow, in the East End of London. From Bow, Watts-Ditchfield went on to study as non-resident student of St John's College, Highbury, an evangelical theological college established for ordinands unable to go to university. He was ordained deacon in 1891 and priest in 1892 in St Paul's Cathedral and served his curacy at St Peter's, Upper Holloway. In 1892 Watts-Ditchfield married Jane Wardell, from Bow, and they had one daughter.

In 1897, the same year that he visited Egypt and the Holy Land, Watts-Ditchfield was appointed as the vicar of St James-the-Less, Bethnal Green, where he revitalised a very poor and deprived parish and showed himself to have a keen social conscience. In 1899 he published *Fishers of Men*, a book about the evangelism of men. Around this time Watts-Ditchfield became a keen worker for the Church Missionary Society, the Church Pastoral Aid Society and a speaker at the Islington clerical conferences, all evangelical bodies. In 1912 he carried out a preaching mission in Australia and New Zealand, and soon he was spoken of in evangelical circles as one who might go far.

The news of Watts-Ditchfield's appointment in 1914 as the first bishop of the new diocese of Chelmsford was far from universally popular in Essex, and fears were expressed about his background and narrow churchmanship. In preparation for his consecration as a bishop in St Paul's Cathedral, he shaved off his moustache, much to the delight of George V.[14] At his enthronement on 21 April 1914, Watts-Ditchfield admitted that he had strong convictions, but he tried to be even-handed in his sermon and pointedly gave thanks for the sacraments as well as the Bible. He said he rejoiced in the Church of England's unbroken connection with the Apostolic Church and three-fold ministry of bishop, priest and deacon, before concluding that his aim and prayer was that 'Essex might be won for her Divine Lord'.[15]

In 2012 parts of some diaries kept by Watts-Ditchfield were discovered the diocesan registry, where they had lain forgotten for many years. One has to bear in mind when reading them that the bishop's diaries are not

---

[14]   Essex Record Office (ERO), Watts-Ditchfield diaries, 26 February 1914. George V here echoed the views of his father, Edward VII, who in 1908 had instructed Cosmo Gordon Lang upon his appointment as archbishop of York that he was to prevent the parties in the Church of England from squabbling and stop the clergy wearing moustaches. In the tradition of the Western Church, priests are usually clean-shaven, unlike the Eastern Church, where they are bearded. Although it was nowhere written down, there was a tradition in the Church of England – rather like the Royal Navy – that the clergy were either clean-shaven or wore full beards, but not moustaches. Some evangelicals grew moustaches as a sign of their churchmanship, though Watts-Ditchfield may have grown his after an accident to his upper lip. Evangelicals also sometimes sported very deep 'jampot' clerical collars (Anglo-Catholic clergy favoured narrow collars) and brown boots instead of black

[15]   G. Hewitt, *A History of the Diocese of Chelmsford* (Diocese of Chelmsford, Chelmsford, 1984), p. 58. Gowing, *Watts-Ditchfield*, pp. 59, 154

continuous, and that some pages are missing; there is also more to a man than what he writes in his diary. Having entered that caveat, the figure that emerges from the diaries is a rather complicated and somewhat angular one. It would be misleading to say that Watts-Ditchfield had a chip on his shoulder about his humble origins, but he was conscious of them and several times recorded that he had sold newspapers in the streets of Patricroft as a boy. He had a strong belief that his life had been shaped by God, and almost a sense of wonder that he now found himself a bishop of the Church of England who was sometimes invited to preach before the king, all of which he put down to the work of Divine Providence.[16] Watts-Ditchfield had a deep and firm evangelical Christian faith – there is no word anywhere of questioning or of religious doubt – and his prayers for his family and friends, his diocese and his own ministry are humbling to read. Rather an austere man – his only relaxation appears to have been smoking cigarettes – Watts-Ditchfield comes across as possessed of a firm and decided character, which some people found attractive. If he had a sense of humour or the ability to laugh at himself, it does not leap out from the pages of his diary. Watts-Ditchfield was not an academic, but neither was he unintelligent. He was also a very hard worker. Watts-Ditchfield did not easily put up with opposition, and one may speculate that there may have been an element of the 'controller' in his psychological make-up. When he arrived in Chelmsford, he seems to have been keen quickly to make his mark upon the bishop of Colchester, as he noted in his diary:

> Had a chat with the Bishop of Colchester – I think we shall get on well together although he is distinctly more in sympathy with things High than is [the bishop of] Barking – after tonight I think he will understand me better.[17]

Watts-Ditchfield could also be sensitive to slights. He felt that Bishop Arthur Winnington-Ingram of London, who had known him for many years, did not quite like or trust him, and he did not much care for Winnington-Ingram in return.[18] In December 1915 Watts-Ditchfield suffered

---

16 ERO, Watts-Ditchfield diaries, 1914, unnumbered fol
17 ERO, Watts-Ditchfield diaries, 8 March 1914
18 ERO, Watts-Ditchfield diaries, 28 January 1914

a bout of depression. After complaining that the Church had not risen to meet the needs of the war and that there was not enough public prayer in churches (neither of which were true, but they reveal something of the state of his mind at that time), Watts-Ditchfield wrote:

> What I want is rest and peace. I am so depressed – terribly depressed – I pray to God to spiritualize me. He knows I want to be all His … I was too tired to go to the Cathedral and am resting at home and am all alone. I am going to pray now. This may be my last year. When I was a boy 2 Phrenologists said I should live to be 55. I don't place reliance [sic] but it is strange I should develop this heart trouble now. Well, in Christ's mercy I am ready, but for the diocese and for my Home's sake [sic] I pray Him to spare me if it be His Will. It shall be God 1st.[19]

The bishop may well have suffered from depression at other times, of which no record remains.

Watts-Ditchfield did also at times display a very warm and caring pastoral heart.[20] During the First World War, he tried by visit or letter to minister to many clergy and laypeople in his diocese who had suffered bereavement. On 4 January 1915, for example, he visited seven families with men killed or wounded, travelling between each by taxi.[21]

At the start of his episcopal ministry in Chelmsford, Watts-Ditchfield wrote that he thought a bishop ought to be 'the biggest soul winner in his Diocese' (which, sadly, is often rather an unrealistic expectation, given the wide range of a bishop's duties). He also wrote, 'I mean with God's help to be a Father in God and not a Prelate.' Unfortunately, Watts-Ditchfield quickly developed an authoritarian and prelatical streak. Some people in Essex thought he did so because he was compensating for his non-Anglican past, or because he was unsure of himself when dealing with clergy who were his academic and social superiors. In fairness, Anglican bishops at the start of the twentieth century were frequently more authoritarian in tone than their successors a century later, but the words 'I cannot permit' appear very often in Watts-Ditchfield's letters in the

---

[19]   ERO, Watts-Ditchfield diaries, 31 December 1915
[20]   For instance, see the rest of his address at the diocesan conference on 27 October 1914, *Essex County Standard*, 31 October 1914
[21]   ERO, Watts-Ditchfield diaries, 4 January 1915

Chelmsford Diocesan Chronicle, and some of the clergy used to dread their monthly appearance.[22]

The question of Watts-Ditchfield's churchmanship is not straightforward. For many years he maintained a warm correspondence with Athelstan Riley, a leading Anglo-Catholic layman, and he surprised many in evangelical circles by ordering a celebration of Holy Communion in all churches in his diocese every Sunday and on all the holy days specified by the Book of Common Prayer. The difficulty was that although the bishop thought that he tried to be even-handed, his background was wholly Wesleyan Methodist and evangelical Anglican, and he had an imperfect understanding of, and little actual sympathy for, other Anglican traditions and churchmanships.

Watts-Ditchfield had a particular distaste for Anglo-Catholic spirituality and forms of worship; he felt that it was his mission to rein in, if not to eradicate, what he regarded as erroneous Anglo-Catholic practices and theology. He frequently noted in his diaries whether the churches he visited or clergy he met were 'high' or were members of the English Church Union.[23] He felt that they were, in many cases, very earnest and sincere, but were misguided, and that it was up to him to show them 'a better way'.[24] He wrote in his diary:

> I fear if I sanction any form of Reservation [of the Blessed Sacrament] I shall grieve my old friends. In my heart I am more strongly convinced of the old Evangelical Doctrinal position but I feel convinced that the sooner we can cease to fight on such questions as Vestments and Incense the better and get to grip with the far greater dangers of compulsory and habitual Confession; of Maridolatry; of Adoration of the Sacred Elements [of Holy Communion] the better [sic]. Does God mean me to lead people that way? May He show me His path and give me grace to follow.[25]

Only sixteen days after being made a bishop, Watts-Ditchfield refused to consecrate a new church unless a crucifix was replaced with a plain cross. He declined to wear a mitre but consented to carry a pastoral staff.

22   ERO, Watts-Ditchfield diaries, 24 February 1914. Hewitt, *Diocese of Chelmsford*, p. 59
23   ERO, Watts-Ditchfield diaries, 10 March 1914, 26 September 1915
24   ERO, Watts-Ditchfield diaries, 25 September 1915
25   ERO, Watts-Ditchfield diaries, 17 September 1915

Before he had even been throned in Chelmsford Cathedral, he had already attempted to ban crucifixes, incense and Tenebrae in the diocese.[26] Later in 1914, Watts-Ditchfield had a row about eucharistic vestments and reservation of the Blessed Sacrament with the Rev. Edward Mears, the rector of Little Bardfield and warden of the Brotherhood of St Paul, an Anglo-Catholic theological college in the village. Mears ordered Watts-Ditchfield to leave his parish and never come back. Watts-Ditchfield never set foot in Little Bardfield again, but he appears to have retaliated by influencing other diocesan bishops to deny ordination to ordinands from the Brotherhood of St Paul, with the result that most of them had to seek ordination overseas at the hands of colonial bishops.[27]

On 24 September 1914, Watts-Ditchfield summoned the Rev. Robert Combe, curate of St Margaret's Church, Leytonstone, and, during an interview of an hour and a quarter, reprimanded him for seeking the heavenly intercession of the Blessed Virgin Mary for the safety of British troops fighting in France and sought to demonstrate to Combe the error of his theological ways.[28] Combe – an Oxford graduate and alumnus of Cuddesdon theological college – presumably found this interview a searing experience. He left Leytonstone the following year and moved to a new post in the diocese of Cariboo, Canada, far away from Watts-Ditchfield.

At his first diocesan conference, on 27 October 1914, Watts-Ditchfield spent half of his address examining questions of liturgy and demanded obedience to his own concept of what the Book of Common Prayer meant. He said – quite incorrectly – that vestments were unlawful in the Church of England, adding that, although he would not take action against clergy already using them, he would not visit any church where vestments were in use, nor permit their introduction elsewhere. Watts-Ditchfield was not entirely satisfied with the worship in his cathedral, complaining, for example, that the watch-night service on New Year's Eve 1915 was too focused on regular communicants and that he disliked the singing of the

---

[26]   ERO, Watts-Ditchfield diaries, 14 March 1914, 18 March 1914, 9 April 1914. For fairness' sake, it should be noted that Watts-Ditchfield's refusal to wear a mitre but willingness to carry a pastoral staff was not at all unusual amongst the bishops in 1914

[27]   R.W.F. Beaken, *Reverence My Sanctuary* (Taverner Publications, East Harling, 2007), p. 46

[28]   ERO, Watts-Ditchfield diaries, 24 September 1914

Litany in procession.[29] Learning in 1915 that the Catholic League (which sought to promote reunion between the Church of England and the Holy See) had 'recommended operations' in St Michael's Church, Walthamstow, Watts-Ditchfield decided, 'I must put it down with a firm hand', though he did also pray for gentleness and a kindly spirit and asked God to take away 'anything that savours of party or self'.[30]

In 1918, Watts-Ditchfield forbad an enclosed community of Anglican nuns at Pleshey to continue reserving the Blessed Sacrament in their chapel, and in the end the community felt constrained to leave his diocese.[31] Nor was the bishop above delivering an unpleasant side-swipe at the Rev. Charles Naters, the Anglo-Catholic vicar of St James's Church, Colchester, with whom he had disagreed, during a controversial sermon which he preached at the unfortunate priest's funeral in 1918.[32] After the First World War, Watts-Ditchfield's outlook broadened slightly, but in 1914 that was still a long way off.

Watts-Ditchfield's wartime pastoral care should not be undervalued, nor should it be overlooked that he was called upon to fashion a new diocese in Essex, a county with many problems and no common identity, at a time of unparalleled national stress. However, it must also be recognised that throughout the First World War the diocese of Chelmsford was led by a controversial bishop who was still finding his feet, and whom, despite his good intentions, many people found hard to get on with. Although his episcopal ministry was certainly not a disaster and had its fair share of successes, the suspicion lingers that Watts-Ditchfield was a better vicar of St James-the-Less, Bethnal Green, than he was a bishop of Chelmsford. Perhaps the attitude of some people in

[29] *Essex County Standard*, 31 October 1914. ERO, Watts-Ditchfield diaries, 31 January 1914, 3 January 1915
[30] ERO, Watts-Ditchfield diaries, 1 November 1915
[31] P.F. Anson, *The Call of the Cloister: Religious Communities and Kindred Bodies in the Anglican Communion* (SPCK, London, 1955), p. 474
[32] 'It would be inappropriate to refer even directly or indirectly to controversial matters, but he thought he knew pretty well something of the inwardness of the life of him whose body lay there. It was not for him (the Bishop) in any way to condemn or to pass judgement as to what had happened in days gone by, but frankly he felt he must in justice to their dear brother, say he thought in his early life he was handled wrongly, and that he developed in him a kind of veneer from which people who only saw that veneer were apt to form a wrong idea of his real character and worth' (ERO, newspaper cutting pasted into St James's, Colchester, register of services, 1918)

7 The bishops of Colchester (the Right Rev. Robert Henry Whitcombe),
Chelmsford (the Right Rev. John Edwin Watts-Ditchfield) and Barking (the
Right Rev. Thomas Stevens), 1914

the diocese towards Watts-Ditchfield is reflected in the highly austere
statue they erected of him above the choir of Chelmsford Cathedral
following his death in 1923.

The suffragan bishop of Colchester in 1914, the Right Rev. Dr Robert
Henry Whitcombe, was a complete contrast to the diocesan bishop.
Whitcombe was born at Milton-next-Gravesend in 1862 and was edu-
cated at Winchester College and at New College, Oxford, where he
obtained a double first in mathematical moderations and natural sciences.
Whilst reading for the Bar, Whitcombe developed a vocation to ordina-
tion in the Church of England. After a spell as a master at Wellington
College, he was ordained deacon in 1888 and priest in 1889 by the bishop

of Oxford and went on to become a master at Eton College, where in 1892 he married Annie Evans, the daughter of the drawing master. In 1899, Whitcombe was appointed the rector of Hardwicke, and in 1903 he became the rector and rural dean of Romford. In 1909 he was appointed suffragan bishop of Colchester and consecrated by Archbishop Randall Davidson in the chapel at Lambeth Palace on 2 February 1909. Bishop Whitcombe was of middle-of-the-road churchmanship, and not of 'High' or Anglo-Catholic churchmanship as Watts-Ditchfield claimed. He soon proved to be a pastoral bishop who was trusted by clergy and laity of all churchmanships. Visitors to Whitcombe's residence, Derby House in The Avenue, Colchester, discovered that the bishop was a good listener, and after his death in 1922 the *Chelmsford Diocesan Chronicle* recorded, 'the clergy never had a more real or true friend. With his wide parochial experience he was able to sympathise with the difficulties of both town and rural clergy.' The bishop's signature – 'R.H. Colchester' – appears in all the surviving service registers of the parishes of Colchester. He also regularly took services in parishes in order that their clergy might go away on holiday.[33]

Whitcombe was an acknowledged expert in finances and pensions and he served on the Chelmsford diocesan board of finance, general purpose, church building and maintenance committees. As there was not yet a diocesan office, these committees met at the Great Eastern Hotel at Liverpool Street Station in London, which was convenient for access by train from all parts of the diocese, as well as for financiers from the City who advised the diocese. Whereas Watts-Ditchfield had a chaplain, secretary and chauffeur, Whitcombe had no chaplain, wrote all his letters by hand and travelled by foot, public transport or in a 'fly' hired from the railway station. As well as being the suffragan bishop of Colchester, he also acted as the archdeacon of Colchester.

When the creation of the new diocese of Chelmsford was announced, many people in Essex had hoped that Whitcombe might be made its first diocesan bishop. The prime minister told Whitcombe that he wanted the new diocese to have an outsider as its first diocesan bishop, but that he hoped to offer Whitcombe another bishopric after a year or two. With

---

[33] J. Foster, *Alumni Oxonienses, 1715–1886* (Parker and Co., Oxford, 1888). 'Obituary', *East Anglian Times*, 20 March 1922. Letter from Christopher J. Whitcombe to the author, 6 July 1998. *Chelmsford Diocesan Chronicle*, April 1922

the benefit of hindsight, Asquith's decision to appoint Watts-Ditchfield instead of Whitcombe was probably right in principle, but wrong in practice. Whitcombe, however, bore no grudges and worked loyally alongside Watts-Ditchfield. By 1920, when Lloyd-George finally offered Whitcombe the bishopric of Hereford, he had been diagnosed with cancer and was obliged to decline. He died nearly two years later.

The suffragan bishop of Barking in 1914 was the Right Rev. Thomas Stevens, a graduate of Magdalene College, Cambridge, and former public school master, but he appears to have played little part in the life of Colchester. The Right Rev. William Harrison, the retired bishop of Glasgow and Galloway, lived on the outskirts of Colchester and was active in the town's churches and on the clergy chapter.

The Parish Churches and their Clergy

Colchester and its suburbs contained seventeen parish churches in 1914, four of which also ran daughter or mission churches. They were staffed by sixteen incumbents and ten curates. Four of the incumbents were aged in their forties, nine in their fifties, two in their sixties and one in his seventies. Four curates were aged in their twenties, three in their thirties, one in his forties and two in their fifties.[34] Twelve priests were graduates of Cambridge, four of Oxford, one of Trinity College, Dublin, and one had attended Durham University without taking a degree. Sixteen of the younger clergy had attended a theological college, but the older clergy were ordained on the strength of a university degree alone, or sometimes without any academic qualification or theological training. At least seven were the sons of clergymen. All were of middle-class or upper middle-class backgrounds, and by their birth and education – if not always by income – they fitted easily into Colchester's social elite.

Before the English Reformation, Colchester was an important centre of monastic life. Several parish boundaries in 1914 reflected the grants of land made to parish churches many centuries earlier by religious communities in the town, with the result that certain districts of Colchester

---

[34] Ages derived from J.A. Venn, *Alumni Cantabrigienses, 1752–1900* (Cambridge University Press, Cambridge, 1951), Foster, *Alumni Oxonienses,* and calculations based upon dates of graduation and ordination in *Crockford's Clerical Directory*

found themselves belonging to a parish church some distance away, with several other parishes in between. Four parishes were Anglo-Catholic: St James's, St Leonard-at-the-Hythe, St Paul's and St Stephen's. Three parishes were evangelical: St Mary Magdalen's, St Nicholas's and St Peter's. The rest were various shades of central, or middle-of-the-road, churchmanship.

St Botolph's was the largest parish in Colchester, with a population of 8,974.[35] The church was built in 1837 next to the remains of the Augustinian priory of St Botolph, off Queen Street. Churchmanship was moderately liturgical and sacramental, though the parish's daughter church of St Stephen's, Canterbury Road, was a centre of advanced Anglo-Catholicism. The vicar was the Rev. Walter Spencer and the curate the Rev. George Behr. St Giles's, next to the remains of Benedictine abbey of St John, which had founded it in around 1097, was the second largest parish with a population of 7,504. The parish had established a mission church of St Barnabas in 1875 in the growing suburb of Old Heath. Both churches were of central churchmanship. The rector was the Rev. John Marsh, who is recalled as a caring and sensitive clergyman whose ministry was somewhat hampered by his rather severe wife.[36] He was assisted by the Rev. William Beale White, an elderly curate with a stammer and a squint, who was kind with children but had a history of never lasting very long in parishes or schools (this was his eleventh post since ordination in 1883).

The best-attended church was St Mary-at-the-Walls, a medieval church built adjacent to the Roman wall, which had been partly destroyed during the siege of Colchester and rebuilt in the 1870s. The parish, with a population of 5,865, included some of the wealthier parts of Colchester and attracted many Anglican members of the town's social elite. In 1914 there were 966 Easter communicants, 300 Sunday school children, and 360 adults attended Bible study classes. The rector was Canon Greville Brunwin-Hales, who was widely popular and gifted with children.[37] He was also the rural dean of Colchester. The parish ran a daughter church of Christ Church in Ireton Road, and Brunwin-Hales held in plurality the

---

[35] Population figures for the parishes of Colchester are taken from the 1914 annual diocesan statistical returns. Other details from C.R. Elrington, ed., *The Victoria County History of Essex, Volume 9* (Oxford University Press, Oxford, 1994)

[36] Mrs Alice Hicks, interview, 18 March 1998

[37] Mr Jack Ashton, interview, 10 February 1998

living of Berechurch, a hamlet on the Mersea Road which had become a suburb of Colchester. Brunwin-Hales was assisted by three curates: the Rev. Stanley Wilson, the Rev. Frank Burnett, a Nonconformist minister who had converted to Anglicanism, and the Rev. Richard Prichard. Under Brunwin-Hales, Mattins and Evensong were said daily in church and there was at least one celebration of Holy Communion each week.

All Saints', near the castle, had a population of 837. The parish was poor and declined through much of the nineteenth century, but its rectors at the end of the century and at the start of the twentieth worked hard to revive parish life, and in 1914 there were 191 Easter communicants. The rector was the Rev. Percival Brinton, formerly a missionary in India. Holy Trinity in Trinity Street was one of Colchester's architectural gems, with a fine Anglo-Saxon tower dating from around the beginning of the eleventh century. The population was 1,450, and parts of the parish were very poor. The rector, the Rev. Espine Monck-Mason, did not live in his parish but in the more salubrious Lexden Road. The churchmanship was very moderately evangelical.

St James's, East Hill, had a population of 1,977. The rector, the Rev. Charles Naters, transformed the church from a large preaching barn into an Anglo-Catholic shrine, introducing incense, vestments, lights and holy pictures. Not everyone liked his ritualistic services, but he was admired as a diligent pastoral visitor. In the summer of 1914, the attention of Colchester was briefly diverted from the war by a consistory court, convoked to investigate a complaint – made by seven Nonconformists living in the parish and one Anglican who had not been to church for thirteen years – that Naters had illegally erected a rood screen.[38] The verdict of the consistory court was that Naters should demolish the screen. The churchwardens supported their rector and complained about the judgement to Bishop Watts-Ditchfield (who, unsurprisingly, was far from sympathetic), and the rood screen remained, in defiance of the court's judgement. From 1907, the parish ran a small daughter church, St Anne's, off the Ipswich Road. Further up the Ipswich Road was St John the Evangelist. The church, designed by Butterfield, served a population of 565. The tradition was fairly moderate, though during the war the vicar, the Rev. Richard Merrett, introduced a votive Eucharist every Thursday, '[with] the special

[38]   *Colchester Gazette*, 29 July and 5 August 1914; *Essex County Standard*, 1 August 1914

intention of asking God's blessing on our ministers and all connected with the war'.[39]

The poorest parish in Colchester was St Leonard-at-the-Hythe, which was also the most Anglo-Catholic. The population of 2,379 was almost entirely poor working class, and the church received financial support from the industrialist James Paxman.[40] The parish developed a Tractarian tradition during the nineteenth century, and the vicar from 1896, the Rev. Henry Carter, reordered the interior of the medieval parish church along Anglo-Catholic lines and from time to time invited the famous Anglo-Catholic priest Father Arthur Stanton of St Alban's, Holborn, to preach.[41] There was a daily Mass and three Masses on Sundays.[42] Henry Carter and his curate the Rev. Gilbert Newcomen had an especially close relationship: they had met at Lincoln theological college in 1884 and were together ordained deacon in 1886 and priest in 1887. Both served their titles in Kettering and went on together to become curates in Hornchurch and then in Brentwood. When Carter was presented to the living of St Leonard's-at-the-Hythe by Balliol College in 1896, Newcomen became his curate and moved into the rectory. Carter is remembered as disliking the local Nonconformist chapel and avoiding its minister.

St Mary Magdalen in Magdalen Street was founded in the twelfth century and was a leper hospital for several centuries. The hospital was refounded as King James's Hospital almshouses in 1610 and the rector, the Rev. Robert Bashford, drew most of his income from the mastership of the hospital. He was also chaplain of the workhouse. The parish's population was 3,423 and the churchmanship very low. St Martin's in West Stockwell Street was a Saxon foundation and before the Reformation had been linked to St Botolph's priory. In 1914 the population was 821. It was a poor and largely working-class parish, though in the years immediately prior to the war there developed a modest economic prosperity.[43] The rector was the Rev. Henry de Courcy-Benwell, who was a member of the

[39] ERO, St John the Evangelist, Colchester, Register of Services, 9 August 1914
[40] Balliol College Library, Oxford, letter from the Rev. H.F.V. Carter to the Master of Balliol, 26 October 1915. Paxman also gave money to Nonconformist chapels in the area of his ironworks
[41] Elrington, *Victoria County History*, p. 321
[42] ERO, Annual Diocesan Statistical Returns, 1914
[43] ERO, report by Dr Maybury, churchwarden, 1912, St Martin's Vestry Minute Book

local Labour and Independent Labour parties.[44] One of his predecessors had begun daily Evensong in the church and de Courcy-Benwell added daily Mattins and a weekly celebration of Holy Communion. He tried to visit his parishioners monthly. South of St Martin's was the parish of St Nicholas, which was of moderate evangelical churchmanship. The church, in the High Street, was of late Anglo-Saxon foundation and was extensively restored and enlarged in 1875–76 by Sir George Gilbert Scott. The rector was the Rev. Joseph Harris, a kindly man who supported the Labour movement and took an interest in social issues.[45] He had a half-time curate, the Rev. James Gardiner, who was also diocesan organising secretary of the Church Mission Society.

Evangelicalism of a more rigorous sort was to be found at St Peter's, North Hill, which had a population of 2,003. The vicar was the Rev. Charles Triffit Ward, an elderly bachelor who surprised his parishioners by marrying during the First World War, and then became ill. Of a mercurial temperament, Ward made a great fuss about wearing a black gown instead of a surplice whilst preaching – a more Protestant practice – until it eventually fell to pieces during the war. He also overworked his unfortunate curate, the Rev. Herbert Hughes.[46]

By way of contrast, the neighbouring parish of St Paul, created in 1879 to serve the working-class housing that had developed round the North Station, was a thriving centre of Anglo-Catholicism. The parish contained 2,143 people, and under its rector, the Rev. Wilfred Courteen, it developed a full complement of Catholic guilds, devotional societies, Bible study classes and a Sunday school with 137 children on the books.

Colchester was edged by five formerly rural parishes which had become suburbs during the nineteenth century. All were of central churchmanship. North of St Paul's lay the parish of St Michael, Myland (or Mile End). The parish's population was 1,693 and the rector was the Rev. Henry Stevens. To the east, St Andrew's, Greenstead, had a population of 1,424 and the rector was the Rev. Clement Worsfold. To the west, St Leonard's, Lexden, contained a population of 1,271 and was a comparatively wealthy parish. Its rector was the Rev. James Evans. All Saints', Stanway,[47] was carved out

---

[44]   Elrington, *Victoria County History*, p. 323
[45]   Elrington, *Victoria County History*, p. 329
[46]   ERO, St Peter's Register of Services and Parochial Church Council Minutes
[47]   The name was changed to Shrub End in the early 1960s

of St Albright's, Stanway, in 1845 and the vicar, the Rev. Henry Stephens, ministered to a population of 469. The parish of St Michael, Berechurch, to the south, as has already been mentioned, was held in plurality by Greville Brunwin-Hales and contained 173 people. Mention must also be made of the Garrison (or Camp) Church, which was built by the army in 1857. In 1914 it served the garrison and their families and was used for compulsory church parades. All its records have unfortunately been lost.[48]

Relations between Colchester's Anglican parish churches and the town's twenty-three Nonconformist chapels or meeting houses and Roman Catholic church of St James-the-Less appear to have been relatively slight. During the late nineteenth century there had been a branch of the Evangelical Alliance in Colchester which had attracted evangelical Anglicans and Nonconformists, but it closed following a change of incumbent at St Peter's. Church life in Colchester in 1914, measured in terms of attendance, was approximately 60 per cent Anglican and 40 per cent Nonconformist and Roman Catholic.[49] This contrasted with the situation in the mid-nineteenth century, when something closer to equality in attendance figures applied. This change may be ascribed to the impact of the Oxford Movement on the Church of England as a whole – resulting in a more vigorous clergy and parish life – as well as to the decline of one or two of the Nonconformist chapels.[50] Some of Colchester's Liberal and prosperous Nonconformist families, such as the Kent and Blaxhill families, attended Lion Walk Congregational Church, but the bulk of the town's social elite were Anglicans, or at least had deserted Nonconformity for the more socially acceptable Church of England by the time they had made their money and settled in Colchester.

During the First World War, Anglican, Roman Catholic and Nonconformist representatives sat on the committee of the Borough of

---

[48] Enquiries at the Garrison Church, the Royal Army Chaplains' Department, the Essex Records Office, The National Archives, Lambeth Palace Library, the National Army Museum and the Imperial War Museums have so far failed to locate any documents or registers

[49] Mr Andrew Phillips, interview, 18 May 2000

[50] Mr Andrew Phillips, letter to the author, 30 May 2000. The Stockwell Chapel had declined most amongst the Nonconformist chapels: in its heyday in the nineteenth century it had regularly attracted a congregation of 1,500 on Sundays, but shortly after the Armistice attendance had declined to such an extent that closure was contemplated

Colchester Social Club for Troops, and Nonconformist ministers were invited to take part in intercession services attended by the mayor in 1916 and 1918.[51] Bishop Whitcombe hosted a devotional afternoon for forty Anglican clergy and Nonconformist ministers at Derby House in 1917, where they heard an address on 'Our Mutual Interest and Converging Tendencies'. This interdenominational event was appreciated by the participants but was not repeated. There was a single exchange of pulpits between Anglicans and Nonconformists to mark the Armistice in November 1918, but otherwise the denominations seem neither to have communicated nor to have cooperated to any great extent.[52]

The Coming of War

Although war with Germany had been widely expected for a number of years, the international crisis which blew up in the summer of 1914 and finally led to the war came as a great shock to much of the population. Colchester was enjoying a period of prosperity, and the three local newspapers – the *Essex County Standard*, *Colchester Gazette* and the *Essex Telegraph* – paint a picture of a self-confident and stable town, proud of both its past and of its more recent achievements. Their news was almost entirely local, with an emphasis on sports, crime, the deliberations of the town council and quite a lot of coverage of church news. There was little mention of national politics, such as the situation in Ireland, nor of international news. The assassination of Archduke Franz Ferdinand in Sarajevo on 28 June 1914 and the subsequent diplomatic and military developments did not rate a mention. Many ordinary people in 1914 did not take a daily newspaper, and so were largely unaware of the situation on the continent until war was imminent.

The reality of the international situation was brought home to the townsfolk of Colchester on Wednesday 29 July 1914, when a garden party at the Colchester Garrison Officers' Club was disturbed by the sound of

---

[51]   ERO, Committee Minutes of the Borough Social Club for the Troops, 8 September 1914. ERO, Colchester Ruri-decanal Chapter Minutes, 28 July 1916 and 5 July 1918
[52]   *Essex County Telegraph*, 13 January 1917

buglers in the barracks repeatedly sounding the 'Alarm!'[53] The party broke up as the officers hurried away to the barracks, leaving their wives and children to get home by themselves. A detachment of nearly 1,000 soldiers was despatched within the hour by train to guard the Royal Naval Base at Harwich, and thereafter the soldiers disappeared from the streets of Colchester as they prepared for mobilisation. The townsfolk, who were accustomed to seeing soldiers in uniform on the streets, found their sudden absence rather unsettling as the news reached them of declarations of war across Europe and the German invasion of Belgium.

Bishop Whitcombe was on holiday in Switzerland as Europe slid into war. Trying to make his way home through France as that country mobilised its troops, he foolishly paused to take some photographs and was arrested by a French soldier as a German spy. The bishop spent several days in prison until his identity could be verified and he was released.[54]

On the morning of 4 August 1914, the public were not allowed to walk through Colchester barracks for the first time. Great Britain eventually declared war on Germany at 11.00 p.m. On 5 August, the 20th Hussars left Colchester by train from the railway station, and were observed having great difficulty coaxing their horses to enter the railway trucks.[55] The infantry and artillery took a little longer to get ready. Some troops left on 14 August, but the bulk of the garrison – the Royal Field Artillery, the Somersets, the Hampshires and the Rifle Brigade – left three days later on 17 August. Led by military bands, the soldiers marched down Mersea Road to St Botolph's Station. The pavements were lined by crowds of cheering and waving townsfolk, and, as they passed, some of the soldiers broke ranks and stole kisses from young women.[56] The troops from the Colchester garrison arrived in France with the British Expeditionary Force in time to participate in the second British engagement with the Germans, on 26–27 August 1914, the battle of Le Cateau.

[53] C. Cockerill and D. Woodhead, *Colchester as a Military Centre* (Essex County Council, Chelmsford, 1978), p. 31
[54] *Colchester Gazette*, 12 August 1914
[55] Mr Jack Ashton, interview, 10 February 1998
[56] Mrs Alice Hicks, interview, 18 March 1998

3

Wartime

In order to understand and appreciate the ministry of the parish churches of Colchester during the First World War, it is necessary to set their wartime experiences in context. No two English towns or cities experienced the First World War in exactly the same way, though anxiety, bereavement, shortages and the widespread dislocation of daily life were universal. Additionally, Colchester's experiences during the First World War were strongly influenced by the town's geographic position in eastern England, the presence of the garrison and the social composition of the town's population.

Geography and Fear of Invasion

Throughout the First World War, the military and civil authorities and ordinary people of Colchester were highly conscious of their town's proximity to the North Sea, and thus to the ever-present menace of the Imperial German Navy, especially after the German bombardment of Great Yarmouth, Scarborough, Hartlepool and Whitby in November and December 1914. In May 1915, the townsfolk were disturbed by rumours that HMS *Recruit* had been sunk off nearby Clacton-on-Sea, and East Anglia was declared a 'danger zone'.[1] On many occasions throughout the war, the sound of artillery fire from France was clearly audible in Colchester, which people found unsettling.[2]

Colchester was in the path of German bombers heading for London and was itself frequently bombed during the war.[3] One of the first bombs

[1]   J. Munson, ed., *Echoes of the Great War: The Diary of the Reverend Andrew Clark, 1914–1919* (Oxford University Press, Oxford, 1985), diary entry for 3 May 1915
[2]   Hunt, *Souvenir*, pp. 56, 60, 67, 68. Christopher J. Whitcombe, letter to the author, 13 April 1998
[3]   Hunt, *Souvenir*, p. 49

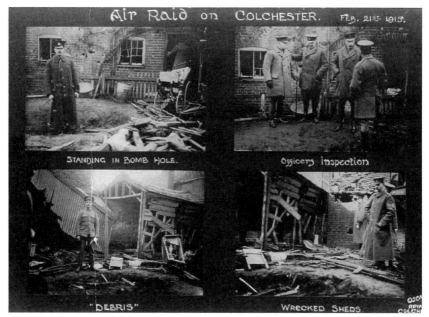

8 The first house in Colchester to be bombed, in Butt Road, on 21 February 1915

fell on 21 February 1915 on Butt Road, where it damaged several houses, mangled a perambulator (mercifully empty of its baby) and narrowly missed ammunition in the nearby ordnance depot. Enterprising locals sold toys fashioned from the debris, and Lady Colebrooke generously replaced the perambulator. Later in 1915, five German Zeppelins were seen over the town.[4] In 1916 the Zeppelin *L33* was brought down at Little Wigborough. In a scene worthy of an Ealing comedy, the Zeppelin crew were arrested by a special constable on a bicycle and taken to Colchester for interrogation.[5] Other wartime bombing went unmentioned in Colchester's newspapers as a result of press censorship.[6]

A rigid blackout was instituted throughout Colchester, the town hall clock was silenced, and at times it was forbidden to ring church bells, so that German aircraft flying at night would not realise they were over

[4]   Mr Jack Ashton, interview, 10 February 1998. Hunt, *Souvenir*, p. 55. A. Phillips, *Colchester: A History* (Phillimore, Stroud, 2004), p. 104
[5]   R.L. Rimell, *Zeppelin! A Battle for Air Supremacy in World War 1* (Conway, London, 1984), pp. 119–26
[6]   Phillips, *Colchester*, p. 104

a town.[7] Churches had either to conclude Evensong before dusk or to erect blackout curtains, and on several occasions worship had to be interrupted or abandoned because of air raids. Bishop Whitcombe insisted that parishes take out air-raid damage insurance. The cost was not negligible: at St Botolph's, for example, blackout curtains cost £9.8.9 and air-raid insurance for 1915–16 added an extra £6.0.0 to the premium.[8]

In November 1914, Colchester Police were advised that 'the Authorities think that a German raid is possible, in which case Germans or proGermans in England will try to help by committing crimes and damage in Essex.'[9] The town's Boy Scouts began systematically patrolling the telegraph lines at night to protect them from sabotage, until a kindly Home Office official packed them off home to their beds with the tactful suggestion that the authorities believed any interference would occur nearer to London.

The authorities took a more serious view of the threat of a German invasion of the east coast, and the Colchester garrison was tasked with the defence of London. The mayor of Colchester was instructed that in the event of a successful German landing, he was to 'evacuate the civil population, and if the grave hour ever comes that compels a surrender, let the enemy find Colchester a barren desert'.[10] A borough Emergency Committee was quickly established, and in January 1915 every household was issued with instructions for the evacuation of the town, which were updated in May 1916.[11] The signal to evacuate Colchester was originally to have been a red poster displayed throughout the town, but this was later changed to maroons fired from the town hall tower at regular intervals and the ringing of church bells. The townsfolk were instructed to leave on foot, along two specified routes, in groups of between fifty and seventy people, carrying clothes, money, food and drink for forty-eight hours. Emergency food was secretly amassed in the town hall basement. The

[7]   Hunt, *Souvenir*, p. 59
[8]   *St Botolph's Colchester Parish Magazine*, May 1916
[9]   ERO, J.A. Unett, 'Orders, Reports and Letters Relating to Essex Special Constabulary, Colchester Division, during the Great War', p. x
[10]   Hunt, *Souvenir*, p. 55
[11]   Colchester Library, Local Studies Department (CL), Colchester Emergency Committee, 'General Instructions to the Inhabitants of Colchester in Case of Invasion' (revised instructions), May 1916. CL, Collection of local material compiled by A.M. Jarmin, during his mayorality of Colchester, 1917–18, fol. N

MAYOR'S PARLOUR,

TOWN HALL,

COLCHESTER,

29th January, 1915.

DEAR SIR, OR MADAM,

Acting under instructions of the Lord Lieutenant and of the Home Office, an Emergency Committee has for some time past, in conjunction with high Military Authority, been considering measures for the safety and welfare of the civil population of Colchester in the event of an attempt by the enemy to land on our shores.

It is not more likely now than it has been at any previous time during the War that a landing will be effected, but in the improbable event of this happening the Military Authorities may find it necessary under certain circumstances to give directions for everyone to leave the Town.

Should such an order be received from the Military Authorities, you will find on the enclosed card directions as to what you should do and along which roads you must go.

The signal mentioned on the card will only be given by express instruction of the General Officer responsible for the defence of this portion of the East Coast, and it is earnestly hoped that, to preserve order and avoid panic, the inhabitants will loyally obey the directions given, as it is only by so doing that help can be rendered to the military and danger to the public averted.

If there is any member of your household who, owing to illness or infirmity, is totally unable to leave the Borough on foot, you are requested to report it in writing to the Borough Police.

Yours faithfully,

W. COATS HUTTON,

Mayor,

(Chairman of Colchester Emergency Committee).

9 Circular letter to the townsfolk of Colchester from the mayor, William Coats Hutton, regarding the possible emergency evacuation of the town in the event of a German landing on the East coast, 1915

Borough of Colchester.

INSTRUCTIONS ISSUED BY THE EMERGENCY COMMITTEE.

January, 1915.

Please insert your name and address here. { Name *Bishop of Colchester*

Address *Derby House.*

This card must be carefully kept, as it shows you what to do if the Military Authorities give an order that everybody is to leave Colchester.

If the Order is given, you will be notified by Signal. The Signal will be as follows :—

1. To prepare to leave:—One rocket sent up from the Town Hall Tower. This signal will be given three times at intervals of five minutes.

2. To leave the Town :—Three rockets sent up from the Town Hall Tower. This signal will be given three times at intervals of five minutes, and Church Bells will be rung.

If the last Signal only should be given, it would mean that you must leave the Town without any delay ; and you should if possible take with you enough food for yourself and your family for 48 hours.

You are told on the back of this card (**which you must take with you**) the direction you are to follow and by which roads you must go.

10 Emergency evacuation card issued to the bishop of Colchester

Colchester refugees' ultimate destination was to have been Oxfordshire, and signs indicating the route were affixed to trees.[12] Livestock, grain stock, hay and straw stacks and petrol were to be destroyed at the orders of the police, though the Emergency Committee sensibly ordered that 'alcoholic liquors need not be destroyed'.[13] Fear of an invasion eased dur-

---

[12]   CL, Colchester Emergency Committee, 'Instructions to Inhabitants, 1915'. Hunt, *Souvenir*, pp. 66–7. ERO, Unett, 'Orders', p. 35
[13]   CL, Colchester Emergency Committee, 'Instructions to Inhabitants, 1915', p. 4

ing 1917, only to resurface during the March 1918 German offensive, when the Emergency Committee was instructed to be vigilant and prepare for a possible invasion.[14]

The Garrison

Colchester's experience of the First World War was governed principally by the presence of many hundreds of thousands of troops undergoing basic training before being sent to the front or specialist military training of various sorts. An average of three ambulance trains a week pulled into St Botolph's Station throughout the war, bringing thousands of wounded soldiers who had been sent home for surgical or medical treatment and rehabilitation.

Following the declaration of war in August 1914, Colchester quickly filled with reservists. Bandsman Victor Shawyer of the Rifle Brigade noted:

> We found Meeanee Barracks full of reservists – many still in civilian dress – and more were flocking in by almost every train. Fitting them out with uniform, boots and equipment was proceeding rapidly, but in some cases was no easy job, as quite a few men had lost that soldierly figure they had taken with them into civil[ian] life at the end of the Colours service [sic] and they were now portly in build. One man in particular, I recall, had becomes so corpulent that the Quartermaster's staff despaired of fitting him out. He must have weighed all of eighteen stone. Out of the corner of my eye I noticed him looking me up and down, as though envious of my long, lean twelve stone. I believe he remained in England for several weeks till rigorous training and less sumptuous feeding tore about four stone out of his bloated carcass.[15]

The barracks could not contain all the reservists, and so tents were erected on Abbey Fields. Reservists attempting to sell their watches and civilian clothes to passing townsfolk for a few shillings – probably to spend

[14]   Hunt, *Souvenir*, pp. 55, 67
[15]   National Army Museum (NAM), Memoirs of Bandsman Victor Shawyer, fol. 154

11 Army recruits in civilian clothing marching up Mersea Road from St Botolph's Station upon arrival in Colchester, 1914 or 1915

12 Recruits in 'Kitchener Blue' uniforms marching along Mersea Road, 1914 or 1915. There were so many new recruits that the army ran out of supplies of khaki cloth and uniforms had to be improvised out of blue cloth, including much blue serge originally woven for General Post Office uniforms.

in Colchester's pubs or brothels – became a regular sight.[16] Colchester also quickly filled with thousands of young men wishing to join up. A recruiting office was established in the Albert School of Art in the High Street, but when this proved inadequate, St Peter's parish room nearby was made available to cope with the overspill. Just over a month later, the *Essex County Standard* reported on 12 September that recruits were still pouring into the town. Many were temporarily billeted in houses all over Colchester and were wistfully remembered decades later as 'nice boys', sleeping in the front room and eating with the family.[17] These were followed in 1915 by the volunteers of Kitchener's Army, and from January 1916 by conscripts.

It is difficult to be very definite about the number of troops in Colchester, but on several occasions the army exceeded the civilian population.[18] The only hard evidence is to be found in the *Annual Report of the Medical Officer of Health*, who assessed the population of Colchester in 1915 to be 38,699 civilians and 12,435 soldiers and in 1918 to be 37,923 civilians and the average daily strength of the army to have been 14,553. Evidence I have gathered from the records of soldiers attending compulsory church parades indicates that the number peaked in 1915–16 as the garrison was swelled, first with volunteers joining Kitchener's New Army, and then with the first conscripts after the introduction of conscription in January 1916. There was a constant ebb and flow of the number of troops in Colchester during the rest of the war.

Daily life in Colchester was punctuated by the sound of bugles, and throughout the war troops leaving for the front would march behind a military band from the barracks to St Botolph's railway station. Troop departures were supposed to be secret, but many townsfolk were employed by the army and knew when a detachment was due to leave. Mersea Road would be lined by civilians as the troops marched past, no longer cheering as they had done in August 1914, but shouting out 'Good luck', and, in the case of some of the women, allowing themselves to be kissed by some of the passing soldiers.[19]

---

[16]   Mr Jack Ashton, interview, 10 February 1998
[17]   Phillips, *Colchester*, p. 101
[18]   Hunt, *Souvenir*, p. 62
[19]   Mrs Alice Hicks, interview, 18 March 1998

The behaviour of the troops in Colchester seems for the most part to have been good throughout the war.[20] The borough medical officer of health reported at the end of 1914 that 'the Troops in Colchester from the beginning of the War have throughout behaved with orderliness and sobriety.' This is corroborated in the annual reports of the Borough of Colchester Social Club for the Troops. The troops may have caused little drunkenness or rowdiness during the war, but there was a significant increase in the number of illegitimate births (see Table 1).

Table 1: Births in Colchester and England and Wales, 1913–21

Year	1913	1914	1915	1916	1917	1918	1919	1920	1921
Colchester									
Live births	885	893	783	859	701	730	718	1,064	904
Illegitimate	40	42	43	52	75	51	62	49	44
Percentage	4.5	4.7	5.5	6.1	10.7	7.0	8.6	4.6	4.9
England and Wales									
Live births	881,890	879,096	814,614	785,520	668,346	662,661	692,428	957,782	848,814
Illegitimate	37,909	37,329	36,245	37,689	37,157	41,452	41,876	44,947	38,618
Percentage	4.3	4.2	4.4	4.8	5.6	6.2	6.0	4.7	4.5

Source: Figures supplied by the Office for National Statistics, 11 October 1999. The figures for Colchester were extracted from General Register Office, *Reports of the Registrar General*, 1913–1919 (HMSO, London, 1915–20) and the *Registrar General's Statistical Review of England and Wales*, 1920 and 1921 (HMSO, London, 1922 and 1923). The figures for England and Wales as a whole were taken from Office of Population Censuses and Surveys, *Birth Statistics, Historical Series FM1, No, 13* (HMSO, London, 1987)

Whereas the national figures for live births declined throughout the war, the number of live births in Colchester declined in 1915, presumably as a result of the departure of the men of the garrison for France in 1914. The number of live births increased again in 1916, which may probably be ascribed to the introduction of conscription – couples wanting to start a baby before the husband went off to France, 'just in case' – and then decreased for much of the rest of the war. The dramatic increase in the number of live births in 1920 is doubtless due to demobilisation.

---

[20]   ERO, Annual Report of the Medical Officer of Health, 1914. ERO, Annual Reports of the Committe of the Borough of Colchester Social Club for the Troops for the years ending 1 October 1916 and 30 September 1918, where the conduct of the troops in the club is described as 'excellent' and 'most exemplary'

The national proportion of illegitimate births declined during the war as men joined the army or navy. In Colchester, the proportion of illegitimate births remained about the same for the first year of the war, increased a little during the second year and then increased greatly between 1917 and 1919, when the town was full of young conscripts anxious to enjoy a 'good time' before they were sent to France and possible death or mutilation. This may be part of the reason why many householders in Colchester were reluctant to leave billeted soldiers alone inside their houses.[21] After demobilisation in 1919, illegitimacy quickly returned to pre-1914 levels, which would suggest that there was largely a return to pre-war sexual morality.

Visits by King George V

One indication of the importance of Colchester as a military centre was the visits made to the garrison by King George V throughout the war. The first visit took place three months after the start of the war on 10 November 1914, when the king noted in his diary:

> I left Liverpool Street [Station] with [Lieutenant Colonel Clive] Wigram by special [train] at 9.50. Sir Ian Hamilton and Major Pollen came with me. We arrived at Colchester at 11.0, where I inspected the Norfolk and Suffolk Infantry Brigade under Genl. Bayard, Genl. Inglefield commands the East Anglian Division [sic]. The 4th and 5th Norfolks and 5 [sic] Suffolks & Brigade of Artillery. Saw the Sandringham Company under [Captain] Frank Beck.[22]

On 14 July 1916 George V travelled to the Clacton peninsula to observe manoeuvres. On his return, the king stopped at Wivenhoe to open a bridge that had been built by the Royal Engineers across the river Colne to Rowhedge, just outside Colchester, and he was the first person to walk

---

21 ERO, St Leonard's, Lexden, Vestry Minutes, 1915
22 Royal Archives, Windsor (RA) King George V diaries, 10 November 1914. Edgar Hunt, *Souvenir*, p. 60, mentions a surprise visit to the garrison made by George V in 1915, but there is no trace of this in the Royal Archives or the local press, and it seems likely that Hunt and the compilers of the *Souvenir*, writing in 1923, confused royal visits

13 King George V in Colchester, 10 November 1914

across it. Crowds from Colchester and the surrounding area lined the streets to see the king drive past but were rather shocked by his appearance: one observer noted, 'The King looked very ill and sad. Sunken cavities under his eyes and black lines.'[23] Perhaps he already knew that the opening stages of the battle of the Somme, which began a fortnight earlier on 1 July, had not gone well, with 60,000 British casualties on the first day.

On 22 February 1917 George V visited Colchester to inspect troops and to present medals. Again, he noted in his diary:

> Left Liverpool Street at 9.35 with Uncle Arthur [the Duke of Connaught] & Lord French for Colchester where I inspected the 66th Division commanded by M. Genl. Sir H. Lawrence who start at once for France. Each brigade marched past in fours on different roads. I also visited the Hospital there. Lunched on the train, home before 3.0.[24]

---

[23]   Munson, *Echoes of the Great War*, diary entry for 4 July 1916. The date in the published version of Andrew Clark's diary appears to have been wrongly transcribed, because the king came on 14 July and not 4 July

[24]   RA, King George V diaries, 22 February 1917

14 Souvenir timetable for the visit to Colchester of King George V on
19 March 1918

George V visited Colchester once more, on 19 March 1918, to inspect
Reed Hall, the hutted 'city' for men in training, and to attend a lecture
with the minister of education, H.A.L. Fisher. In many ways, this was the
king's most interesting visit.

> Went to Colchester by special at 9.50 where Genl. Pulteney recevd. me &
> I went to the camp of 67 Division Genl. Cis Bingham to see the system
> of educational training of the troops [sic]. Visited many classes and heard
> the lectures, Mr Fisher (Education) came with me, he was pleased. Left
> at 1.30.[25]

Illness and Disease

Jack Ashton recalled that the troops brought a degree of prosperity to
Colchester's shops and pubs, for which the townsfolk were grateful, but
they also brought illnesses and diseases with them.[26] By the end of 1914,
1,454 troops were accommodated in 1,043 civilian billets, and the borough
Inspector of Nuisances, Thomas Wells, instituted the regular inspection
of billets 'in order to see if the premises were overcrowded, dirty, or if any
sickness existed which might prove to be of an infectious nature'. Troops
arriving in Colchester were frequently found to be verminous, and the
borough made arrangements for their blankets, clothing and paliasses to
be disinfected free of charge at the Mile End Isolation Hospital.[27] The
troops were responsible for bringing a variety of illnesses to Colchester,
such as diphtheria and scarlet fever, and the provision of additional
beds for soldiers and civilians in the isolation hospital was a source of
anxiety to the borough council throughout the war.[28] The troops also
helped spread measles: in 1918, for example, there were 443 civilian cases

---

[25]   RA, King George V diaries, 19 March 1918
[26]   Mr Jack Ashton, interview, 10 February 1998
[27]   ERO, Annual Report of the Medical Officer of Health, 1914, pp. 49–50
[28]   The *Essex County Standard* reported on 6 January 1916 that there were four cases of
        scarlet fever and one case of diphtheria amongst the garrison. On 5 February 1916
        the *Essex County Standard* reported that there were now twenty cases of diphtheria
        amongst the troops and five amongst the civilian population. ERO, Special report
        attached to the minutes of the meeting of the Borough and Port Health Committee,
        12 November 1914, and minutes for 18 January 1917

of measles and 22 military cases, and 28 civilian cases of German measles and 247 military cases.[29]

Venereal Disease

Prostitution and venereal disease were a cause of concern to the army and borough medical officers of health throughout the First World War. Mrs Parker Bird, a Voluntary Aid Detachment (VAD) nurse at Colchester Military Hospital, recalled:

> [There was] a tremendous lot of venereal disease amongst the troops. So many of the young boys who'd never been away from home, or experienced that sort of thing, sexually got venereal disease [sic]. There was quite a lot of it in the town, because, of course, it was a military town, and there were prostitutes in some of the streets, which eventually were put out of bounds. So many of these boys came back from France with venereal disease … [that] we had to build extra huts in the grounds for them. [It was] very difficult to explain to their wives – some of them were married, of course – over the telephone, what was the matter with their husbands.[30]

Outline notes survive in the papers of Bishop Whitcombe for a speech about venereal disease, though they do not make it clear when or where he delivered the speech. The bishop – himself the father of six boys and two girls – asserted that the object of sexual appetites was the preservation of the human race; he went on to mention the dangers of venereal disease, and concluded that consideration for others ought to lead to self-discipline rather than sexual indulgence.[31]

Official army figures reveal that on average thirty-two men per thousand caught venereal disease per year during the war and were unavailable for duty for between twenty-eight and thirty-seven days whilst they underwent treatment. Forty-two per cent of all military cases of venereal

---

[29] ERO, Annual Report of the Medical Officer of Health, 1918, p. 19
[30] Imperial War Museums (IWM), Sound recording, interview with Mrs Parker Bird
[31] Archive of Mrs Sarah Bradley, papers of the Right Rev. Dr R.H. Whitcombe, notes marked 'Amateur speech'. The bishop also preserved a detailed newspaper article about the identification and treatment of syphilis, though the name of the newspaper and its date are missing

disease were contracted in Great Britain, 45 per cent were contracted in France and the rest were contracted in other countries or were of unknown origin.[32]

In Colchester, the Essex County Hospital, an early-nineteenth-century foundation with a strong Anglican ethos, was obliged to change its rules during the war to permit the treatment of venereal disease, which previously had been forbidden.[33] The army never quite made up its mind whether to regard contracting venereal disease as a self-inflicted wound, which should be punished, or as a disease like any other, which should accordingly be medically treated. Fear of punishment sometimes caused soldiers to conceal venereal disease until it became untreatable. The army announced that warrant officers and non-commissioned officers who contracted venereal disease might be reduced to the ranks, and officers might be required to resign their commissions.[34]

Spanish Influenza

The most serious medical problem of the war was the Spanish influenza pandemic of 1918–19. There are many theories and much uncertainty about the origins of Spanish influenza. The United States of America, Austria-Hungary and the Far East have all been suggested as its place of origin. The pandemic's Hispanic name owes much to the Allied censorship of newspapers, which played down the spread of the influenza in order not to damage morale. Newspapers were free to utilise press reports of the influenza pandemic in Spain, where King Alphonso XIII was amongst those suffering from it, and it was accordingly soon referred to as 'Spanish influenza'.

Modern research by Professor John Oxford has suggested Étaples, a port on the northern French coast, as an immediate source of the influenza for the British Army in 1918. Étaples was used as the British Expeditionary Force's principal base transit camp, through which millions of troops passed – undergoing infamously gruelling and demoralising training in

---

[32]   Corrigan, *Mud, Blood and Poppycock*, pp. 94–5

[33]   J.B. Penfold, *The History of the Essex County Hospital, Colchester (formerly the Essex and Colchester Hospital), 1820–1945* (Lavenham Press, Lavenham, 1984), p. 201

[34]   Corrigan, *Mud, Blood and Poppycock*, pp. 94–5

the 'Bullring' – and it also contained several military hospitals, the largest of which was run by the St John Ambulance Brigade. At its peak, this contained 744 beds, and treated 35,000 patients between 1915–18. Unsurprisingly, given the huge numbers of troops at Étaples, there were periodic outbreaks of fever and illness throughout the First World War, including influenza in 1916, which may have mutated into the 1918 virus. The 1918 influenza virus made its first appearance at Étaples, and Professor Oxford has suggested that it might be more appropriate to rename it 'English influenza'.[35] On 31 May 1918 German aeroplanes bombed and machine-gunned the hospital at Étaples, causing many deaths and injuries amongst the patients and the St John Ambulance Brigade staff. Several of the surviving patients were transferred and the hospital was later re-established at Trouville, which ironically probably helped to spread the virus.

There were two distinct outbreaks of Spanish influenza in 1918. The first, in the spring or summer, was sometimes known as 'three-day fever', and was a milder strain. Troops who acquired it generally recovered and developed immunity to later strains. By the autumn, the influenza virus had mutated into a more potent and deadly form. Most deaths from influenza are normally amongst the sick and elderly. The 1918 pandemic tended to prove fatal for younger men and women, usually aged between their twenties and forties, apparently by overwhelming their immune systems. Whereas the average incidence of deaths from influenza is around 1 per cent, the 1918 Spanish influenza outbreak proved fatal for some 20 per cent of patients. The influenza was spread by sick troops evacuated from the front amongst the war-weary and undernourished civilian population. Ironically, soldiers with mild doses of influenza who managed to stay in the trenches often fared better than their comrades who were sent to hospital.

One of the first indications of the arrival of the influenza virus in Colchester is an entry in the service register of St Peter's Church: 'June 30, 9.45. No Parade Service owing to illness in the camp.' As one might expect, there were two distinct influenza epidemics in the town in 1918, in the summer and the autumn. Serum was used with some degree of

---

[35]   Professor John Oxford, letter to the author, 14 June 2013

success to treat the first outbreak but proved useless during the second.[36] The assistant medical officer of health recorded:

> Energetic measures were adopted to cope with the epidemic as far as possible. Two whole time nurses were engaged to visit patients in their own homes. At one time the severer cases were taken into a ward in the Infirmary and later on into the Infectious Hospital. In many instances where a whole family was attacked, domestic assistance was obtained, or the family as a whole removed to the hospital. Circulars *re* precautions, etc., were distributed by the Boy Scouts to every house in the town, all Elementary Day Schools, Evening Classes and Sunday Schools were closed from October 21st, until December 4th. Cinemas, etc., were closed to all persons under 16 years of age, and the hours and intervals were arranged in accordance with L.G.B. [Local Government Board] orders. Cinemas and Theatres were disinfected after every entertainment. Disinfectants and gargles were supplied free of charge at the Health Offices.[37]

Despite all these efforts, the virus was not contained. Influenza was not a notifiable illness, and no record exists of the numbers of soldiers and civilians who contracted it but survived. Mrs Bird recalled the impact of Spanish influenza at Colchester Military Hospital:

> We also had the Spanish 'flu epidemic during my stay [as a VAD nurse] in the hospital, and the funerals were going on all day long. The boys were dying off like flies … Every morning before we went on duty we had to go through the fumigation department and also before we left at night. The mortuaries were so full [that] we had the patients [i.e. the dead] lying one on top of another. It was a terrible time for everyone. Going home to my digs [for a break at lunchtime] … we had to stand with bowed head while the funerals were passing by [up Mersea Road to the cemetery], and sometimes it took so long to get there [that] I had to give up.[38]

By late 1918, the situation at Colchester Military Hospital had become desperate. Many of the doctors and nurses – including Mrs Bird – suc-

36   ERO, Annual Report of the Medical Officer of Health, 1918, p. 19
37   ERO, Annual Report of the Medical Officer of Health, 1918, pp. 19–20
38   IWM, Sound recording, interview with Mrs Parker Bird

cumbed to the virus, and the death rate from influenza was over ten per day. The general medical officer appealed to the mayor of Colchester to call for volunteers from the town to run the hospital. Seventy women volunteered and looked after the patients until the staff recovered.[39]

In total, 268 people died of Spanish influenza in Colchester in 1918: 141 civilians and 127 soldiers. The assistant medical officer of health noted:

> The majority of deaths occurred in adults in their prime and were generally the result of Pneumonia or Broncho-Pneumonia … It is perhaps worthy of note that out of 141 deaths of civilians in the Borough, only four occurred in the better class houses; all the other deaths occurred in the houses of the artisan or labouring classes.[40]

There was a third outbreak of influenza in the spring of 1919 but it was not as severe as that of the previous autumn: fifty-five people died and the epidemic ceased after the spring.[41] It has been estimated that globally at least 70 million people died of Spanish influenza; in India alone more people died of influenza than were killed during the First World War.

In Colchester the death rate from Spanish influenza exceeded that from cholera in the 1834 epidemic, but its impact was not felt as strongly as in other parts of the country because the proportion of men killed in the war was much greater. For the clergy of Colchester – already over-stretched by 1918 – the Spanish influenza meant a considerable increase in the numbers of funerals and of pastoral work amongst the sick and bereaved.

Soldiers recovering from the effects of shell shock were sometimes to be seen on the streets of Colchester. Mrs Bird recalled that at the military hospital, the worst cases were kept naked in padded cells, so they could not harm themselves, under regular observation from a non-commissioned officer. She was particularly moved by one very handsome young soldier suffering from shell shock, who thought he was Jesus Christ and 'who knelt all day and half the night on the floor of his cell, praying for the deliverance of mankind', in a beautiful voice. Mrs Bird was very sympa-

[39] Hunt, *Souvenir*, pp. 64–5
[40] ERO, Annual Report of the Medical Officer of Health, 1918, pp. 19–20
[41] ERO, Annual Report of the Medical Officer of Health, 1919, pp. 35–6

thetic towards the shell shock patients she encountered in the hospital and thought that many of them tended to be the braver – or perhaps more conscientious – soldiers, who had 'bottled up' their experiences until they became ill. Patients suffering from shell shock might suddenly lurch from being perfectly reasonable to being highly excitable, with uncertain reactions. With time and care, many of them improved, and they were allowed to go out into Colchester to tea or to visit the shops. Only one soldier, she recalled, went into the town and did not return – much to the worry of the nurses, who in the end were compelled to inform the military police, who found him and brought him back.[42]

Munitions and War Materiel

The war brought large orders from the government – and full employment – to Colchester's factories and engineering firms. Mumford's produced specialised equipment for warship construction, whilst Paxman's manufactured tens of millions of items for the war, including equipment for submarines and warships, naval guns, field gun parts, parts for aircraft engines and military vehicles. They also produced a quarter of a million shells of various types.[43] Tanks were developed by Major T.G. Hetherington at Berechurch, and it is not unreasonable to surmise that he took advantage of the engineering expertise to be found in Colchester.[44]

Many skilled workmen from Colchester volunteered for the army at the outbreak of war, and in some cases it proved necessary for them to be withdrawn and sent back from France to carry out war work in their factories.[45] As the war dragged on, Paxman's recruited hundreds of women to replace the male workers serving in the army or navy.[46] All over Colchester, small workshops and garages began to produce shells for the Ministry of Munitions, and the town's clothing firms started making military uniforms, including heavy army greatcoats. Despite the carefully controlled prices paid by the government for war materiel, many people

[42] IWM, Sound recording, interview with Mrs Parker Bird
[43] Hunt, *Souvenir*, pp. 82–4
[44] *St Mary-at-the-Walls Parish Magazine*, November 1916
[45] Hunt, *Souvenir*, p. 84
[46] Hunt, *Souvenir*, p. 82

in Colchester managed to do rather well out of the First World War. So, too, did Colchester borough council: soldiers in uniform were given a discounted tram fare of a penny per journey, no matter what the distance, and the profits poured into the town hall.[47]

Food

Lloyd George reflected in his memoirs that 'the food question ultimately decided the issue of the war'.[48] In 1915 there was an unusually good harvest, but the following year saw a poor harvest in Britain, as well as in the United States and Canada, which had previously supplied much of the grain used for bread in Britain. Bad weather prevented much winter sowing, and the prospects for 1917 were further darkened by the loss of many ships to German submarines.[49] In 1915 the government had rejected proposals put forward by a committee under Lord Milner for the regulation of agriculture, but from 1916 there was ever-greater government control of food production and distribution, particularly after Lloyd George succeeded Asquith as prime minister on 9 December 1916.

Getting enough to eat was a problem for the civilian population of Colchester for much of the war. The shortage of food was exacerbated by the presence of the army: there was a limit to the amount of food that could be harvested from the countryside around Colchester, and during the war there were many thousands of extra mouths to feed, particularly at those times when the garrison equalled the civilian population in size. In the early part of the war, the borough established a Food Economy Committee at the request of the government to prevent waste, but their experiment with a war kitchen run by volunteers proved a failure.[50]

Many foodstuffs became more expensive: by 1918, for example, apples were selling at 10d each, potatoes reached one shilling per pound, and the 4lb loaf, which cost 5d before the war, then cost one shilling.[51] Queues for

[47] Phillips, *Colchester*, p. 103
[48] D. Lloyd George, *War Memoirs of David Lloyd George* (Odhams Press, London, 1936), p. 755
[49] Lloyd George, *War Memoirs*, pp. 756, 759–6
[50] Hunt, *Souvenir*, p. 62. CL, Return to Food Control Campaign by A.M. Jarmin, April 1917
[51] Hunt, *Souvenir*, pp. 61, 64

food frequently formed outside shops as early as 6.00 a.m.[52] As the situation worsened, many foodstuffs became unobtainable, and the borough instituted a Food Control Committee on 5 September 1917, with authority to ensure a fair distribution of food and to enforce the use of 'Standard' flour, which had been adulterated with other ingredients to make it go further, and unfortunately sometimes made people ill in consequence. A black market for food sprang up in Colchester, run in part by children. Cant's famous rose beds were given over to agriculture, and 2,200 allotments covering 200 acres were begun all over the town. Elaborate arrangements were made for schoolchildren to gather hundreds of tons of blackberries one autumn weekend.[53] The nadir was reached in the winter of 1917–18, when the Food Control Committee displayed posters with slogans such as:

> When Christmas is over, the war will last –
> And the greater the Feast, the longer the fast.
>
> Don't leave the sacrifice to the Boys.
>
> Just think this Christmas when you carve:
> The Nation's S.O.S. is *Save or Starve!*[54]

A few tales have survived showing the desperation of the hungry townsfolk in late 1917. A van delivering cheese in Crouch Street was raided by women shoppers and on at least one occasion clamorous crowds frightened shopkeepers into selling them what they demanded, so that supplies were exhausted and other people went without.[55] The most dramatic incident occurred shortly before Christmas in 1917 when a crowd of 2,000 people gathered at 7.30 a.m. in Long Wyre Street to await a delivery of margarine to the Maypole Dairy. The mood turned nasty and the mayor, A.M. Jarmin, summoned special constables to control the crowd. Several members of the Food Control Committee then clambered onto the delivery van and commandeered half of the margarine, some

---

[52]   CL, Jarmin Collection, fol. 20
[53]   Phillips, *Colchester*, p. 104
[54]   Hunt, *Souvenir*, p. 62
[55]   Hunt, *Souvenir*, p. 64

15 Elementary school teachers writing ration cards for Colchester in the town
hall, February 1918

two tons. This was then distributed to twelve other shops in Colchester
in order to disperse the crowds, where it was promised that it would be
sold at the official price. The atmosphere lightened, a possible food riot
was averted, and the crowds applauded the mayor.[56] Early in 1918, King
George V issued a proclamation appealing for economy in foodstuffs.
'Practically all the responsible citizens' in Colchester signed the king's
pledge to abstain from certain foodstuffs and passed their pledges on to
the mayor; these were later deposited beneath the town war memorial.[57]

There was further trouble early in February 1918 when a deputation
of trade unionists threatened to down tools, complaining to the mayor
about alleged unfairness and the length of time their wives spent in
queues.[58] On another occasion, a crowd of indignant mothers with
babies stormed the Food Control Office and were appeased by the

[56] CL, Jarmin Collection, fols 24, 32
[57] Hunt, *Souvenir*, p. 56
[58] CL, Jarmin Collection, fol. 40

mayor, who himself sold them half-pounds of margarine. In February 1918 the government rationing scheme finally got underway and the unrest ceased in Colchester. The town's schools were closed for a week whilst 180 elementary school teachers sat in the town hall writing ration cards by hand, which were then distributed to 10,000 households by Colchester's Boy Scouts.[59] After the Armistice, A.M. Jarmin observed: 'if ever the heraldic symbols of Colchester are altered, one thinks surely a half-a-pound of margarine (Blue Band) should somehow be incorporated into the design.'[60]

The picture that has emerged of Colchester during the First World War is of a town with a population which was relatively socially cohesive and stable. Colchester had a strong civic identity, to which the war added full employment and prosperity. The town's wartime experiences – fear of invasion, bombing, illnesses, food shortages, the presence of troops and wounded soldiers – were hardly unique. Many other towns in eastern England experienced bombing or shelling by the Germans, everyone in Great Britain found food increasingly hard to obtain during the war, and military service, injury and death were ubiquitous. The difference was one of scale: Colchester had an unprecedented number of troops in the town throughout the war.

Many of the civilians who volunteered to join the army in 1914–15, or who were conscripted after 1916, were regular and committed churchgoers. It is estimated that at least 70 per cent of troops were Anglicans – in 1915, the chaplain-general (an Anglican bishop) thought that it was nearer 75 per cent – whilst other Christian denominations and Jews accounted for the rest.[61] This meant that Colchester contained a flood of what might be termed civilians-in-uniform, of various degrees of Christian devotion, experience and sophistication, who not infrequently sought comfort and reassurance from the Church of England as they grappled with the newness of military life and faced the prospect of being sent to France. Many thousands of wounded civilians-in-uniform were sent from France to the hospitals in Colchester throughout the war,

[59]   Phillips, *Colchester*, p. 104
[60]   Hunt, *Souvenir*, p. 63
[61]   M. Snape, *God and the British Soldier: Religion and the British Army in the First and Second World Wars* (Routledge, London, 2005), pp. 142–5

and they were in need of pastoral care from the Church of England. If I may resort to a metaphor, the presence of so many troops turned up the gas beneath the parish churches of Colchester and presented them with challenges, opportunities and a level of stress which, as the war went on, became particularly acute.

4

The Clergy

Most of my clerical readers will agree, I am sure, that being a priest is the best job in the world, and that one would not swap it for anything. Except, that is, on the bad days, when being a priest can be a very tough vocation indeed. It is our privilege to minister to people in the happiest moments of their lives, and also when the bottom has fallen out of their world, and things cannot get better, only worse. One sees rather more of the painful and seamy side of life than most laypeople realise; and for this reason a priest's life can sometimes be rather a lonely existence, because only one's fellow clergy, or perhaps those married to the clergy,[1] fully understand.

There is no reason to believe that the clergy of Colchester a century ago would have had markedly different ministerial experiences, or that they would have disagreed with this description of priestly life. Following the Evangelical Revival and the Oxford Movement, expectations of pastoral care gradually rose throughout the Church of England during the nineteenth century. Just as significantly, the clergy came to have higher expectations of themselves.[2] We find this expressed, for instance, in addresses delivered to ordinands. Bishop Arthur Winnington-Ingram of

---

[1] Herbert Hensley Henson (Dean of Durham 1912, Bishop of Hereford 1918, Bishop of Durham 1920) once observed that in his experience, half of his clergy were saved by their wives, and the other half were ruined by them. T. Beeson, *The Bishops* (SCM Press, London, 2002), p. 103

[2] O. Chadwick, *The Victorian Church, Part Two, 1860–1901* (SCM Press, London, 1987), pp. 171–6. A. Hastings, *A History of English Christianity, 1920–2000* (SCM Press, London, 2001), pp. 34, 72.

There were, of course, pastorally effective clergy with a self-sacrificial view of ministry in the early nineteenth century Church of England – see, for example, Richard Hawker's *Four Sermons on Particular Occasions* (T. Williams, London, 1804) – but the difference by 1914 seems to have been predominantly one of clerical culture and practice: priests were more consciously and practically pastoral figures. Better ministry – including sacramental ministry – to the sick and dying, and improved provision for hospital chaplaincy, are good examples of this

London, to take one example from a man whom we shall encounter later, delivered a series of addresses to the Leeds Clergy School in 1896 which were published under the title *Good Shepherds* and ran to several editions. He held up very high standards of ministry and self-expectation to those shortly to be ordained:

> What made more impression on me as an undergraduate at Oxford than all the sermons I ever heard in Chapel, was a young [ordained] don insisting, at the risk of his life, on ministering to an undergraduate dying of a most infectious disease. That, then, is the life and work that lies before you – to which you will say on your Ordination day that you are 'truly called' … Are you prepared for a life of toil, and of toil to the end, for a life, it may be, of obscurity … are we prepared to give ourselves to the work? To give up all extraneous aims in life, such as to be popular, or famous, or rich, and to offer ourselves on the altar on our Ordination day … Shepherds are to gather in, tend, guide and feed their sheep, and whatever interferes with this must be put aside.[3]

It was the lot of the Colchester clergy to have to live out their vocations at a time of intense stress and suffering, perhaps unparalleled since the English Civil War in the seventeenth century. After the passage of a century, their story deserves to be told, because – despite their foibles, mistakes and failures – they met the challenges of 1914–18 rather successfully, though often at considerable personal cost.

Coping with the Outbreak of War

The people of Colchester threw themselves into supporting the war with vigour from the very outset. The Prince of Wales' National Relief Fund was widely promoted in the town. Most churches held services of intercession

---

[3] A.F. Winnington-Ingram, *Good Shepherds* (Wells Gardner, Darton and Co., London, 1904), pp. 19, 22, 86. *Good Shepherds* was first published in 1902 and ran to at least three editions, and Winnington-Ingram published four other collections of similar addresses in the early twentieth century. Nor was he alone: some broadly similar ideas about priestly ministry can be found in C.G. Lang's *The Opportunity of the Church of England: Lectures Delivered in the Divinity School of the University of Cambridge in 1904* (Longmans, Green, London, 1905)

for victory, and parish study groups examined the origins and aims of the war. For their part, the clergy appear to have felt obliged to say something about the war to their congregations. Their attitude was universally sober: a mixture of sadness at the unfolding tragedy combined with support for their country's cause, without any obvious jingoism or triumphalism.[4] On 5 August 1914, the day after the declaration of war, Brunwin-Hales preached a sermon in St Mary-at-the-Walls entitled 'The Community of Pain'.[5] Spencer, the vicar of St Stephen's, prepared a short letter for his parish magazine, asking for intercessions for victory, adding, 'War is evil. But this good may come of it, that we may be bound closer to each other by its discipline, and that we may feel the Comfort and know the Power of Prayer as we have never felt or known them before.'[6] Monck-Mason wrote a longer letter for *Holy Trinity Parish Magazine* on 29 August 1914:

> It is exceedingly difficult to know how and what to write at the present time. It is hard to realize that when I last wrote, all was peaceful. We seem to have lived through months, though it is scarcely four weeks since War was declared. Even now we are receiving news which will make history, and by the time these lines are read, a long list of casualties will probably have been received.
>
> It only remains for us to keep calm, strengthened by the knowledge that the cause for which our country is fighting is a just and honourable one. For this reason, I am certain that our earnest prayers which are being offered up daily for the success of our arms and the safety of our dear ones, will be heard, though not always answered in the way we wish; but the end is not yet and we are called on to make sacrifice of some kind, some greater, some less. There is work for our brave men at the front, and there is work for us all at home who 'abide by the stuff'.
>
> I am anxious to have an accurate list of all those who have gone from this Parish to serve their King and Country, either abroad or at home, and should be grateful to any who will help me to make the list complete.

4   *Essex County Standard*, 15 August 1914. *St Mary-at-the-Walls Parish Magazine*, September 1914. *Holy Trinity Parish Magazine*, September 1914. *St Peter's Parish Magazine*, September 1914. *St Botolph's Parish Magazine*, September 1914
5   ERO, St Mary-at-the Walls Register of Services, 5 August 1914
6   *St Botolph's Parish Magazine*, September 1914

Services of Intercession at our Church will be continued daily at 12.30, and after Evensong on Sundays. There will also be a Service on one evening in the week which will be announced in Church each Sunday.[7]

The clergy explained the war as a just conflict which was worthy of support. Bishop Whitcombe, for example, preaching before the mayor and corporation at the borough intercession service on 21 August 1914, told his congregation:

they had entered this great war with clean hands. Their leaders had striven for peace, and they had only taken up arms in the cause of national honour, for the defence of the rights of smaller states against oppression, and to relieve Europe from the strain of an intolerable despotism … they embarked on this awful enterprise with clear consciences, as to the justice of their cause.[8]

Monck-Mason, writing again for his parish magazine on 28 October 1914, urged his parishioners,

not [to] neglect the constant prayers for our brave men at the Front, who are fighting to protect our land from bloodshed and devastation, and secure freedom for the brave little State of Belgium which has suffered so terribly from the inroads of the enemy, who has broken treaties in such a dastardly manner.[9]

Military Service and the Clergy

From the start of the war, the Colchester clergy were confronted by a mesh of interwoven problems concerning military service and their own attitudes and involvement. Unlike many other European countries – where conscription was practised – Great Britain had a long tradition of a voluntary army and navy. The question of volunteering for military service occupied many minds during the first eighteen months of the war,

[7]   *Holy Trinity Parish Magazine*, September 1914
[8]   *Essex County Standard*, 21 August 1914
[9]   *Holy Trinity Parish Magazine*, November 1914

until Britain was eventually obliged to adopt conscription in January 1916. Many priests were approached by young men asking, 'Ought I to fight?'[10] There are occasional tales of bloodthirsty preachers, such as the Rev. Thomas Sadgrove of Fairstead in Essex, who, in August 1914, 'preached a horrifying sermon on the horrible scenes of the battlefield and exhorted all the young men to join the army. He had a big union jack hung in front of the pulpit, instead of the pulpit hanging.'[11]

The Colchester clergy seem to have been too conscious of the tragedy of the war to engage in such histrionics, although they widely appealed for volunteers to enlist in the army. Ward, for example, announced that a visiting preacher at St Peter's on 7 March 1915 would preach on the subject of 'The Volunteer, the Procrastinator, and the Irresolute'.[12] Brunwin-Hales wrote in *St Mary-at-the-Walls Parish Magazine* in September 1915:

RECRUITING. – Window cards, showing the number of members of a household who have responded to the call for King and Country, can be obtained, free of charge, from any of the Clergy or District Visitors, who will gladly supply them. They are of a handsome design, with a picture of the King and of the British Isles, and we should like to see them displayed in every house that has sent a man or men to the Colours. The Rector had been trying experiments with cards of this sort for some, when he came across the one published by the Parliamentary Recruiting Committee alluded to above. This is an official one, and each copy bears an official stamp vouching for the use of the card.[13]

Support for the war and appeals for volunteers for the army and navy inevitably had an effect on the clergy themselves. They were exhorting their fellow Christians to join the army and fight in a war which might see them wounded or killed. Ought their pastors to accompany them? If the war was indeed a just one, ought the clergy to serve as combatants? There was a long tradition in Christianity forbidding the clergy from shedding blood, and the possibility of Christian priests taking up arms and perhaps

[10]   W.R. Matthews, *Memories and Meanings* (Hodder and Stoughton, London, 1969), p. 86
[11]   Munson, *Echoes of the Great War*, diary entry for Sunday 16 August 1914
[12]   *St Peter's Parish Magazine*, March 1915
[13]   *St Mary's Parish Magazine*, September 1915

killing or wounding people – some of whom might have been Christians – was extremely emotive and controversial.[14] From the outset, the bishops of the Church of England opposed combatant service for their clergy. The archbishop of Canterbury, Randall Davidson, having consulted Sir Lewis Dibdin, the dean of the Arches and a leading ecclesiastical lawyer, sent a letter to the diocesan bishops on 2 September 1914 affirming that combatant service was incompatible with ordination.[15] This view was shared by Bishop Watts-Ditchfield, who refused several applications from diocesan priests for permission to serve as combatants.[16]

On 21 January 1915, Watts-Ditchfield wrote to the archbishop of Canterbury with a connected problem: questions were 'coming in from all sides of Essex' as to whether the clergy might be allowed to enlist for combatant service in the Home Volunteer Corps – a sort of militia, or 'Home Guard'– which was intended to fight in the event of a German invasion. Davidson replied on 24 January that the bishops could not approve of clergy enlisting for any sort of combatant service, whether in their own parishes or overseas.[17]

Episcopal wires must have become crossed in Essex, because four days earlier, on 20 January 1915, Bishop Whitcombe had positively advised the Colchester clergy to join the Home Volunteer Corps: 'He thought it an excellent movement and one that the clergy might help by their example. It also offered solid advantages of personal intercourse with the men.'[18] The Colchester Volunteer Corps regularly contained over 200 men, and at its peak it had 700, and so there would have been important pastoral opportunities for the clergy.[19] There is no evidence, however, that any priests from Colchester joined the Home Volunteer Corps, either as combatants or as chaplains.

Although the bishops disapproved of the clergy enlisting as combatants, they could not actually prevent them from doing so, and a small number of priests and deacons defied them and volunteered, either because they felt this was the best way they could support their country in a just cause or because they believed they could get alongside the

---

14   St Thomas Aquinas, *Summa Theologica*, II-II, question 40, article 2
15   Lambeth Palace Library, London (LPL), Davidson Papers, volume 201, fols 75–7
16   *Essex County Standard*, 5 September 1914
17   LPL, Davidson Papers, vol. 201, fol. 98–9
18   ERO, Colchester Ruri-decanal Chapter Minutes, 26 March 1915
19   Rusiecki, *The Impact of Catastrophe*, p. 138

men in the trenches more effectively as ordinary soldiers than as chaplains.[20] The bishops were not of one mind themselves about conscription. Watts-Ditchfield described a meeting of bishops at Lambeth Palace on 27 October 1915:

> [The] Bishop of London moved a resolution practically permitting the clergy to enlist. He spoke feelingly and well. The Bishop of Birmingham seconded. I immediately spoke against and emphasized first that the spirit of the Ordination Service could not permit such and that if the resolution was passed it meant that *all* clergy of military age to go [sic] for it was all or no[ne]. There was a long and excellent discussion. [The] Bishops of Oxford, Winchester, Ely and [the] Archbishop of York spoke strongly against the resolution. [The] Bishops of Birmingham, [St] Asaph, [and] Manchester in favour. The final voting was 6 for, 25 against.[21]

In January 1916, the Military Service Bill introduced compulsory conscription. The spectre of clergy being compelled by the state to take combatant service was distressing to many. Watts-Ditchfield wrote again to Archbishop Davidson on 31 December 1915:

> I do hope that steps will be taken to Exempt clergy from Conscription. The more I view it in relation to national needs and the state of the Church today the more I feel the clergy must not be allowed into the fighting line. I suppose you notice in the 'Telegraph' correspondence, the number of laymen who objected to the Enlistment of the Clergy. I am sure that we shall do more good in the end by standing firm on the question.[22]

The clergy were eventually exempted from conscription by Parliament when the Act was passed.

Many priests, whilst unhappy about enlisting as combatants, were nevertheless anxious to take service as non-combatants. When the war began in 1914, the peacetime army contained only 117 chaplains, and the need for more quickly became clear as recruits flocked in their

---

[20]   A. Wilkinson, *The Church of England and the First World War* (SCM Press, London, 1996), pp. 42–5

[21]   ERO, Watts-Ditchfield diaries, 27 October 1915

[22]   LPL, Davidson Papers, vol. 339, fols 357–8

thousands to join Kitchener's New Army.[23] Clergy could also serve as non-combatants with the Royal Army Medical Corps, and later with the Church Army and in the Young Men's Christian Association rest huts behind the lines. From the outset, Watts-Ditchfield was hostile to clergy abandoning their churches and parishioners to serve as non-combatants. He made this clear in his charge delivered at the diocesan conference on 27 October 1914:

> He felt it his duty to refuse consent for the clergy to join the fighting line. He was convinced that the great body of the laity as well as the clergy realised that at a time like this the priest could serve his nation better in another place than in the firing line. He had, however, given permission in some cases for clergy to join the Royal Army Medical Corps, but even here a word of caution was needed. Before volunteering, each clergyman should consider carefully the claims of his particular parish. If the hundreds of troops quartered there were to be left without adequate provision for their spiritual and social welfare, if women and children bereaved of the bread-winner were to lack help and comfort in their great loss, then it was a serious question whether his place was not at home among the people committed to his care. Each case must be decided on its merits, but generally speaking he was persuaded that the parish priest could best serve his country by remaining, as, for instance, Lord Kitchener, at his post away from the firing line.[24]

This was clearly an important consideration in Colchester, where there were more troops than in any other town in the diocese of Chelmsford, or indeed in the whole of East Anglia. At times during the First World War, there were over 40,000 soldiers in Colchester – as many as the civilian population – and once, in February 1917, an entire division numbering over 20,000 officers and men, the 66th East Lancashire Territorial Division, left Colchester for France and was almost immediately replaced.[25] Many of these soldiers sought help and support in various forms from Colchester's churches and clergy whilst stationed in the town.

[23] Major Margaret Easey, Royal Army Chaplains' Department Depot, letter to the author, 2 June 1998. By the Armistice in 1918, there were some 3,500 chaplains
[24] *Essex County Standard*, 31 October 1914
[25] Hunt, *Souvenir*, p. 59

The public seldom understood the awkward position in which their parish clergy found themselves in wartime, and attitudes towards them were sometimes hostile: priests were every so often accused of being 'shirkers' – even in Parliament on occasion – and the controversial journalist Horatio Bottomley grumbled that French Roman Catholic priests were being conscripted into the trenches, whilst strapping Anglican curates were to be seen at parish tea parties.[26] In industrial areas, small boys sometimes followed the clergy in the streets shouting, 'Kitchener wants you!'[27] Many of the clergy found such criticism unfair and hurtful; others grew restless.[28]

The most notable example of a Colchester clergyman suffering from wartime conflicts of loyalty is that of the Rev. Edward Strangeways Morton. Morton was a graduate of Worcester College, Oxford, and, after only a single term's theological training at Bishop's College, Cheshunt, he was ordained deacon by Watts-Ditchfield on 4 October 1914 to serve as assistant curate at St Giles's, Colchester. The first few weeks after ordination are always apt to be somewhat unsettling, and it should be recalled that Morton began his ministry in a parish containing the barracks, into which he could see large numbers of recruits of a similar age to himself flocking daily. Morton began his parish ministry, but his heart was not in it, and he felt drawn towards military service. After three weeks, he could bear the inner conflict no longer; he ran away from the parish and enlisted in the Royal Army Medical Corps. Bishop Watts-Ditchfield was far from sympathetic when the news reached him and wrote immediately to Lord Kitchener, the secretary of state for war:

> I am sorry to trouble you but I feel it my duty as Bishop of Chelmsford to express to you the following facts relating to Edward S. Morton who this week enlisted in the Royal Army Medical Corps and has, I believe, gone to Aldershot.
>
> 1st He was ordained by me only three weeks ago on October 4th

---

[26] A. Marrin, *The Last Crusade: The Church of England and the First World War* (Duke University Press, Durham, NC, 1974), pp. 190–1

[27] F.A. Iremonger, *William Temple, Archbishop of Canterbury* (Oxford University Press, Oxford, 1949), p. 193

[28] LPL, Davidson Papers, vol. 201, fol. 135, Archbishop of York to Archbishop Randall Davidson, 11 May 1915

2nd Before his Ordination I had a long conversation with him about the Royal Army Medical Corps and he told me definitely that he ought to be ordained.

3rd He was sent as curate to Colchester which is crowded with troops and to a parish where help is urgently required.

4 [sic] This week he has enlisted without the permission of his Vicar and without even communicating with me at all.

As your Lordship is aware every Candidate for Ordination takes an Oath of Canonical Obedience to the Bishop and promises to remain in his curacy for two years. Such conduct as Morton's, if allowed to be passed over, [*indeciph.*] contrary to all discipline and I wonder what his Oath to his King and Country can be worth when he easily breaks the one made three weeks ago at the most solemn time of Ordination. I may add that I have gladly permitted and approved of clergy joining the Royal Army Medical Corps but this is a case of defiance of all authority and I am sure your Lordship will interfere in a case of this kind.[29]

Lord Kitchener passed the letter on to the archbishop of Canterbury, who replied on 5 November 1914, saying that he thought the matter might be rightly left in his and Watts-Ditchfield's hands.[30] Davidson also wrote on the same day to Watts-Ditchfield:

A letter of yours, dated October 22nd, to Lord Kitchener has been sent to me with a request for an expression of my opinion and advice. The facts as I gather them are that the Rev. Edwd S. Morton, who was ordained by you a month ago, after you had talked to him about the rival claims of his Ordination and Army work, has now, without the permission of his Vicar and without telling you, rushed off to take service with the Royal Army Medical Corps, and this from a Parish where in War time the clerical staff has quite exceptional duties laid upon it and his services are especially wanted. Such behaviour seems to me reprehensible in a high degree. But I wonder whether the proper course is that Lord Kitchener should interfere to refuse to accept him. You rest the request for such action on Lord Kitchener's part upon the Oath of Canonical Obedience taken by Mr Morton. I a little doubt whether this is the most substantial ground on which to

[29] LPL, Davidson Papers, vol. 192, fol. 393
[30] LPL, Davidson Papers, vol. 192, fol. 393

proceed. Would it not be better that you should write to Mr Morton or send for him and talk things over, showing him in the fatherly way which would be yours, that he has in his enthusiasm lost his head, and that he is placing himself in a wholly false position as regards his future life and his best use of this (I do not mean promotion but opportunity of service.) Very likely you would find him amenable to fatherly advice and ready to tell you that he would like to withdraw from the position he has taken up. In that case you would be in a position to write to Lord Kitchener to obtain leave from him to do so. If he takes the other line and says that he would be miserable in Colchester, and wishes to retain the Army position he has taken up, it ought to be gravely pointed out to him that in that case he is really showing himself not to have the vocation which a few weeks ago he solemnly assured you that he felt God had given to him. In that case I should be inclined to tell him that you do not propose to interfere further, but that a careful record of what has passed must be placed in my hands for preservation here, so that the facts may be known should he at any time hereafter entertain the idea of trying to re-enter the ministry. Sometimes young fellows of this sort are simply acting with an unbalanced enthusiasm without having adequately weighed up what it all means.[31]

What followed is uncertain, because Morton's military records were destroyed by enemy bombing in 1940, and Watts-Ditchfield's daughter burnt or threw away many of the bishop's papers following his death in 1923.[32] Morton must have managed to make a good impression on Watts-Ditchfield, because upon his demobilisation from the Royal Army Medical Corps in 1919, the bishop allowed him to return to the ministry and ordained him to the priesthood in 1920. The bishop took good care, however, to send Morton to a parish in Barking, on the other side of the diocese of Chelmsford from Colchester.[33]

As the war continued, the policy evolved in the diocese of Chelmsford that incumbents should remain in their parishes, but that curates might be allowed to volunteer to become chaplains or for other non-combatant service, provided they could be spared. Not all curates who offered their

[31]   LPL, Davidson Papers, vol. 192, fols 394–5
[32]   Christopher Gowing, Bishop Watts-Ditchfield's grandson, letter to the author, 19 January 1998
[33]   *Crockford's Clerical Directory*, 1920

services were accepted, as was the case with the Rev. Stanley Wilson from St Mary-at-the-Walls, who volunteered in late 1915 or early 1916. His parish magazine announced:

> The Rev. Stanley Wilson some time ago offered his services as a Chaplain to the Forces, and he was recently summoned to London by the Chaplain General (Dr Taylor Smith) for an interview on the subject. After careful consideration of all the circumstances, the Chaplain General came to the conclusion that Mr Wilson would best do his duty by remaining where he is at present. The Parish will be glad that this is so, though they will feel that it was right for him to offer his services, since he is an unmarried man of military age. The fact is, since the War began, the work of the Clergy of our Parish has been so much increased that it is no exaggeration to say that calls made on them in connection with military undertakings, and not least the wounded soldiers, are enough to absorb the full time of one man. We mention this for several reasons – one being that we like the Parishioners to know that the Clergy have their place in the dislocation of business, which is so general now – and another being that we are anxious to ask members of our congregations to bear with us if the systematic visiting, which is of such great importance, and other normal work suffer during the war. Had Mr Wilson gone, it would have been necessary to find someone else to have taken his place, or to have abandoned much of the work now being done (especially with the soldiers) on week days as well as Sundays. All the Clergy regard their special work in connection with the war as a great privilege and as of prime importance as at this time, and we deeply regret any curtailment of it.[34]

The chaplain general's reasons for rejecting Wilson, and the references to military undertakings in the magazine article, are further indications of the way in which by 1916 ministry to the troops and the wounded had become a very important part of the wartime work of the Colchester clergy.

The controversy surrounding the clergy and combatant military service flared into life once again during the final months of the war. On 21 March 1918, the Germans launched an offensive to try to capture Paris and force the war to a conclusion before the Americans landed troops in France in

---

[34] *St Mary-at-the-Walls Parish Magazine*, February 1916

any large number. For several weeks, the outcome of the war seemed to hang in the balance. British troops were rushed to the front and a new Military Service Bill was hurriedly introduced to Parliament on 9 April 1918, which raised the age of military service from forty-one to fifty and in some cases to fifty-five, and made no provision for clerical exemption from conscription.[35] Two days later Sir Douglas Haig issued an Order of the Day revealing the gravity of the situation: 'Every position must be held to the last man: there must be no retirement. With our backs to the wall, and believing in the justice of our cause, each one of us must fight to the end.'[36] Randall Davidson very reluctantly agreed to conscription of the clergy for combatant service, though he was privately relieved when the government reintroduced clerical exemption on 15 April, for fear of what the reaction to the forcible conscription of Roman Catholic priests might be in Ireland. This, however, placed the clergy of the Church of England in a very invidious position: they had already received much criticism concerning their exemption, and emotions now ran high, especially when the Germans recaptured the old battlefield of the Somme and the British were forced to evacuate Passchendaele Ridge, which had been captured at great cost.

Speaking in the House of Lords, Davidson stressed that neither he nor any other of the Anglican bishops had had anything to do with reintroducing clerical exemption: 'Let no man say hereafter that the clergy of the Church of England have asked for exemption at this hour … the very contrary is the case.'[37] He promised 'to see what we can do voluntarily under conditions so different – and this is the real point – from those of 1915–1916 as to justify a different attitude on our part from that which we took at that time.'[38] Watts-Ditchfield remained unhappy about the clergy being conscripted for combatant service, but he told Davidson on 20 April 1918 that he would not oppose priests from enlisting as combatants if their consciences permitted them to do so.[39] Two days later, the bishops met at Lambeth Palace and unanimously agreed to appeal to the clergy of military age to offer themselves for enlistment as though they had been

[35] Marrin, *Last Crusade*, p. 193
[36] M. Gilbert, *First World War* (HarperCollins, London, 1994), p. 414
[37] Wilkinson, *Church of England*, pp. 40–1
[38] Marrin, *Last Crusade*, p. 194
[39] LPL, Davidson Papers, vol. 341, fol. 80

included in the new Military Service Act, making no distinction between combatant and non-combatant service.[40]

The prospect of clergy enlisting willy-nilly and causing chaos in the parishes led Bishop Watts-Ditchfield to set up a tribunal in March 1918 to coordinate all offers of service, 'subject to ministerial efficiency being maintained'.[41] The tribunal consisted of a panel of clergy and laity, under the chairmanship of the bishop of Colchester. It advised the Colchester clergy that, with so many troops and wounded soldiers in the town, they could best aid their country during the new emergency by remaining in their parishes. The only priest from Colchester we can be certain became a military chaplain during this period was James Gardiner, the part-time curate of St Nicholas's.[42] George Behr of St Stephen's wanted to become a chaplain and was disappointed to be told by the tribunal that he should remain in his parish and continue his work as an officiating clergyman to the troops in Colchester.[43] Herbert Hughes, the overworked curate of St Peter's, was directed by the tribunal to undertake other work in Colchester, much to the chagrin of his vicar.[44] Percival Brinton of All Saints' wished to become a chaplain and was advised by the tribunal that the best way to achieve this was to go to work with the Church Army in France and then to apply for a commission.[45] He left his parish in September 1918 and was away until Easter 1919.[46]

Perhaps the most surprising clergyman from Colchester to become a military chaplain was Bishop Whitcombe, who was then aged fifty-six. He had offered his services in 1915, but had been turned down because he was a bishop. Learning early in 1918 that there was a backlog of soldiers in France waiting to be confirmed, Whitcombe wrote once more to offer his services. The Army Chaplains' Department replied rather unhelpfully that they could not see their way to let him go to France with the rank of a bishop. Whitcombe replied that he was happy to go as a chaplain fourth

[40] *Chelmsford Diocesan Chronicle*, May 1918. LPL, Davidson Papers, vol. 201, p. 75
[41] LPL, Davidson Papers, vol. 341, fol. 108
[42] Entry in Venn, *Alumni Cantabrigienses*
[43] *St Botolph's Parish Magazine*, June 1918
[44] *St Peter's Parish Magazine*, June and August 1918
[45] Balliol College Library, Oxford. Brinton to the Master of Balliol College, 14 September, 1918
[46] ERO, All Saints' Register of Services, 1918–19

16 Bishop Whitcombe in army chaplain's uniform, Lexden Road,
Colchester, 1918. Although the bishop was only permitted to serve as a chaplain
fourth class by the Army Chaplains' Department, he appears to have worn an
episcopal purple stock beneath his clerical collar, rather than an
ordinary chaplain's black stock.

class. He served on the Western Front between 1918 and 1919, though it appears that he returned to the diocese from time to time.[47]

Throughout England, the numbers of clergy offering themselves for military service of any sort in 1918 were extremely low. Many priests were too old, whilst others of military age had already enlisted or were engaged in additional war work outside their parishes. The numbers of ordinations declined rapidly during the war as ordinands volunteered or were conscripted into the armed forces. The bishops agreed that, after Trinity Sunday 1915, they would not normally accept for ordination any able-bodied men of military age. This policy inevitably led to a shortage of new priests to replace those who left their parishes. By the spring of 1918, the parochial clergy were spread thinner than ever before, and the Church of England was scraping the bottom of the manpower barrel.

The burden of the parochial clergy during the First World War was further increased early in 1917 with the introduction of a scheme of National Service evolved by Neville Chamberlain and Archbishop Lang of York. During 1916, a number of priests had voluntarily begun working on the land and in munitions factories, in addition to their normal parochial work. A scheme was set up in 1917 to establish this on a regular basis and to seek to involve as many able-bodied priests as possible. The whole of the Colchester ruri-decanal chapter volunteered for additional war work when they met on 9 February 1917 and sent four resolutions to Watts-Ditchfield:

1 That the Bishop of Chelmsford be asked to appoint commissioners to submit a scheme to him with a view to releasing as many of the clergy of the Deanery as possible to take part in the new system of National Service.

2 That the Chapter ventures to suggest to the Bishop that the Bishop of Colchester, Bishop Harrison, with two or three laymen might be invited to form the Commission.

3 That the Chapter, irrespective of the National Service age limit, pledges itself to co-operate as far as possible in any re-arrangement of work which may be necessary.

---

[47] Obituary in *Chelmsford Diocesan Chronicle*, April 1922. Christopher J. Whitcombe, letter to the author, 13 April, 1998. Major Margaret Easey, Royal Army Chaplains' Department Depot, letter to the author, 2 June 1998

4   That this chapter offers to supply a sufficient number of chaplains for the troops in Colchester as part of its contribution to the scheme of National Service.[48]

The fourth point was a late addition, after the chapter had been told that the chaplain general would be grateful if they would undertake to minister to a division that was shortly to arrive in Colchester; it is significant that they did not feel able to take on additional wartime work until they had made provision for the troops in their own town.

Watts-Ditchfield set up a commission as they had requested, and its decisions took effect from 11 April 1917. As expected, ministry to the troops formed the bulk of the national service for the Colchester clergy. Behr, Burnett, Brunwin-Hales and the Rev. John Francis Hewitt, rector of St Mary Magdalen from 1916, were appointed as 'Officiating Clergymen to the Troops'. They were informed that 'this appointment does not carry with it the title of chaplain or give the right to wear uniform', but were told that they were to do the full work of chaplains and that the troops were to have the first call on their services. Courteen, Monck-Mason and Marsh were appointed to help with the wounded at the Essex County Hospital; Gardiner, Harris, Worsfold and the Rev. T.J.L. Davies, chaplain of Severalls Hospital, were to help in the two Young Men's Christian Association huts, and the Rev. William Beale White and the Rev. Walter Alexander Limbrick, curate of St Peter's from 1916, in the lecturing huts.[49] This, as expected, restricted the amount of time that they were able to devote to their parishes, and the remaining clergy had to plug the gaps as best they could. Brunwin-Hales appears to have become a temporary chaplain to the forces later in 1917: he is described as a temporary chaplain in his post-war entries in *Crockford's Clerical Directory* and in his obituary, and a photograph exists of him in chaplain's uniform, but other records do not seem to have survived. As far as one can tell, he remained in his parish throughout this period, so perhaps he was appointed as a temporary chaplain in order to work amongst the troops in Colchester.

---

48   ERO, Colchester Ruri-decanal Chapter Minutes, February 1917
49   ERO, Colchester Ruri-decanal Chapter Minutes, April and May 1917. List by Brunwin-Hales appended to Colchester Ruri-decanal Chapter Minutes, 1 June 1917

G.T.B-----Hales
1918.

17 The Rev. Canon Greville Brunwin-Hales, rector of St Mary-at-the-Walls and rural dean of Colchester, wearing the uniform of a temporary chaplain to the forces

Pastoral Work in Wartime

The pastoral work of the Colchester clergy between 1914 and 1918 may be divided into three categories: pastoral work with parishioners; work with the troops training in Colchester; and work with wounded soldiers in the military hospitals in the town. In the first category, the Colchester clergy were in the same position as other parochial clergy except that they probably had a higher ratio of parishioners in the army at the start of the war. Their subsequent experience of ministering to the troops and to the wounded on such a large scale during the war was probably unique to a garrison town and set them apart from the rest of the diocesan clergy.

The Impact of the War: Anxiety and Stress

The impact of the First World War upon European society has been compared with the Black Death in the fourteenth century.[50] The British experience of war for over a century and a half prior to 1914 was largely of conflicts in distant lands or parts of the empire waged by a small, professional army, backed up by the Royal Navy. The general public might have followed the progress of a particular campaign with interest, such as the conflicts in the Sudan or South Africa, but unless they had relatives in the army, these conflicts hardly impinged upon their everyday lives. The First World War, by contrast, was completely different: the British Army found itself fighting the principal enemy in the main theatre of the war. It was also a total war, in which armies used modern weapons with their vastly increased firepower and utilised the latest scientific and industrial techniques, of which poison gas – used first in 1915 by the Germans and later by the Allies – is a particularly gruesome example. The First World War encompassed the civilian population in new and unfamiliar ways, as Britain's social, economic and agricultural life was changed by the demands and exigencies of waging what soon became a worldwide conflict.

For this reason, the 1914–18 generation named it the 'Great War'. Virtually every household came to have some family member, friend or colleague in the army or navy, and all lived in fear of the postman or telegram boy bearing news of death or injury. The public mood was further darkened by British propaganda, which portrayed the German troops – not always untruly – as baby-slayers, rapists, mutilators of women, destroyers of libraries and churches.

Parish magazines from Colchester from the First World War often refer to 'anxiety'. Monck-Mason, for example, wrote in October 1914:

> There is scarcely a house in the Parish where anxiety is not felt for some relative or friend, whose welfare, we know, is entirely in the hands of the All-

---

[50]   A. Gregory, *The Silence of Memory: Armistice Day, 1919–1946* (Berg, Oxford, 1994), p. 1

powerful God. The lists of those for whom we pray gradually grow, and we have already to mourn the loss of some – killed and wounded … Another thing that brings the difficulties of war home to us is the billeting which is going on at the present time. To some it is a help, to many it is a hardship borne quietly, as all are anxious to take their part in the present distress.[51]

The population – civilian and military – experienced stress on an unparalleled scale between 1914 and 1918. The task of the parish clergy in wartime was to minister to their frightened and anxious parishioners as best they could, and to bring them the comfort and reassurance of the Gospel. In Colchester in the late summer of 1914 this mainly meant ministering to the troops from the garrison departing for the front and to their families. Brunwin-Hales wrote in *St Mary-at-the-Walls' Parish Magazine* shortly after the declaration of war:

> The Clergy will most readily arrange for Celebrations of the Holy Communion for any families which have relations going to the war, and of course they would esteem it a privilege to call and see all who are in special anxiety and sorrow at this time. We remember in the South African War some of our most solemn moments were spent with soldiers going to the front, and their relations, and the Services then held can never be forgotten.[52]

The commonest way in which the clergy ministered to the families of soldiers – at least in the first years of the war, before they became overstretched – was by visiting them at home, and by praying for their menfolk serving at the front or at sea. Prayers were sometimes said in houses, but additionally each parish church in Colchester arranged to hold a weekly intercession service (see below). An intercession service for the whole of Colchester was kept up daily throughout the war at Holy Trinity Church in the town centre, so that any passer-by could drop in to pray or ask for special intercessions.

Many of the Colchester clergy attempted to try to keep in touch with their parishioners serving in the army or navy. Some priests, at least to begin with, endeavoured to write to each man on a monthly basis. Others sent cards at Christmas and Easter, and there were periodic requests in all

---

51 *Holy Trinity Parish Magazine*, November 1914
52 *St Mary-at-the-Walls Parish Magazine*, September 1914

church magazines for the clergy to be kept informed of soldiers' changes of address. Sometimes the soldiers' replies to their vicars' letters were also printed.[53]

What we see here are the clergy adapting well-known pastoral methods – which, importantly, were also familiar to their parishioners – to meet new demands during the war. Pre-war clerical training emphasised the importance of regular parochial visiting, summed up in the adage that 'a house-going parson makes a church-going people'.[54] It was also common in those days, when telephones were a comparative rarity, for the clergy to keep in regular touch with their parishioners or former parishioners by letter, one well-known example being Bishop Edward King of Lincoln.[55]

Ministry to the Bereaved

It also fell to the clergy to minister to the families of those wounded and killed during the war. During the First World War, 1,248 men from Colchester lost their lives.[56] If Colchester replicated the national trend, probably about twice that number were wounded: this would mean around 3,750 men from Colchester were either killed or injured, most of whom would have had distressed or grieving families in the town. The Colchester clergy did not have to cope with whole streets of terraced houses in which almost every family suffered a bereavement, which was the lot of some clergy when locally recruited 'Pals' battalions perished together,[57] but nevertheless they had to cope with an above-average casualty rate and the highest ratio of deaths in East Anglia during the war (see Table 2).

---

[53]   For instance, *St Peter's Parish Magazine*, May 1915, April 1916, April 1917, December 1918

[54]   Winnington-Ingram, *Good Shepherds*, p. 37

[55]   See B.W. Randolph, ed., *Spiritual Letters of Edward King, DD, Late Lord Bishop of Lincoln* (A.R. Mowbray and Co. Ltd, London, 1910)

[56]   Hunt, *Souvenir*, pp. 44, 99–107

[57]   I remember meeting an old lady in July 1987 in St Bartholomew's Church, Netherthorpe, Sheffield, who recalled that seventy-one years earlier, almost to the day, she had been playing in the street with some other children when the postman appeared and delivered letter to almost every house in the street. A few days earlier the 'Sheffield Pals' had gone 'over the top' during the battle of the Somme and suffered enormous casualties. One by one the children were called in by weeping relatives until the street was left silent and empty

Table 2: War deaths in eastern counties and similarly sized towns, 1914–18

Town	Population	Number killed	Percentage killed
Eastern counties			
Norwich, Norfolk	120,653	2,892	2.40
Southend, Essex	106,021	1,352	1.28
Ipswich, Suffolk	79,383	over 1,400	1.73
Ilford, Essex	78,188	1,127	1.44
Great Yarmouth, Norfolk	60,710	1,472	2.42
Cambridge, Cambridgeshire	55,812	1,420	2.54
Lowestoft, Suffolk	44,326	722	1.63
Colchester, Essex	43,377	1,248	2.88
Chelmsford, Essex	20,761	over 200	0.95
Other towns of a similar size			
Hove, Sussex	46,519	750	1.61
Crewe, Cheshire	46,447	over 1000	2.15
Leigh, Lancashire	45,545	705	1.55
Eccles, Lancashire	44,237	670	1.51
Wallsend-on-Tyne, Northumberland	43,013	450	1.05
Keighley, Yorkshire	41,942	700	1.67
Lancaster, Lancashire	40,212	850	2.11
Darwen, Lancashire	37,913	1,387	3.66

Source: Hunt, *Souvenir*, p. 96

The first news of a death was usually conveyed in a telegram or letter to the next of kin from Lord Kitchener or from the Army Council.
The families of officers were informed by telegram. The families of 'other
ranks' were sent a standardised letter, army form B.104-82.B, which began
bluntly, 'It is my painful duty to inform you that a report has been received
from the War Office notifying the death of [gap for typed name]', before
proceeding to mention in a fairly matter-of-fact way arrangements for
the disposal of any personal effects and unpaid money. This letter was felt
to be too harsh, and it was modified in the middle of the war to include a
paragraph expressing the sympathy of the king and queen and the regret

of the Army Council.[58] This was followed by a letter of condolence from the king, and usually by a letter from the dead man's commanding officer or from a chaplain.

The parish clergy usually tried to visit bereaved families living in their parishes.[59] It should be remembered that the established status of the Church of England, and its internal culture and self-understanding, meant that it was never a gathered church in the sense that Roman Catholic churches or Nonconformist chapels in England were: the Church of England and its clergy believed themselves to exist for the whole English people, whether they were churchgoers or not. Thus, the clergy of Colchester would routinely have visited not just members of their congregations who had suffered bereavements, but all bereaved families living within the geographical boundaries of their parishes. The system of parochial lay district visitors (see below) doubtless played a significant part in keeping the clergy informed about wartime bereavements, and district visitors probably followed up visits by the clergy and kept an eye on bereaved families, a task which became increasingly important after 1917 when the clergy had to devote more time to their national service amongst the troops and wounded. Even allowing for Roman Catholics, Nonconformists, cases who slipped through the net and families who did not want a visit from a clergyman, the twenty-six Anglican priests in Colchester still had a great many grieving families to visit, as well as the families of wounded soldiers. A number of families were bereaved of several sons during the war – or sometimes a father and his son were killed – and the clergy would not infrequently have had the melancholy task of visiting the same family on a number of occasions following different deaths.

It would be interesting to know what the clergy said to comfort the bereaved. Bereavement is always a shock, for which one can never adequately prepare. No two people have the same patterns of grieving, and one not infrequently reacts to different deaths in different ways. During the First World War, grief was made more burdensome when the

---

[58]   R. Van Emden and S. Humphries, *All Quiet on the Home Front: An Oral History of Life in Britain during the First World War* (Headline, London, 2003), p. 90

[59]   Mrs Alice Hicks, interview, 18 March 1998. Mrs Hicks thought that the rector or curate of St Giles's had visited her mother following the death in 1917 of her brother, Sergeant Alfred Mann, but she had no personal recollection of the visit because she had been at school at the time

deceased died violently or of wounds and was buried overseas in a grave which the next of kin could not normally expect to visit. Worse still were the cases of the men whose bodies were completely destroyed or lost forever beneath the mud of Picardy or Flanders. Unfortunately, no diaries or letters containing information about the visits survive, and bereavement visits are, by their very nature, private and personal. A clue to the sort of sentiments expressed may perhaps be found in a letter which Brunwin-Hales published in his parish magazine when his first son was killed in October 1915:

> I want to tell you how deeply my wife and I (as well as my children and household) appreciate the sympathy which you have abundantly bestowed in the overwhelming grief that has come upon us through the death of a much-loved and loving son on the field of battle. Ours is a life-long sorrow, and life can never be the same again for the lad's parents, whatever the consolations that the healing action of time may bring to us. We quite realize that, and so the thought that you feel for us and with us is really helping us to shoulder our burden and work on again. Thank you so much.
>
> Will you do one thing more, please? Pray for us that walking in our path of sorrows we may come nearer to the 'Man of Sorrows', and so nearer to the dear son who, we humbly trust, has departed to be 'with Christ', and may also have within us the blessed hope that through Christ we shall one day see him again and part no more.[60]

On Sundays, prayers were more frequently said for parishioners killed whilst serving in the army or navy (see below). Their names were often displayed on 'rolls of honour' in churches and published in parish magazines, sometimes with details of their deaths.

Ministry to the Troops

The clergy spent a very great deal of their time ministering to the troops who passed and re-passed through Colchester during the war. There were, quite simply, too many soldiers for the army chaplains to cope with, and so the parish clergy were asked to hold parade services for the troops

---

[60]   *St Mary-at-the-Walls Parish Magazine*, November 1915

at five churches – All Saints', St Mary-at-the-Walls, St Nicholas's, St Leonard's, Lexden, and All Saints', Stanway – with greater or lesser regularity throughout the war.[61] Interestingly, none of these churches was Anglo-Catholic: perhaps wartime complaints by Anglo-Catholics that they were marginalised by the army – or at least by senior figures in the Army Chaplains' Department – had some basis in fact. As well as attending compulsory Sunday morning church parades, many of the troops voluntarily attended Evensong in different churches around the town.[62]

The parochial clergy, acting on their own initiative, arranged many special services and events for the troops, such as Harris's 'Talks to Troops' at St Nicholas's in 1915, or the Sunday afternoon teas and Bible classes held by Ward at St Peter's during 1917–18.[63] Special celebrations of Holy Communion were also sometimes held in Colchester's churches – interestingly, at the request of the troops – before they departed for the front.[64] Soldiers were also occasionally presented for Confirmation – the usual route to becoming a communicant in the Church of England – before they went to France.[65] Brunwin-Hales did what he could to welcome and help Jewish soldiers stationed in Colchester in 1915, making St Mary-at-the-Walls' parish room available to them for a club, and explaining their religious practices to his parishioners.[66]

Colchester became an important army medical centre during the First World War, and the parish clergy quickly became involved in ministering to the wounded, their families and the hospital staff. The clergy of St Mary-at-the-Walls were most affected, with three hospitals in their parish. They began regular Friday afternoon services at Gostwycke Hospital in November 1914, and at the Essex County Hospital on Sunday afternoons in December 1914. Services were also held Hamilton Road Military

[61]   *St Mary-at-the-Walls Parish Magazine*, November 1914. ERO, All Saints' Register of Services, 23 July 1915, St Nicholas's Register of Services, 30 May 1915, St Leonard's, Lexden, Register of Services, 27 September 1914. Other churches may have held parade services but their registers of services are missing

[62]   *St Peter's Parish Magazine*, October 1914, November 1914, November 1916, October 1918

[63]   ERO, St Nicholas's Register of Services, 6 January 1915. *St Peter's Parish Magazine*, March 1917, March 1918

[64]   ERO, St Nicholas's Register of Services, 13 November 1915. *St Peter's Parish Magazine*, April 1918

[65]   For example, ERO, St Peter's Confirmation Register, 22 February and 29 March 1917

[66]   *St Mary-at-the-Walls Parish Magazine*, February and June 1915

Hospital.[67] With time, the clergy became accomplished scroungers on behalf of the wounded, successfully obtaining musical instruments, sunshades, umbrellas, deck-chairs, bath-chairs, books, illustrated newspapers and sheet music. Brunwin-Hales even managed to acquire the fittings for a mortuary chapel, so that the next of kin could view the bodies of dead soldiers in decent surroundings.[68] The Colchester clergy sometimes officiated at the funerals of wounded soldiers who had died in hospital in Colchester, which were held in the borough cemetery on Mersea Road.[69]

As well as their additional duties occasioned by the war, the clergy had to continue with all their usual parochial work of administering the sacraments, preaching sermons, pastoral care, baptisms, weddings, funerals, Bible classes, Lent study groups, confirmations and day-to-day parish administration. Church magazines reveal that many pre-war activities continued throughout the war, such as Sunday school treats, missionary missions, rummage sales, sales of work, flower festivals (called 'flower missions'), Boy Scouts and Girl Guides, harvest thanksgivings (curtailed but never abandoned) and all the services and activities of the Church's liturgical year.

The Effect of the War upon the Clergy

As the war dragged on, the clergy of Colchester began to suffer from the effects of their increased workloads, and from an accumulation of stress. Many factors affected this, such as the size and location of each parish,

---

[67]   *St Mary-at-the-Walls Parish Magazine*, June 1917
[68]   *St Mary-at-the-Walls Parish Magazine*, November 1914, December 1914, June, 1917, July 1917, August 1917, April 1918, September 1918
[69]   Colchester Cemetery and Crematorium, Borough of Colchester Burial Registers, 1914–18. The registers contain the names of the deceased, their dates of death and burial, and the ecclesiastical parish in which their deaths occurred. There are no details of military unit and rank. The parishes of St Giles and St Mary-at-the-Walls are given as the places of death for a great many men in their twenties and thirties throughout the war. As these two parishes contained the Military Hospital, Essex County Hospital and Gostwycke Hospital, it is reasonable to adduce that many of these young men were soldiers. Additional evidence may be drawn from the fact that army chaplains officiated at most of these burials – including a British Roman Catholic chaplain at the funeral of a German Roman Catholic prisoner – but the clergy of St Giles's and St Mary-at-the-Walls officiated at a significant number of others

the age, experience and stress level of the individual priest and the support available to the clergy throughout the war.

It is a fact of clerical life that many church congregations contain troublemakers: gossips, backbiters, parishioners who try to play the curate off against the vicar, people who 'project' onto the clergy their own sorrows, problems and inadequacies, and so forth. The priest, mindful of his own sins and of the high demands of his vocation, deals with these troubled and troublesome members of his flock as best he can, but sometimes he can be deeply wounded, or be left feeling a failure, by their antics. Most parishioners in Colchester were profoundly grateful for the ministrations of their clergy between 1914 and 1918, but nerves became frayed as the war dragged on, and the clergy sometimes became a soft target for troublemakers or people with grudges. Priests were occasionally sent abusive letters. Some people complained that the clergy were neglecting their parishioners.[70] Brunwin-Hales tried to explain in his magazine why they he was unable to visit so frequently:

> We do hope that parishioners will be merciful with their Clergy if they receive fewer visits just now, as the increased population in the County Hospital makes a considerable demand on their time. Our congregations are always indulgent and overlook many shortcomings, but this note will perhaps excuse us from unnecessary blame. Visiting we have always regarded as most important, and every member of the staff is always wishing he had double the time for it.[71]

The clergy were daily exposed to scenes of acute grief and suffering in their parishes and in the hospitals. Sometimes, parishioners with serious problems, knowing how over-stretched their priests were, did not contact them for help until it was too late, and the clergy became upset and downcast when they found out.[72] Like everyone else, the clergy were undernourished, overworked and short of sleep because of air raids. They also began to suffer money worries as inflation grew, whilst their stipends

[70]   *St Mary-at-the-Walls Magazine*, November 1915, February 1918
[71]   *St Mary-at-the-Walls Magazine*, January 1916
[72]   *St Mary-at-the-Walls Magazine*, January 1918

remained unchanged.[73] The war threw up a multitude of small problems in parish administration, not the least of which was the frequent commandeering of church halls by the army, often at short notice, which meant that many activities had to be rearranged and ruffled feathers smoothed.

A significant number of army officers in the First World War came from clerical families – it was estimated in 1916 that as many as 30 per cent of officers were the non-ordained sons of the clergy – and the casualties they sustained were proportionally high.[74] Bashford, Spencer and the Rev. John Crampton Triphook, curate of Great Horkesley, each had one son killed, and Brunwin-Hales lost both his sons.[75] There are no details of any sons of Colchester clergy who were wounded. Bishop Whitcombe had three sons in the army, which must have caused him daily anxiety, though all survived the war. To state the obvious, the clergy had to bear their own sorrows and anxieties as well as try to help their parishioners shoulder theirs.

Stress usually expressed itself in illness. De Courcy-Benwell was ill for much of April 1916.[76] The Rev. Montagu Cecil Dickenson, rector of Myland from 1916, was confined to bed for three weeks in March 1918 and wrote later that, 'being overworked and very poorly', he got behind with his paperwork and then lost his register of services.[77] Merrett and his wife were also ill on and off for long periods during the war.[78]

Ward wrote to the parishioners of St Peter's on 25 June 1917:

> It is with great regret I write to say that the stress and strain of war conditions, which we all feel so acutely, have overtaxed my strength. An eminent London specialist, whom I have consulted, takes a serious view of my present state of health, and has ordered me to leave home without delay, but

---

[73]   Figures in *Crockford's Clerical Directory*, 1914–20. Easter offerings varied slightly from year to year, but the rest of the stipends remained largely unchanged

[74]   Marrin, *Last Crusade*, p. 187

[75]   Triphook also helped in other parishes in Colchester during the war. The sons of the Colchester clergy killed during the war were Charles Bashford, Edmund Spencer, Owen Triphook, Henry Brunwin-Hales and Greville Brunwin-Hales

[76]   ERO, St Martin's Vestry Minutes, 1916

[77]   ERO, St Michael, Myland, Vestry Minutes, 1918. Note in the Register of Services

[78]   ERO, St John's Vestry Minutes, 1918

he is quite hopeful that with complete rest and specific treatment I shall, please God, be quite ready to resume work in the autumn.'[79]

The newly married Ward went to Derbyshire with his wife and was able to return to St Peter's on 17 October. Marsh's health also suffered and in the autumn of 1917 he was compelled to leave the large and demanding parish of St Giles's for the much smaller living of Nayland in Suffolk.

Brunwin-Hales suffered a physical or psychological breakdown on Sunday 18 August 1918, when he was taken ill after baptising two babies in the afternoon: perhaps they reminded him of his own sons, Henry and Greville, killed in the war. He slipped away to Eastbourne with his wife and did not return to the parish until the spring of 1919, although he still undertook a certain amount of deanery correspondence. It seems that, at first, Brunwin-Hales's curates tried to conceal his illness, but when the news eventually broke, his congregation realised how greatly they were indebted to him, and he was helped on the way to recovery by a letter of good wishes bearing hundreds of parishioners' signatures.

Two priests died during the war: Bashford was taken ill after Evensong at St Mary Magdalen's on 27 February 1916 and died four days later, aged seventy-three. Naters died on 4 October 1918, aged fifty-nine. Although they were both reasonably long-lived by the standards of the day, their deaths may perhaps have been hastened by grief and the war.

Support for the Clergy in Wartime

From whom did the clergy of Colchester receive support, help and encouragement during the war? The answer would appear to be largely from each other. Bishop Whitcombe was a very pastoral bishop and a patient listener, and Brunwin-Hales, as the rural dean of Colchester, spent a good deal of time supporting his fellow clergy. Registers of services show that the town's clergy were good at providing each other with cover for holidays and in times of illness. From time to time they also exchanged pulpits on Sundays and delivered devotional addresses during Lent in each others' churches. Churchmanship does not seem to have been much of a problem: registers of services reveal that the clergy

---

[79] *St Peter's Parish Magazine*, July 1917

preached and conducted services in parishes of different churchmanship to their own.

The ruri-decanal chapter proved important in maintaining clerical morale during the war. The chapter was a forum for conveying information, taking decisions on deanery matters and exchanging views and information; membership was open to all parochial clergy, hospital and army chaplains stationed in the town. The chapter also organised an annual devotional day for the clergy.

The ruri-decanal chapter met seventeen times during the war, usually chaired by Brunwin-Hales, but sometimes by bishops Watts-Ditchfield, Whitcombe or Harrison. A special meeting was convened three days after the outbreak of war, and an emergency committee consisting of Brunwin-Hales, Spencer, Ward, Harris and the Rev. Frederick Theobald, rector of Great and Little Wigborough, was established to liaise with the borough council, although they appear only to have reported back once.[80] A further sub-committee was established in June 1916 to coordinate preparations for the National Mission of Repentance and Hope, which occupied a good deal of the chapter's time (see below). The chapter also discussed liturgical matters, cooperation with army chaplains, the National Register (the list of all persons aged between 15 and 65, created by the National Registration Act of 1915) and war savings, the national service and the military service of the clergy, plans for Good Friday, church finance, Sunday school work, arrangements at Colchester cemetery and the annual exchange of preachers in June. In July 1917 members were anxious to discuss the controversial introduction of women police constables with the Colchester Watch Committee. In December 1917, the chapter unanimously resolved 'to resist by every means in its power the passage into law of any Bill to make three years separation whether by mutual consent or by legal separation order a ground for divorce'.[81]

Meetings were occasionally ill-tempered, such as rumpus that broke out on 4 June 1915 when the chapter discussed Harris's suggestion that they all ought to follow George V's example and pledge total abstinence from alcohol during the war, or the meeting of 26 October 1916, when Harris's further suggestion that the clergy might meet fortnightly at

[80]   ERO, Colchester Ruri-Decanal Chapter Minutes, 7 August 1914, 16 June 1916
[81]   ERO, Colchester Ruri-Decanal Chapter Minutes, 17 December 1917

different churches for Holy Communion was greeted with 'not quite the spirit of brotherhood and equanimity'.[82] A sub-committee chaired by the ever-tactful Brunwin-Hales came up with the compromise that they would meet for Holy Communion followed by breakfast at different churches on Tuesdays in Ember weeks.[83]

The Colchester and District Clerical Society was a nineteenth-century foundation. It met almost monthly throughout the war at different vicarages and enabled the clergy to discuss a variety of topics, and probably also to get things off their chests. Mornings were spent in Bible study, whilst afternoons were devoted to talks given by the members or by visiting speakers. Subjects covered included 'Prayer Book Revision', 'Prayers for the Dead', 'Foreign Missions and the War as Viewed by the Swanwick Conference', 'Dean Inge and Prayer', 'The Church and the Country Labourer', 'Hinduism, Historically Reviewed', 'Immortality as Treated by Canon Streeter', 'The Housing Problem in National Re-construction', 'The Training of the Clergy', 'A Parson's Air-Craft War Work' and Bishop Whitcombe on 'With the Troops in France'. It had been the custom for the host to provide lunch, but as the war progressed members were asked to bring their own food. They were also somewhat irked by the need to obtain military permission when they met near Harwich.[84]

Nothing in the previous experience of the clergy of Colchester could have prepared them for the enormity of the task that confronted them between 1914 and 1918. They were used to dealing with pain, illness and death in their everyday parochial ministry, but not on such a scale. For four and a half years, the clergy found themselves repeatedly walking up garden paths and ringing doorbells, wondering what would confront them when the door was opened and they were faced with the families of the killed or injured.

The clergy also spent many thousands of hours ministering to the wounded in hospital, preparing some soldiers for their deaths, helping those who would recover and, more tragically, ministering to troops who would never get over their physical or psychological injuries. We know from Brunwin-Hales's concern to fit up a decent mortuary chapel that it

[82]   ERO, Colchester Ruri-Decanal Chapter Minutes, 4 June 1915, 26 October 1916
[83]   ERO, Colchester Ruri-Decanal Chapter Minutes, 9 February 1917
[84]   ERO, Colchester and District Clerical Society, Annual Reports 1914–19

also fell to the Colchester clergy to try to comfort the grieving relatives of soldiers who had died in the town's military hospitals. At the same time, the clergy had to continue to look after their own parishes and bear their own anxieties and sometimes bereavements. It is no wonder that they were sometimes ill; what is surprising is that they coped as well as they did.

It is regrettable that, although much primary material remains, no diaries written by Colchester's clergy during the First World War have survived. Vicars and rectors tend to be on their best behaviour when writing monthly letters for publication in their church magazines – there is no point in upsetting the congregation unnecessarily – but it would have been interesting to have seen a little more of the ebb and flow of their lives in wartime. Nevertheless, enough material has survived over the past century to help us build up a picture of the clergy of Colchester in 1914–18 as a rather mixed group of men, of varied temperaments and abilities, who nevertheless responded to the challenges of the First World War with courage, imagination and self-sacrifice, and who enjoyed a fair degree of success. They seem – perhaps unsurprisingly – mostly to have adapted pre-war forms of ministry and mutual support to meet wartime needs, rather than to have discovered or evolved new ones.

By the time of the Armistice in 1918, the clergy of Colchester were over-stretched, tired and frequently ill, but they were not broken. If any priests took refuge in alcohol, or went off the rails in other ways, no stories have come down to us. It is interesting to observe from the subjects discussed by the ruri-decanal chapter and by the Colchester Clerical Society that the clergy appear to have kept up their reading – to a certain extent, at least – and continued to discuss a variety of issues, and not just those con-nected with the war. It is also significant that, whilst supporting the war from the pulpit, the clergy of Colchester were shrewd and judicious in what they said: they did not emerge from the war saddled with extremist sermons which they hoped would be quietly forgotten. If letters in parish magazines are anything to go by, the wartime ministry of the Colchester clergy was not unsuccessful and was widely appreciated by many of their parishioners, as well as by many of the troops and wounded soldiers.[85]

[85] *St Peter's Parish Magazine*, January 1918, *St Mary-at-the-Walls Parish Magazine*, June 1918

5

The Laity

Archbishop Cosmo Gordon Lang once expressed the view that the years 1890–1914 were the 'Golden Age of parochial work in the towns of England'.[1] To ascribe golden qualities to any age is to court controversy, but the picture that emerges of parish life in Colchester in the years immediately before and during the First World War is one of great busyness, involving many people.

It was occasionally alleged later in the twentieth century – sometimes as a result of friction between different Anglican churchmanships – that parish life in the recent past had been over-clericalised, and character- ised by a dominant clergy and a passive laity[2] whose members were under-used, seldom consulted, and of whom the clergy had limited expectations.[3]

Like all generalisations, this claim contains an element of truth: the clergy a century ago were accorded a greater deference in a more class- conscious society, where – by status, and not infrequently by birth – they formed a part of the social elite. In many parishes in 1914–18, the clergy were better educated than the bulk of their parishioners. It is also true that the lives and contribution of the clergy are better documented than those of the laity. Worship a century ago was almost entirely the preserve of the clergy, particularly in those parishes where the principal service was Mattins, at which the vicar officiated, read the lessons from the

---

[1] J.G. Lockhart, *Cosmo Gordon Lang* (Hodder and Stoughton, London, 1949), p. 155

[2] Strictly speaking, 'laity', from the Greek *laos*, means the whole people of God, both ordained and non-ordained. For the purposes of this work, the word will be used in its commonly accepted meaning of every Christian who is not a bishop, priest or deacon

[3] L. Paul, *The Deployment and Payment of the Clergy* (Church Information Office, Lon- don, 1964), pp. 148–9. The Church of England Board of Education's *All Are Called: Towards a Theology of the Laity* (Church Information Office, London, 1985), essays produced by a working party of the General Synod Board of Education chaired by the Bishop of Oxford, pp. 13–17. R. Greenwood, *Transforming Priesthood: A New Theology of Mission and Ministry* (SPCK, London, 1995), pp. 31–2, 51

Old Testament and New Testament, said the prayers and preached the sermon. Lay participation was usually limited to handing out the books, singing in the choir and taking the collection; though in a few churches a prominent layman might occasionally be invited by the vicar to read a lesson. Ironically, in Anglo-Catholic parishes – where there was usually a much higher doctrine of the priesthood – laypeople tended to be more involved in worship. This was because the principal service was a Sung Eucharist instead of Mattins, and laymen usually acted as altar servers, acolytes, thurifers, and so on.

However, this generalisation about the role of the Anglican laity ought to be treated with a degree of caution. The evidence from Colchester indicates that laymen and laywomen played a very important part in the daily life of all parishes before and during the First World War; it provides grounds for questioning, as over-simplistic, the picture of an over-clericalised Church and an under-valued or under-used laity.

The participation of the laity in church life in Colchester in 1914–18 was characterised by two principal features. Firstly, it was well organized and vigorous. Secondly, it reflected the class-conscious and deferential society of the town. These two aspects played an important part in determining the nature and scope of the laity's response to the needs and opportunities of the First World War. A further noticeable feature is that of sex: men, on the whole, tended to become involved in activities to support the war effort, whilst women were more concerned to minister to the needs of the troops and wounded in Colchester.

Class-Consciousness, Social Obligation and Good Works in Colchester

Before 1914, there was an established tradition of Colchester's social elite taking the lead in good works of various kinds. A good example was the Essex County Hospital, which was founded in 1820 and enjoyed a good deal of support from the town's parish churches. Fundraising and associated good works for the hospital were established on lines of social class. A Ladies Linen League was established in 1910 to provide linen for the hospital, under the patronage of Queen Victoria's daughter, Princess Louise. This was run by local ladies, under a series of vice presidents who found 'associates' from whom money was raised to purchase linen:

in other words, upper middle-class ladies ran it and collected money from middle-class women. In the same year, a Workers' Committee was set up to collect money from the 'artisan class' and was run by the workers themselves. In 1911 other ladies established the Colchester Ladies' Collection Association, in which upper middle-class women were appointed 'presidents' of districts, and organised house-to-house collections by rather more lowly women.[4] We shall see similar patterns emerging during the war, with upper middle-class townsfolk setting up schemes to be run by the middle-class or respectable upper working-class bulk of the population.

The social elite of Colchester probably took the lead in good works for a mixture of reasons. For some people, there was a sense of *noblesse oblige*: they were conscious of their privileged position, and in consequence they more or less expected to set an example in helping those less fortunate. Other members of the elite may have engaged in good works to further their social aspirations – to 'get on' in Colchester society – or to buttress their social position in the town.

Two women we shall encounter who exemplified these differing attitudes were the Honourable Mrs Mary Maxse, who seems to have tried to help the wounded out of Christian compassion, and possibly also because she felt that, as a general's wife, it was expected of her; and Mrs Ethel Coats Hutton, a regular churchgoer, and later the wife of a mayor of Colchester, who was nonetheless judged by some members of the Colchester social elite to be a pushy arriviste.

The Honourable Mrs Mary ('Tiny') Maxse was the wife of Major General Ivor Maxse, who commanded XVIII Division for much of the war. She was the daughter of Lord Leconfield and was well connected in aristocratic high society, well above Colchester's rather provincial elite. She moved to Colchester in 1915 and lived at Kingswode Hoe in Sussex Road. Mary Maxse was a devout and thoughtful Anglican laywoman who became a churchwarden in Sussex after the war. She was very patriotic and had a strong sense of duty; her character was described as 'forceful'. Mary Maxse was a born organiser who took an active interest in the welfare of the families of troops under her husband's command, and it is entirely characteristic that she should have wished to help the

---

[4]   Penfold, *History of the Essex County Hospital*, pp. 195–6

18 The Hon. Mrs Mary 'Tiny' Maxse

19 Mrs Ethel Coats Hutton

thousands of wounded soldiers passing through Colchester's hospitals.[5] As her husband's biographer has written:

> In respect of good works and patriotic duties, Mary Maxse would have had great influence on the middle-class elite of the town. As a very grand lady in her own right (Petworth, etc), as well as a General's wife, all those with social aspirations would have been anxious to help her and join her committees.[6]

William Coats Hutton made his money in the cotton trade in Liverpool and Manchester, and, following his retirement from the family firm of Hutton and Company, he and his wife Ethel settled in Lexden in 1908. They built a large neo-Tudor house, which they named Lexden Manor. Ethel Coats Hutton was an imposing figure who struck some people as being anxious to get herself known in the town. Some members of the social elite were disdainful of her as someone who had bought her way into Colchester society, and they referred to her simply as 'Mrs Hutton'.[7] However, William and Ethel Coats Hutton's willingness to spend their money in Colchester – of which they seem to have had a good deal – was widely appreciated, with the result that William soon became a magistrate, was found a place on the town council and became mayor within four years of settling in the town. He was elected mayor again in 1914.

William and Ethel Coats Hutton attended St Leonard's Church, Lexden, where William served as churchwarden from 1914 to 1926 and where Ethel was one of the first members of the parochial church council when it was constituted in 1923.[8] Ethel Coats Hutton may well have felt, both as a Christian and also as the mayoress of Colchester, that she ought to engage in patriotic good works during the First World War – and, in fairness, we all have mixed motives for doing things – but the suggestion of some that she may have seen wartime activities as a way of consolidating her place in Colchester society cannot entirely be excluded.

[5]   J. Baynes, *Far from a Donkey: The Life of General Sir Ivor Maxse* (Brassey's, London, 1995), p. 230. J. Gore, *The Life of Mary Maxse* (Rolls House, London, 1949), pp. 71, 117, 123

[6]   Lieutenant Colonel Sir John Baynes, letter to the author, 23 January 1999

[7]   Miss Mary Beattie, interview, 1 February 1999

[8]   ERO, St Leonard's, Lexden, Vestry Minutes, 1914–29

Mrs Coats Hutton was certainly quick to call a meeting within a week of the declaration of war to set up the War Work Depot (see below), and she worked exceedingly hard in a variety of schemes in Colchester throughout the First World War, suffering a serious illness in the spring of 1918, probably as a result of overwork.[9] Both William and Ethel Coats Hutton's names appear on a list of thirty names recommended by the mayor of Colchester, A.M. Jarmin, to the government in 1918 for decorations for wartime service. Without exception, all were members of the town's social elite.[10]

---

[9]   ERO, Committee Minutes of the Borough of Colchester Social Club for Troops, 13 May 1918

[10] CL, WW1, local material, box 1, letter from A.M. Jarmin, 6 October 1918. The letter does not give the name or address of the recipient, though there is a reply from the Foreign Office dated 8 October 1918 with an indecipherable signature, suggesting that different names should be sent to different government departments for recommendations for decorations. The surviving list of recommended names is: Alderman Wilson Marriage, Cllr. W. Coats Hutton, Cllr. Allen G. Aldridge, Cllr. John T. Bailey (all Mayors of Colchester during the war); Alderman R.W. Wallace, Chairman, Borough War Loan Association; Mr F.G. Mills, Borough Accountant; Cllr. J.L. Burleigh, Chairman, Advisory (Recruitment) Committee; Alderman E. Alec Blaxhill, for work organizing the National Register and recruiting; Alderman W. Gurney Benham, Commanding Officer of the Colchester Battalion, the Local Volunteer Force; Mr A.A. Appleton, Recruiting Officer, the Local Volunteer Force; Mr Horace H. Holloway, Quartermaster, the Local Volunteer Force (all three held temporary commissions); Cllr Ernest S. Beard, Mr Frank Grimwade and Mr A. Whitworth, who all organized and ran the Colchester Special Constables; Cllr A.J. Lucking, Chairman, Borough of Colchester Social Club for Troops, work with war loan and food economy; Mr A.H. Cross, Secretary, Borough Social Club for Troops; Mr S.C. Turner, President, Borough Social Club for Troops; Mrs Hines and Mrs W.G. Benham, prominent organizers, Borough Social Club for Troops; Mrs Renny and Mrs Alderton, Hon. Secretaries, Ladies Committee, Borough Social Club for Troops; Mrs Hunt, for work with the Soldiers' and Sailors' Families Association and the Enquiry Bureau for (military) Pensions; Miss Digby and Miss Harrison, for work with the Soldiers' and Sailors' Families Association; Mrs Coats Hutton 'is Chairman of the Ladies Committee of the Borough Social Club for Troops. One of the most prominent workers in connection with the Mayoress' War Workers (needlework) Depot, which has provided very large supplies of garments and necessaries to the Troops. Has raised funds and given generously to its funds. Has also organized many recent flag days' [the longest recommendation on the list – author]; Mrs Tyler and Mrs R.B. Beard, for 'prominent' and 'splendid' work at the Mayoress' War Work Depot; The Rev. Edward Spurrier, Chairman of the Committee of the Essex County Hospital; Mrs Dickinson, Hon. Superintendent of the County Hospital. The list says it recommends the following doctors who gave of their time and

Working-Class Parishioners

Having established the role played by social elite of Colchester, it is important to make another point which could easily be overlooked: during the First World War, Colchester's parish churches were attended by the town's working-class population in considerable numbers. The upper middle-class social elite provided only a handful of worshippers in each church. The rest of Colchester's middle class – middle-middle and lower-middle class – accounted for quite a few more, but by far the majority of people in the pews were drawn from the working classes, who formed the bulk of the population in 1914–18. This is evident from the large numbers of churchgoers in Colchester: there were simply far more worshippers than there were members of the elite and the middle classes, and so they can only have been drawn from the working classes.

Additionally, all the survivors from the parish churches of Colchester in 1914–18 whom I managed to trace and interview before their deaths were drawn from the town's working classes. For them, there appeared to be nothing strange or usual about working-class townsfolk attending their local parish churches. Whether the working-class churchgoers resented the part played by the social elite in their parish churches, or simply accepted it as the way things were, remains unclear. An education in the borough's elementary schools had hardly equipped most working-class townsfolk to exercise much in the way of leadership. Many parishioners drawn from Colchester's social elite felt a sense of responsibility towards their less well-off fellow worshippers: it was a world in which it was perfectly natural for a churchwarden owning a business to offer a job to a boy from the church choir when he left school, or for an upper middle-class couple to present a canteen of cutlery to a working-class woman parishioner upon her marriage.

services, but the last page is missing from the file. It is unclear how many received decorations

Lay Involvement in Parish Life

District Visitors

Each year every parish had to submit an 'annual statistical return' to the diocese of Chelmsford, and these give a fascinating picture of lay life in Colchester between 1914 and 1918.[11] The laity may not have played an important role in leading worship, but they had a significant place in the regular pastoral ministry of many parishes in Colchester. With three exceptions (St James's, St Martin's and St Paul's), all parishes operated extensive systems of 'district visitors'. Each parish was divided into a number of districts, and each district was allocated a member of the congregation as a 'visitor', who undertook to visit the parishioners in the district on a regular basis, and to report serious or difficult pastoral problems to the parish clergy. At Lexden, for example, there were regular meetings of all the district visitors in the rectory, and it is probable that this pattern was replicated in other parishes.[12] In 1915–16 there were 157 district visitors in Colchester. The number grew to 189 in 1916–17, but shrank slightly to 161 by 1917–18. Throughout the First World War, details of districts and their visitors were printed in church magazines, and it is probable that the system of district visitors played an important part in the Church's ministry to bereaved and anxious families.

Parochial Church Councils

Colchester's laity were involved in the administration of a number of parishes in the town through parochial church councils. These were not mandatory in the Church of England until the Enabling Act of 1919, but some progressive clergy and parishes began them during the late nineteenth century. By 1914, parochial church councils were held in seven parishes in Colchester – St Botolph's, St James's, St Mary Magdalen's, St Mary-at-the-Walls, St Nicholas's, St Paul's, St Peter's – which between them were representative of all shades of Anglican churchmanship.

[11] ERO, Annual Summaries of Church Work and Finance, 1912–18
[12] *Lexden Parish Magazine*, April 1917

The laity in all parishes – whether they had parochial church councils or not – were able to attend annual vestry meetings, held after Easter, during which they elected the people's churchwarden (the other church-warden was appointed by the vicar) and heard reports on the finances, goods, fabric and ornaments of their church. Some laypeople attended the Colchester ruri-decanal conference – the precursor of the rural deanery synod – which comprised lay and clerical representatives from all the town's parishes. There are no surviving minutes of the ruri-decanal conference;it would appear not to have met between November 1914 and February 1919.[13]

Parish Organisations

The bulk of lay activity for the average churchgoer in Colchester was centred on the wide variety of groups and societies to be found in their parishes. These were a mixture of local branches of national organisations and home-grown parochial groups. National organisations, such as the Church of England Men's Society or the Mothers' Union, straddled the spectrum of churchmanship and often united laypeople from very differ-ent parishes. Choirs were another important element of lay participation in the life of many churches. Every parish in Colchester had a choir, usually comprising men and boys. Singers were largely voluntary, except at St Martin's and St Mary Magdalen's, where – surprisingly, for poor parishes – a few choir men were paid. Anglo-Catholic parishes, with their emphasis on the Eucharist as the principal act of worship, additionally ran Anglo-Catholic devotional groups for communicants and servers, such as branches of the Guild of Servants of the Sanctuary, the Confraternity of the Blessed Sacrament, the Confraternity of Our Lady and the English Church Union.

Parishes of more moderate or evangelical churchmanship, such as All Saints', Holy Trinity, St Botolph's, St Giles's and St Nicholas's, held communicants' classes to prepare laypeople for the sacraments. Eleven parishes held Bible classes for laypeople, which were frequently divided according to sex. The Mothers' Union had a few branches in Colchester,

---

[13]   ERO, Colchester Ruri-decanal Chapter Minutes, 9 October 1914 and 19 December 1918

though many other parishes preferred to continue their own independent Mothers' Meetings. St Botolph's and St Stephen's ran parochial troops of Boy Scouts and Girl Guides, whilst St Mary-at-the-Walls was home to a company of the Church Lads' Brigade, and to another Girl Guide troop from 1918. The Band of Hope, which encouraged abstinence from alcohol, had branches in some parishes, though its membership was not large.

Anxiety about the Troops

Traditionally, civilians did not greatly care for the rank and file of the army. Officers were viewed differently – especially in Colchester, where many married and settled in the town – but the 'other ranks' tended to be drawn from the unskilled working classes and were often treated with caution, if not hostility. Rudyard Kipling made much of this in his *Barrack Room Ballads*. There was a widespread fear amongst civilians that soldiers, when outside their barracks, might get up to no good, which principally meant swearing, drunkenness, brawling, theft and sexual vice. There was also an anxiety that wartime recruits from respectable families would be coarsened or brutalised by their time in the army.[14] Put simply, Mrs Coats Hutton, for example, wanted to be able to walk home at night and know that she was safe, and to return to Lexden Manor without discovering that some light-fingered Tommy had made off with the silver.

There is no surviving evidence that the troops caused many serious problems during the war for Mrs Coats Hutton or any other citizens of Colchester. Common sense suggests that there were probably incidents from time to time, but they appear to have been very minor and were not reported in the newspapers (which admittedly were censored), and have not survived in local tales and reminiscences about the First World War. We know that the townsfolk were somewhat anxious about the influx of troops in the summer and autumn of 1914, but this was probably to do with the military authorities billeting them in civilian houses until the barracks could be expanded. After this problem of accommodation was resolved, the people of Colchester appear to have become more relaxed about the troops. This would have been aided by the fact that the troops of Kitchener's New Army in 1915–16 were all volunteers and were mostly

---

[14] Snape, *God and the British Soldier*, pp. 189–200

men of a much higher calibre than most pre-war soldiers. However, when we read of the efforts made by the churches and laypeople of Colchester to help the troops, we should bear in mind that one motive, competing with others, was to keep them out of the town's pubs, and thus to try to head off bad behaviour.

Lay Support for the War Effort

Promoting Recruiting and Keeping in Touch with the Troops

The laity of Colchester's parishes, like their clergy, appear generally to have supported the First World War from the outset. In the first eighteen months of the war, Anglican laypeople played an important role in the drive to recruit soldiers. In the early part of the war, there was a wide-spread reluctance to introduce conscription, which was felt to be somehow un-British: 'Prussianism and conscription are synonymous terms,' avowed the *Essex County Telegraph* in 1915.[15] Thus, from the declaration of war in August 1914 until the introduction of conscription in January 1916, the British Army and Royal Navy relied for recruits upon volunteers.

By the end of August 1914, some 300,000 men volunteered for military service, and a further 700,000 had joined-up by the end of December 1914, but this so-called 'Rush to the Colours' was always patchy, and by January 1915 the rate of enlistment had begun to decline. As the campaign on the Western Front settled down into the stalemate of trench warfare, it quickly became apparent that Great Britain would need large numbers of recruits in order to prosecute the war, and that steps had to be taken to encourage enlistment. Municipal authorities and commercial firms began to sponsor 'Pals' battalions, comprising men from the same locality, who were promised that they could serve together if they volunteered together. The unmentioned corollary, of course, was that they could be killed together.

In some districts the supplies of men of military age and fitness quickly became exhausted, whilst in other areas recruitment was sluggish. It became clear that further action was needed to promote enlistment. Some men and women sought to shame or humiliate men into enlisting.

---

[15]   *Essex County Telegraph*, 21 September 1915

The handing out by women of white feathers – signifying cowardice – to men of military age but not in military uniform has entered legend. Colchester's MP, Laming Worthington-Evans, sought to pressurise young men into enlisting at a public meeting in September 1914, during which he dramatically claimed that men who did not answer their country's call would spend the rest of their lives finding excuses for their conduct, whilst those who volunteered would be honoured forever. To the west of Colchester, Lexden and Winstree Rural District Council passed a resolution protesting against the employment by Essex County Council of able-bodied men of military age as road menders. Major Cecil Sebag-Montefiore refused to employ men aged between nineteen and thirty-five on his estate at Stisted.[16]

To promote enlistment, Lord Kitchener, the secretary of state for war, appointed the Earl of Derby as national director general of recruiting in 1915. In October 1915, Lord Derby introduced a half-way house to conscription known as the 'Derby Scheme', whereby men aged between eighteen and forty were personally canvassed and invited to 'attest' their willingness to serve in the army or navy if called upon to do so. Tribunals were created to adjudicate appeals for exemption on personal or occupational grounds. A significant proportion of eligible men declined to attest. It became necessary to appeal for volunteers for the army and navy, and even after the introduction of conscription in January 1916, appeals were still made for men to enlist before they were conscripted.[17]

The Church of England Men's Society (CEMS) Federation in Colchester was active in the drive to recruit troops. As far as one can tell, the CEMS did not seek to shame men into enlisting, but rather exhorted them to offer themselves for military service for altruistic reasons. Parochial CEMS meetings took on an increasingly patriotic hue, and in August 1915 the Colchester CEMS Federation held a large open-air service outside Colchester Castle to encourage recruiting and to support the war effort.[18] They invited Bishop Watts-Ditchfield to preach, and he proved a good choice for their purposes:

[16] Rusiecki, *The Impact of Catastrophe*, pp. 74, 78
[17] J.M. Winter, *The Great War and the British People* (Macmillan, London, 1987), p. 30. Wilkinson, *Church of England*, p. 32. *St Mary-at-the-Walls Parish Magazine*, March 1916
[18] *St Mary-at-the-Walls Parish Magazine*, August, September, November, December 1915

The grim old walls of the Castle looked down on a notable gathering on a recent Sunday afternoon. Centuries ago those walls echoed to the martial tread; this time to the martial voice. The gathering was noticeable for the reason that a Bishop of the Church, constrained by an imperative sense of duty, was heard advocating the cause of the great war, and urging men to enlist: That fact itself explains the origins of the war, and justifies every move in the widespread campaign. The occasion was an assembly of the Church of England Men's Society, Colchester Federation, the speaker being the Bishop of Chelmsford. Each society in the federation was well represented, some members cycling in from a distance. The chairman was the Right Hon. J. Round, P.C., who was accompanied by Sir Mark Stewart. The Lord Bishop of the Diocese traversed the origin of the war, and with eloquence and downright common sense, allied with the best of reasons, urged every man present to thrift, to total abstinence, to intercession, to be thoroughly alive to the opportunities of service which the days were bringing.[19]

The Church Lads' Brigade

Another church organisation in Colchester which actively encouraged men to enlist was the Church Lads' Brigade. Founded in 1891 as an Anglican response to the Nonconformist Boy's Brigade, the Church Lads' Brigade clothed boys between thirteen and eighteen in a version of the army's khaki uniform and trained them in godliness, as well as drill, signalling, first-aid, field-craft and, in some cases, musketry; evidently they did not see any incompatibility between these activities. Such attitudes were to prove important when war was declared in 1914. Appeals by the Church Lads' Brigade for recruits for the army from amongst its members were sown in well-prepared soil.

The Church Lads' Brigade had a formal link with the Territorial Force, and the branch at St Mary-at-the-Walls maintained a close connection with the 16th Battalion, the King's Royal Rifle Corps. News of the battalion was carefully reported most months in the parish magazine and congratulations were expressed for promotions and decorations. Much was made of the battalion's good record of conduct, the absence of swear-

---

[19]   *St Mary-at-the-Walls Parish Magazine,* August 1915

ing and crime, and the favourable impression they created when they attended church parades. In December 1915, for instance, it was reported:

> Inspiring accounts of the Church Lads' Brigade Service Battalions reach
> us from several quarters. In two Parishes, at least, we have heard that their
> devout Churchmanship and good behaviour have produced marked reli-
> gious results and led the Parishioners among whom they were stationed to
> be more earnest in their religion and regular in their worship. Field Mar-
> shal Lord Grenfell, in asking for more C.L.B. recruits, writes as follows:– 'I
> have lately inspected and taken leave of the 16th Battalion on its going
> up to the Front, and I can say it would be hard to find another Service
> Battalion so well set up, smart, and with so fine a record as to conduct,
> there having been absolutely no crime in the Battalion, thus showing what
> C.L.B. training has done in the past when put to the test.' All this testi-
> mony must be most encouraging to the parents of the lads, and above all, to
> the officers who have bestowed unstinted prayer and work on this branch
> of the Church's organisations. As a Parish we congratulate the C.L.B. and
> are proud to think that members of our Company are doing their duty to
> God as well as 'King and Country' in such large numbers in this time of
> supreme trial.[20]

This rosy picture ought to be taken with a small pinch of salt: in the summer of 1916 one army chaplain complained to the soldiers of the 16th Battalion that he had no difficulty finding them because of the swearing and foul language emanating from their section of the trenches. In fair-ness, these former members of the Church Lads' Brigade were involved at the time in the ongoing battle of the Somme, so perhaps the good chaplain might have been a little more understanding.[21]

The Church Lads' Brigade also sought to inculcate a martial spirit in boys too young to enlist. Use was made of the rifle range at the cavalry barracks, and on Easter Monday 1917 thirty boys took part in an exercise to capture Olivers, the residence of Bishop Harrison at Stanway, from other boys defending it. They then marched home in a fierce blizzard, singing songs and 'proved the senior as well as the junior section of our

---

[20] *St Mary-at-the-Walls Parish Magazine*, December 1915
[21] Snape, *God and the British Soldier*, p. 198

lads to be British to the bone'.[22] The Church Lads' Brigade insisted that its members regularly attended church, held its own Bible study classes and occasionally laid on treats for the boys such as a trip to the theatre.[23]

Civilian distrust of soldiers changed during the First World War, but perhaps more slowly than we have traditionally assumed. The Church Lads' Brigade's portrayal of the decent side of military life may perhaps be understood as an attempt to overcome any lingering reluctance in respectable working-class and middle-class families to let their sons volunteer for the army.

Keeping in Touch with the Troops

Both the Church of England Men's Society and the Church Lads' Brigade sought to keep in regular contact with their members in the army and navy, though with 1,200 men serving in the 16th Battalion of the King's Royal Rifle Corps this was no easy task. Branch secretaries and officers tried to keep up a personal correspondence with individual members, and their families were asked to pass on changes of address. The articles in parish magazines reveal that St Mary-at-the-Walls branch of the Church Lads' Brigade was reasonably successful at keeping in touch with its former members, and in October 1915 it published a booklet containing the names of all former Church Lads' Brigade members in the army or navy, together with a foreword by the bishop of Colchester, who was honorary chaplain to the 16th Battalion of the King's Royal Rifle Corps, and a prayer for those who were serving.[24]

The Colchester Church of England Men's Society sent cards and duplicated letters to all its members in the armed forces on a number of occasions such as Christmas 1916. In June 1917 letters were sent to each member of St Mary's Men's Club in the army or navy:

> TO THOSE ON *Active* SERVICE,–
>
> Although you are absent from our fellowship at St Mary's Club, you are not absent from our thoughts.

[22]   *St Mary-at-the-Walls Parish Magazine*, May 1917
[23]   *St Mary-at-the-Walls Parish Magazine*, February 1917
[24]   *St Mary-at-the-Walls Parish Magazine*, October 1915

20 Bishop Whitcombe, probably at a camp of the 16th (Territorial Force) Battalion of the King's Royal Rifle Corps, of which he was chaplain

Your name is inscribed on our Club Roll of members on Active Service. It is not our privilege to serve as you are serving, but it is our privilege to pray for you. And we do it.

You are fighting for freedom, just as brave Britons have done before you.

You are fighting for international right, for the safety and well-being of smaller nations, for the immunity of non-combatants from lustful cruelty and murderous slavery.

You are fighting to bring about the failure of the most atrocious methods of war that ever disgraced even a German government.

With thankfulness to God we think of your steadfast daring and your unquenchable faith. You are of the blessed company of peacemakers, and it is written 'Blessed are the peacemakers.' May the day of battle ere long draw to its close and peace sure and abiding be the happy lot of us all. To that peace you will have contributed with a willing heart. God have you in His keeping until you come home again.

TO THOSE ON *Home* SERVICE,–

You hardly need to be assured that we – your fellow members of S. Mary's Club – are thinking about you. But we are giving ourselves the privilege of writing and telling you so. Your name is often on our lips and your needs are not forgotten at the Place of Help.

Whether you stay in the homeland or go across the seas, and whatever you may be called upon to do, you are helping onward the greatest cause of right the world has ever seen.

The object of your serving is as clear as the day; that object is – the overthrow of despotism, the emancipation of the people's liberties and their very life. The conflict is long and the demands upon your endurance are great. But you will endure, because of the righteousness of your cause, because of the hopeful signs that the day is breaking, and because it is ever true that in the long run right is greater than might.

Be sure that we never forget you in thought and prayer.[25]

War Savings Bonds

As the war dragged on, it proved more expensive than anyone in the government had foreseen. Various schemes were tried to raise money, including War Savings Bonds, which were introduced in the spring of 1916. The public were encouraged to invest in special bonds, with a modest financial return, to help the government pay for the war. In July 1916, with the sound of artillery on the Somme audible in Colchester, Ward appealed to the parishioners of St Peter's:

At the present moment our thoughts are centred on the brave deeds of our countrymen on the western front, and those of us who perforce remain at home are naturally anxious to second their efforts in every possible way. Some, as munitions workers, are doing all that lies in their power to help, and to these Sir D. Haig writes from the General Headquarters on July 13th: 'At this moment we are engaged on the greatest battle the British Army ever fought. Our daily progress has been continuous since the battle opened, but the successes of our gallant troops have only been made possible by the guns and ammunition turned out in the factories at home … The

---

[25] *St Mary-at-the-Walls Parish Magazine,* June 1917

troops are prepared and eager to maintain 'this pressure,' but the continuous supply of ammunition is a vital factor.' The response to this appeal has been most striking throughout the country, munitions workers generally giving up their August holidays with the utmost willingness, and, in some cases, devoting to the Red Cross Society or other charitable purposes, the "bonus" promised to them by their employers for their work in the holidays.

With such a noble example before us, surely we who are not munitions workers must do all that lies in our power to assist in the conduct of the war, and an opportunity of so doing is not only open to us, but is urgently pressed upon us, i.e., by lending to the Government not only our savings but all that we can possibly spare. 'The war will be won, well won, and quickly won, if behind the firing line the people at home stand and offer their money to their Country. Money cannot be used more patriotically.' It has been stated in the House of Commons that the cost of the war is now £6,000,000 a day and that the borrowing powers of the Chancellor are being rapidly exhausted. As a Parish and Congregation we have shown our interest by our prayers, let us now respond to the appeal for help by our acts of self-denial, and by our gifts or by offering to the Government on loan at interest, what we can, all we can – pence, shillings, or pounds – for the defence of our Country and the cause of right.

We propose to hold a meeting in the Parish Room on the evening of Thursday, August 10th, to consider the appeal of the National War Savings Committee, to which we invite all our Parishioners, as well as all the members of our Congregation, and we sincerely hope that our patriotism will be manifested by the presence of large numbers, all willing and ready to help.[26]

In fact, the response at St Peter's was disappointing: fewer than a dozen parishioners attended the meeting and Ward was unable to form a parochial War Savings Association.[27]

Two War Savings Associations did operate in Colchester during the war: one run under the auspices of the borough council, and the other by the comparatively wealthy parish of St Mary-at-the-Walls. The branch in St Mary-at-the-Walls was begun in July 1916 and was run in the parish room on Tuesday evenings by volunteers from the congregation with

26   *St Peter's Parish Magazine*, August 1916
27   *St Peter's Parish Magazine*, September 1916

banking or financial backgrounds; needless to say, they were all middle-class men.[28] The minimum deposit was 6d, and parishioners could save for War Savings Certificates which cost 15s 6d. A certificate could be cashed at any post office for 15s 6d during the first twelve months after the date of issue and for 15s and 9d at the end of the first full year. There-after, the certificate increased in value at the rate of a penny per month until it reached a maximum value of £1 at the end of five years. No one was allowed to hold more than 500 certificates.[29] Parishioners from other churches used the St Mary-at-the-Walls War Savings Association, as did many Freemasons.[30]

The public's overall response to the war savings scheme was patchy, and early in 1917 the government asked the clergy to urge their congregations to invest in war savings.[31] The difficulty was that although working-class men and women employed in munitions factories, and so on, enjoyed better wages as the war continued, few of them were accustomed to save money, and many tended to spend their increased wages on luxury goods. The middle classes saw their own spending power, and thus their ability to save money, greatly diminished by wartime inflation. Despite these prob-lems, by August 1918, 163 members of St Mary-at-the-Walls War Savings Association had subscribed £6,605 9s 6d. There was no let-up with the Armistice in 1918: parishioners were urged to continue buying War Savings Association certificates to help the government with the cost of demobili-sation, and in January 1919 the scheme was renamed 'peace savings'.[32]

Care of the Troops in Colchester

Colchester War Work Depot

The laywomen of Colchester's parishes tended to be practical when it came to wartime good works. Shortly after the start of the war, Queen Mary appealed for garments for sick and wounded soldiers. Mrs Edith

[28]   Names in *St Mary-at-the-Walls Parish Magazine*, 1916–18
[29]   *St Mary-at-the-Walls Parish Magazine*, March 1917
[30]   *St Peter's Parish Magazine*, September 1916. *St Mary-at-the-Walls Parish Magazine*, October 1916
[31]   *St Mary-at-the-Walls Parish Magazine*, November 1916, February 1917
[32]   *St Mary-at-the-Walls Parish Magazine*, August 1918, December 1918, January 1919

Marriage, the mayoress of Colchester, who was leaving office, and Mrs Ethel Coats Hutton, the deputy mayoress, arranged a meeting of about half a dozen wealthy ladies on 10 August 1914 at which £50 was subscribed on the spot to establish a Colchester War Work Depot to organise the manufacture of clothing for the troops by the middle- and working-class women of the town.[33]

Ethel Coats Hutton and her committee established a workroom in the Albert School of Art in Colchester High Street, but the bulk of the work was done by women at home. Two firms of tailors cut cloth to the right patterns, and this was distributed to be sewn into shirts, underclothes, and so forth. Colchester's churches recruited needlewomen from amongst their congregations, distributing the cloth and collecting the finished garments. Church magazines kept members of congregations informed about the output of their parish's needlewomen. In December 1914, for example, Ward reported that in four months the ladies of St Peter's congregation had made fourteen flannel shirts, eleven bed jackets, seven vests, seven scarves, twenty-four pairs of gloves, eighteen pairs of socks, and other unspecified garments.[34] These were much appreciated by the troops at the front, as a letter from Lieutenant H.A. Tyler of the Royal Field Artillery, published in Holy Trinity magazine in June 1915, shows:

> I want to thank you all very much on behalf of myself and the whole battery for the really magnificent contribution of shirts and socks for the men. When you realize that the men had had no change of any description for a month at least, and had had no time to wash on at least half the days, you will realize what it meant for them. Please thank all the workroom [staff] in our names, too.[35]

Within a week or two of the establishment of the War Work Depot, an appeal for help was received from the matron of the military hospital. The needlewomen began to sew clothes for wounded soldiers, as well as for those at the front, and they also made large numbers of bandages and

---

[33]   Mrs Ethel Coats Hutton was mayoress of Colchester in 1912–13 and 1914–15. At the outbreak of war she was deputy mayoress until her husband took over the mayoralty from Alderman Wilson Marriage in the autumn of 1914. Hunt, *Souvenir*, p. 69

[34]   *St Peter's Magazine*, December 1914. *Holy Trinity Parish Magazine*, December 1914

[35]   *Holy Trinity Parish Magazine*, June 1915

padded splints for use in the hospitals. Other women formed the Soldiers' Laundry and Mending Guild to wash and repair soldiers' clothes, and one anonymous needlewoman was retained discreetly to make good the mistakes of others.

Caring for Troops in the Town

A good deal of time and effort was devoted by the laity to ministering to the troops who were training in Colchester before going off to the front. The number of troops in Colchester ebbed and flowed throughout the war. Following the declaration of war, the town was swamped by reservists and members of the Territorial Force. They were soon followed by the volunteers of Kitchener's Army. Towards the end of 1915 there was a lull as many of these men completed their training and were sent to France, but following the introduction of conscription in 1916, the town began to fill up with troops once more.

In the late summer of 1914, hundreds of soldiers were to be seen wandering around the streets of Colchester every afternoon and evening, and Brunwin-Hales wrote that he was frequently asked 'What is being done for the troops in the way of recreation?' and 'What is the Church doing?'[36] Hospitality is, of course, a Christian virtue, but many of Brunwin-Hales's questioners were doubtless motivated by the desire to keep the soldiers out of public houses, and to keep prostitution and its attendant problems at bay. The answer seemed to be social clubs for the troops, run on respectable lines, with no alcohol or other temptations.

The people of St Mary-at-the-Walls secured premises in Colchester High Street and had made arrangements to open a club, when it was announced that the borough council had made plans to open a club of its own opposite. The parishioners dropped their plans in support of the council's club. In all, thirty-five social clubs for the troops were established in Colchester during the war. Some existed for the duration of the conflict, whilst others opened for just a few months. Seven were run by Anglican parishes: St Paul's, St Nicholas's, Holy Trinity, St Stephen's, Myland, and St Leonard's, Lexden. The others were run by Roman Catholics, Nonconformists, religious organisations, political parties, the

---

[36]   *St Mary-at-the-Walls Parish Magazine,* October 1914

Co-operative Society and even – rather surprisingly – by the workhouse. Separate clubs were also established for soldiers' wives in St Botolph's Street and in the High Street.

The Borough of Colchester Social Club for the Troops

By far the largest club was the Borough of Colchester Social Club for Troops, which operated under the aegis of the town council in the Albert School of Art and in the Essex and Suffolk Fire Office in Colchester High Street between 24 September 1914 and 31 May 1919. The club was open free of charge to all soldiers, and, in principle, it was non-sectarian, but in practice it was strongly supported and influenced by the town's parish churches. The club committee contained three Anglican priests (Brunwin-Hales, Ward and the Rev. John Holyoak, curate at St Mary-at-the-Walls) and only one Nonconformist minister (the Rev. K.L. Parry).[37] The bishop of Colchester was invited to participate in the opening of the club, and many Anglican parishioners were involved in its day-to-day running, including Ethel Coats Hutton, who became the chairman of the ladies' committee for refreshments.[38] Much support was given to the club by the parishioners of St Mary-at-the-Walls and St Peter's. The club provided a canteen, baths, a soldiers' help bureau, a games room, a writing room where writing-paper, postcards and envelopes were provided free of charge, a reading room, a post office and a savings bank run by Barclays Bank. The club was open between 6.00 p.m. and 9.30 p.m. on weekdays, and between 2.00 p.m. and 9.30 p.m. on Sundays.[39]

The committee originally expected to cater for 1,000 visits per day, but the club found itself coping with between 25,000 and 30,000 visits per week.[40] The canteen sold huge amounts of food: in 1916, for instance, the

---

[37] *Essex County Standard*, 26 September 1914. Holyoak left Colchester shortly after the Borough Social Club for the Troops was set up to become vicar of Holy Trinity, South Woodford

[38] ERO, Committee Minutes of the Borough of Colchester Social Club for the Troops, 14 September 1914

[39] *Essex County Standard*, 26 September 1914. ERO, Annual Reports of the Committee of the Borough of Colchester Social Club for the Troops, 1916, 1917, 1918

[40] ERO, Annual Report of the Committee of the Borough of Colchester Social Club for the Troops, 1917

club used 10,804 quartern loaves of bread, 6,139 pounds of butter, 1,645 gallons of milk, 6,973 pounds of sugar, 1,557 pounds of tea, 449 pounds of coffee, 917 pounds of cocoa, 21,672 bottles of mineral water, 11 tons of cake, 311,515 pastries, and 2,404 pounds of meat for sandwiches. A full-time caretaker, Mr Crosby, was employed, assisted part time by his wife, but the combination of his unreliability and her frequent demands for pay rises would seem to have caused the committee more worry than anything else throughout the war.[41]

The bulk of the work of running the club was carried out by about 200 volunteers and largely followed class lines: middle-class ladies formed the catering committee and served the soldiers at the canteen counter, whilst working-class women were more likely to be found buttering bread or washing up.[42] Such social divisions were probably also to be encountered at the other wartime social clubs in Colchester. Additional help was provided by the St Mary-at-the-Walls Church Lads' Brigade and by the Boy Scouts, though the committee were asked to intervene when some of the boys were upset by the contradictory instructions and sharp tongues of several of the women helpers.[43] The committee had also tactfully to dispose of unwelcome ideas from some of the volunteers, such as repeated suggestions that they should hold joint afternoon tea parties for troops about to depart for the front to mix with wounded soldiers from the hospitals, and provide a room for the wounded, which would have helped neither group of men.[44] The club pursued something of a Sabbatarian policy: it opened early on Sundays to keep the men off the streets, but card games were discouraged and packs of playing cards, which on other days were freely available, were locked in a cupboard and only made available when specifically requested. At one stage in April 1915 playing cards were forbidden owing to gambling. Details of religious services in the

---

[41]   ERO, Committee Minutes of the Borough of Colchester Social Club for the Troops, December 1914, 9 August 1915, 12 June 1916, 12 July 1916, 14 August 1916, 18 September 1916, 13 November 1916, 14 October 1918

[42]   ERO, names in the Committee Minutes of the Borough of Colchester Social Club for the Troops, 1914–19

[43]   ERO, Committee Minutes of the Borough of Colchester Social Club for the Troops, letter from S.C. Bensusan Butt, Hon. Secretary of the Boy Scouts Association, to Harry Barton, Hon. Secretary of the Club, 1 April 1915

[44]   ERO, Committee Minutes of the Borough of Colchester Social Club for the Troops, 8 July, 9 September 1918, 14 October 1918

town's churches were prominently displayed on one of the noticeboards and the piano was not allowed to be played between 7.30 p.m. and 8.30 p.m. on Sundays, to encourage the men to attend an evening service.

By the time the Borough of Colchester Social Club for the Troops closed in 1919, it had been open seven days a week, including Christmas Day, for 1,711 days and had been greatly appreciated by many ordinary soldiers, whose behaviour during the whole of the war was exemplary.[45] Together with the other social clubs for troops in Colchester, the Borough Social Club may have helped to preserve military discipline in the town. Keeping busy in the club and having a sense of purpose may have helped many of the volunteers to cope with their own wartime anxiety and bereavement.

Welcoming the Troops to Parish Churches

Colchester's laity tried to help the troops when they came to church. At St Mary-at-the-Walls, for example, the Men's Club elected the sergeants of the Manchester Regiment, who were temporarily using their club room as a mess, as honorary members of their club. Parish branches of the Church of England Men's Society welcomed the troops to their meetings, and some branches, such as that at St Peter's, arranged special meetings for members of the CEMS serving in the army, which were greatly appreciated by the troops.[46]

With the active encouragement of their commanding officers, soldiers with musical skills were invited to play during services in Colchester's parish churches. In July 1917, for example, an army drummer and a sergeant who was a doctor of music played duets after Evensong in St Mary-at-the-Walls, and when the church organist was conscripted in 1918, a company quartermaster sergeant, who was a Fellow of the Royal College of Organists, took his place. At both St Mary-at-the-Walls and St Peter's, troops helped from time to time with the Sunday school and with Sunday afternoon children's services.[47]

[45] *Essex County Telegraph*, 17 June 1919
[46] *St Mary at the Walls Parish Magazine*, April 1917. *St Peter's Parish Magazine*, July 1916, September 1916, April 1917
[47] *St Mary-at-the-Walls Parish Magazine*, April 1917, August 1917, June 1918, November 1918. ERO, Minutes of St Peter's Parochial Church Council, 13 November 1918

Care of the Wounded

Hospitals

The laity spent much time, effort and money throughout the war trying to help the wounded soldiers in Colchester's hospitals. In the early part of 1914, the Red Cross reached an agreement with Brunwin-Hales that, in the event of a war, they might use St Mary's parish room as a hospital. When war with Germany was declared in August, the parishioners of St Mary-at-the-Walls quickly rallied around and donated beds, sheets, blankets, furniture and medical equipment. The parish room was soon set up as a small hospital and staffed by Red Cross nurses, but, before the first wounded soldier could arrive, the military authorities pronounced the sanitary arrangements inadequate. As an alternative, the parishioners and Red Cross were offered the use of the public hall of the Essex and Suffolk Fire Office in the High Street, and all the beds, medical equipment and furniture was moved there from the parish room, but, before they were unpacked, the army once again declined to approve the sanitary arrangements. At length, Gostwycke House, an imposing residence in Cambridge Road, was spotted as being empty and was deemed suitable. This time, the parishioners and Red Cross first ascertained that the sanitary arrangements met with military approval before raising the money to rent the house. Gostwycke House functioned as a hospital for troops throughout the First World War, together with Hamilton Road Military Hospital, which was set up in an empty school. Both these hospitals were run by the Red Cross, with active support from parishioners from St Mary-at-the-Walls and other churches. In addition, Colchester Military Hospital and the Essex County Hospital were run by the Royal Army Medical Corps, with help from local doctors and surgeons. The people of Colchester quickly became accustomed to the sight of wounded soldiers, and before long, the laity of the town's parishes were trying to help the wounded in whatever ways they could.[48]

An average of three ambulance trains arrived in Colchester every week throughout the First World War, bringing wounded soldiers, in many cases direct from France, and sometimes still covered with dried mud and

---

[48]   Hunt, *Souvenir*, pp. 75–80.

21 Unloading wounded soldiers at St Botolph's Station

blood. The army provided no official transport to take the wounded from St Botolph's Station to the hospitals, and so week after week, townsfolk who continued to run motorcars drove to the station and conveyed the wounded to hospital. Clearly someone – or several people – must have taken charge of the arrangements and probably organised a rota, and the supply of cars never failed at any point during the war. This indicates that there were a significant number of wealthy townsfolk who could continue to afford to run cars, and who were possessed of a strong sense of duty.[49]

Comforts for the Troops

In early 1915 each of Colchester's parishes received the following appeal:

Owing to the frequent arrival of wounded soldiers from the front and the large size of the garrison, the Colchester Military Hospital contains more than double its usual number of patients. Comforts and small luxuries are needed for these sick men, and a Receiving Room has been opened by the Hon. Mrs Maxse and Mrs Harvie Scott at the Albert School of Art,

[49]   Hunt, *Souvenir*, p. 60

High Street (in the same building as the Recruiting and Relief Offices), where gifts for the Hospital will be gratefully received, acknowledged and forwarded on. The room is open on Tuesdays from 11 to 1, and on Saturdays from 10.30 to 1.

The following are among the articles most welcome: cakes, cheese, cigarettes, cut flowers and plants, fruit, games and playing cards, jam, magazines and weekly papers, new laid eggs, potted meats, sardines, stamps and stationery, sweets.[50]

The laity responded with enthusiasm to Mary Maxse's appeal. At Holy Trinity, a special collection of oranges, bananas, eggs and honey was held on Trinity Sunday 1915 and sent to the Military Hospital. St Stephen's sent the fruit and flowers from their harvest thanksgiving services to the wounded throughout the war, as did other churches. The people of St Mary-at-the-Walls, St Peter's and St Botolph's churches organised receiving centres for gifts for the troops from the townsfolk.[51]

Most parishes printed appeals for comforts for the wounded in their parish magazines, and branches of the Church of England Men's Society encouraged their members to support this cause. At St Mary-at-the-Walls, the CEMS branch canvassed the whole of the parish and arranged for parcels to be collected. Each month from November 1915 until the Armistice, they published an account of their progress in the parish magazine and an appeal for further donations, of which the following is typical:

When we say that a 'Comforts Committee' was appointed, everyone will know that we are referring to food comforts for the wounded soldiers, who, while they are the patients at the County Hospital, happen to be our parishioners. Anything in the way of jam, potted meat, tinned fish, kippers, cakes, fruit, etc., will be much appreciated. This is a bit of real patriotic work and is worth doing well. Arrangements are being made for the canvas of the whole parish, then for the systematic and regular collection of whatever

[50]   *St Botolph's Parish Magazine*, May 1915. Mrs Harvie Scott was the wife of Colonel Harvie Scott, the Principal Medical Officer of the Colchester Garrison

[51]   Gore, *Mary Maxse*, p. 75. *Holy Trinity Parish Magazine*, June 1915. *St Botolph's Parish Magazine*, November 1915, December 1915, November 1916, November 1917, November 1918. *St Mary-at-the-Walls Parish Magazine*, November 1915, November 1917. *St Peter's Parish Magazine*, December 1915

22 Wounded soldiers and nurses at Colchester Military Hospital

comforts householders desire to give. Both kinds of help will be valued – in kind and in cash – and givers will have the joy of knowing they are making some slight return to the valiant fellows who are daring everything in the cause of Right. The Parish Hall will be open every Saturday from 6 to 8 for the receiving of comforts, whence they will be despatched to the Hospital.[52]

A committee was formed to oversee the distribution of collected food to the hospitals and to buy further comforts with donated money. All Colchester's parish churches organised appeals, special collections and fund raising events. At St Botolph's, for instance, members of the congregation went carol-singing and held parish entertainments to raise money for the wounded.[53]

Money was collected by the laity for many other purposes connected with the war. There were, for example, collections, fundraising events and sales of work in aid of the Army Scripture Readers Association, the Essex Regiment and for prisoners of war. Appeals for help to provide CEMS

---

[52] *St Mary-at-the-Walls Parish Magazine*, November 1915
[53] *St Botolph's Parish Magazine*, September 1917, January 1918, February 1918, May 1918

huts for the troops in France received widespread support, and the branch at St Mary-at-the-Walls appealed for half a crown from each of its members.[54] Names or articles in parish magazines indicate that, once again, these collections tended to be organised by middle-class members of congregations and supported by working-class parishioners.

Music

The wounded soldiers in Colchester's military hospitals commonly underwent a variety of psychological reactions once they were brought home from France. Many exhibited symptoms of shock, anxiety and guilt that they had survived whilst their comrades had been killed. Some soldiers exhibited anger; others became shy, depressed and introverted. Many men had difficulty sleeping, or experienced disturbing dreams. Most soldiers had not been a patient in a hospital before the war, and some found it embarrassing to be cared for by nurses, who were usually drawn from a higher social class. Many wounded soldiers found hospital life and routine frustrating from time to time.[55]

It was soon discovered that music helped: patients relaxed, and this helped their physical and psychological healing.[56] Before long, the laity of Colchester's parish churches were trying to help. St Mary-at-the-Walls parish magazine, for instance, announced in November 1915:

> The men need something more than marmalade and medicine – they need music; we are therefore hoping our choirs may find it possible to assist at the Sunday afternoon Hospital service, and also perhaps to give a concert occasionally. Musicians disposed to help may communicate with our choirmasters.[57]

Before long, choirs and musicians from Colchester's churches were singing at services in the military hospitals, and helping to organise 'smoking concerts' and other entertainments for the wounded, usually at

[54]   *St Mary-at-the-Walls Parish Magazine*, September 1915, October 1915, January 1916
[55]   Van Emden and Humphries, *All Quiet on the Home Front*, pp. 124, 132, 139
[56]   Van Emden and Humphries, *All Quiet on the Home Front*, p. 145
[57]   *St Mary-at-the-Walls Parish Magazine*, November 1915

weekends. Musical instruments, including pianos and even a small organ, were borrowed from parishioners' houses, and money was raised to buy sheet music for the troops. Other wounded soldiers enjoyed listening to music on gramophone records.

The Place and Role of Children and Young People during the First World War

The way that children are treated in Great Britain has changed enormously in the century since the First World War. In working-class and middle-class households in 1914–18, the requirements of the husband were usually met first, because he was the breadwinner, followed by the needs of any other adults in the family, and finally those of children. If food was scarce or difficult to afford, the best part of it would often be given to the husband, simply because his wages were needed to support everyone else. Infant and child mortality rates remained stubbornly high until the 1950s.[58]

The children of 1914–18 inhabited a world in which the aphorism that 'children should be seen and not heard' was frequently cited, even if this was only an aspiration. Discipline both at home and at school often involved corporal punishment, and teachers sometimes controlled classes by belittling pupils in a way that would horrify their successors a century later. Parents of all social classes were more formal and reserved in their behaviour towards their children, and few fathers would have helped to look after their children in a very 'hands-on' way.[59] None of this should be interpreted as meaning that parents did not love or care for their children; merely, as L.P. Hartley famously observed, 'the past is a foreign country: they do things differently there'.

Most children in 1914–18 left school at the earliest opportunity and went out to work, because their wages were needed to support the rest of the family. A university education or entry into the professions was, for

[58] As a curate in Gosport in the 1980s, I remember being told by the local undertaker that until the 1950s, the firm of funeral directors had a couple of hearses which had been specially adapted to take the small coffins of children, because the funerals of children were so frequent. These were eventually done away with as the funerals of infants and babies became rarer in the second half of the century

[59] Lockhart, *Cosmo Gordon Lang*, p. 16

the most part, the preserve of the middle and upper classes who could afford the fees. The occasional gifted working-class boy made it to university with the aid of bursaries, but these were very rare. More fortunate working-class boys might secure an apprenticeship, leading to a skilled trade. There was no distinct teenage culture: this did not emerge until after the Second World War.

The Experience of Children during the First World War

It has been estimated that a little over 340,000 children lost one or both parents during the First World War, with a greater number losing a brother or close relative. Roughly double this number of children had a close relative wounded. Many younger children were old enough to share in their family's anxiety, without really understanding what was going on. Many children bottled up their feelings in order to 'be strong' for their mothers and siblings, and sometimes harboured feelings of guilt or insecurity for the rest of their lives.

The war intruded into children's experience at school. Former pupils and fathers home on leave from the army or navy, wearing their uniforms, would sometimes visit their children's classes. A more dreaded experience was the arrival of the headmaster or headmistress to withdraw a child from a lesson because news had come that his or her father had been killed. When pupils' fathers or brothers, or schoolmasters and former pupils, were killed, they were often commemorated in school assemblies with hymns and special prayers. Many schools erected 'rolls of honour' of fallen old boys, and these sometimes formed the basis for school war memorials after the war.[60]

Supporting Children in Wartime: Sunday Schools and Other Organisations

Throughout the First World War, the parish churches of Colchester devoted a great deal of effort to continuing their activities for children. The adults who ran church organisations for children were frequently tired and over-stretched, and had to bear their own burdens and anxieties.

---

[60]   Van Emden and Humphries, *All Quiet on the Home Front*, pp. 100–9

Nevertheless, there was a sense of 'business as usual' with children's organisations: the adult leaders probably realised that this was one way in which they could help and support the children of their parishes.

The most common church organisation for children was the Sunday school. In 1914 the sixteen churches in Colchester each held Sunday schools, which were attended by 2,429 children and run by 280 teachers.[61] The largest Sunday schools were at St Botolph's, which had 515 children, and at St Mary-at-the-Walls and St Mary Magdalen, which had 300 each. The smallest was at St John's, which had a modest 46. The numbers of children and of Sunday school teachers remained fairly constant throughout the war.[62] Soldiers with experience of teaching in Sunday schools were sometimes recruited to help in Colchester's Sunday schools, thus filling the places vacated by male Sunday school teachers who had joined the army. The popularity of Sunday schools may not have been wholly religious: for families living cheek by jowl in 'two-up and two-down' terraced houses in parishes like St Paul's (107 children, 12 teachers), the Sunday school got the children out of the house and provided their parents with an hour or two's peace and quiet.

The average Sunday school met in a church hall or vicarage during the principal Sunday morning service, and in some parishes such as St Giles's the children joined the congregation at the end of Mattins for the final hymn. They were usually divided into infant and junior classes, and learnt the collects from the Book of Common Prayer, the Catechism, the Ten Commandments and passages of Scripture.[63] In every parish in Colchester there was additionally a children's service in church at 2.00 p.m. or 2.30 p.m. on Sunday afternoons.[64] The children's records of attendance were published in some church magazines as an encouragement to them to attend Sunday school regularly, though the principal incentive was the annual Sunday school treat. Treats for the infants tended to take the form of tea parties, whilst the juniors were usually taken on an outing to Clacton-on-Sea or West Mersea. In most parishes, adults were invited to donate money to pay for the treats, but as the war continued, food became

[61]   ERO, Diocese of Chelmsford Annual Statistical Returns, 1914–15
[62]   ERO, Diocese of Chelmsford, Annual Statistical Returns, 1914–18
[63]   Mrs Alice Hicks, interview, 18 March 1998
[64]   Details in surviving registers of services, parish magazines and annual statistical returns

23 Members of the Church Girls' Brigade from St Giles's parish, before 1914. Two boys from the Church Lads' Brigade are in the foreground. The clergy are the rector, the Rev. John Marsh (left), and the curate, the Rev. William Beale White (right), who had an unfortunate tendency of not lasting very long in parishes or schools.

scarce and treats were curtailed, though never abandoned.[65] A Sunday School Teachers' Ruri-decanal Association was formed in Colchester in July 1917 for teachers from all the parishes. The association met twice a year for discussion and the dissemination of new ideas and held an annual service in a different church each year. Training classes were also organised for teachers.[66]

A variety of organisations and groups catered for older children: Boy Scouts, Girl Guides, the Church Lads' Brigade, the Church Girls' Brigade, the King's Messengers (the junior section of the Society for the Propagation of the Gospel), assorted parish guilds, clubs and church choirs. All of these were used by the parishes as means of instructing the young in Christianity. Behr was an enthusiastic scoutmaster at St Stephen's and insisted that his scouts attend church. Scouts from St Botolph's marched to church parades at their annual camp. The Church Lads' Brigade held

[65]   *St Botolph's Parish Magazine*, October 1915, February 1918
[66]   *St Mary-at-the-Walls Parish Magazine*, July 1917, October 1918

Bible classes, and junior members of many church choirs were expected not merely to sing but also to study the sacraments and the liturgy and to take written examinations, the results of which were published in parish magazines.[67]

Young Women

In 1914 Ethel Coats Hutton helped to organise a Girls' Patriotic League, together with the wife of the Rev. K.L. Parry, a Nonconformist minister, and other prominent – and principally Anglican – laywomen from the town's social elite. This was aimed at older girls and young women. The members each swore an oath: 'I promise, by the help of God, to do all that is in my power to uphold the honour of our nation and its defenders in this time of war, by prayer, purity, and temperance.'[68]

The aim of the Girls' Patriotic League was to help preserve sexual purity, and by 1915 there were 700 members in Colchester and over 220,000 across the country. In 1916 the Colchester branch opened a club for women munitions workers in the town.[69] This was doubtless a practical response to the wartime rise in illegitimate births and venereal disease in the town.

Babies of the Empire Society

In July 1917, Bishop Winnington-Ingram of London wrote to the *Daily Telegraph* about the plight of babies during wartime: 'while nine soldiers died every hour in 1915, twelve babies died every hour, so it was more dangerous to be a baby than a soldier … the loss of life in this war has made every baby's life doubly precious.'[70] Winnington-Ingram was a pastoral bishop and knew the realities of life in many of the poorer parishes of his diocese. His letter helped to start the Babies of the Empire Society, whose middle-class leaders sought to train predominantly poorer mothers in

---

[67] *St Botolph's Parish Magazine*, November 1914, September 1917
[68] *Essex County Telegraph*, 21 November 1914
[69] Rusiecki, *Impact of Catastrophe*, pp. 222–3
[70] Van Emden and Humphries, *All Quiet on the Home Front*, pp. 228–9

'mothercraft'. The society established offices at the Aldwych in London. In 1918 it launched a 'Save the Babies' poster campaign, warning of the dangers of summer diarrhoea; on 9 July 1918, W.F. Massey, the prime minister of New Zealand, opened the Babies of the Empire Mothercraft Training Centre in Earls Court, London. The society received widespread support from Church leaders and former army personnel. No evidence of the Babies of the Empire Society has survived from Colchester, but it would be very surprising if the society had not received support in the town.

Children and the War Effort

The experience of children during the First World War mirrored that of adults. The war was explained to them at Sunday schools and in children's services, and they were encouraged to play their part. We read of the following, for example, at St Mary-at-the-Walls in 1915:

> On Sunday May 16 the Rector showed everyone at the Children's Service the Military Cross won by Lieutenant J.K. Keyes of A.O.D. [Army Ordnance Depot], the father of one of the children. 'We are all proud of this honour that has fallen on a parishioner of S. Mary's with Christ Church – and we hope it will inspire us all to do our duty the better.'[71]

Other children were encouraged to follow the example of their parents and help the wounded. Bishop Whitcombe's children frequently accompanied the bishop and Mrs Whitcombe on their trips to see the wounded and made a special point of visiting the wards on Christmas Day. One of the bishop's sons, Christopher, recalled eighty years later that he was told by his parents to invite wounded soldiers instead of his friends to his birthday parties; twenty soldiers came to one party and took part in games.[72] Other children collected fruit, flowers, and so on, or gave money to buy things for the wounded. At Berechurch, the Sunday school children agreed in June 1917 to give up sweets and to save pennies for the CEMS fund for the wounded in the Essex County Hospital. The children's gifts

---

[71]   *St Mary-at-the-Walls Parish Magazine*, June 1915
[72]   Christopher J. Whitcombe, letter to the author, 13 April 1998

were usually taken to the receiving room in the Albert School of Art, but carefully prepared visits to the hospitals were sometimes arranged for the children to present their gifts to the wounded in person. From time to time cigarettes and other gifts were sent by Sunday school children to the troops at the front.[73] At St Stephen's, the catechism class further emulated the example of the adults, offering in March 1917 to purchase a War Savings Bond, and their names and individual contributions were subsequently published in the parish magazine.[74] Members of the Church Lads' Brigade and of the Boy Scouts helped at the Borough of Colchester Social Club for Troops. The scouts practised ambulance work and signalling during the war,[75] and when it was discovered that nutshells were required to make the charcoal for gas masks, the children of Colchester, including many Sunday school children, collected eight tons of chestnuts.[76]

The Impact of the War upon the Laity

No attempt to understand the work of the laity during the First World War will be successful unless it takes account of the significance of social class in the relatively cohesive society of Colchester. By way of contrast to the wartime experience of Colchester, one has only to look to the West End of London, where there were examples of drunkenness, high living and licentious behaviour by the 'leisured classes' throughout the war, which many people in the provinces found deeply shocking.[77] The social elite of London could get away with that sort of behaviour in a large metropolis; in a town the size of Colchester it would not have gone unnoticed. In Colchester, the social elite seem to have a strong sense of public duty. What seems to have happened in Colchester during the First World War was not that a number of new people began organising good works for the first time, but rather that those who were already accustomed to take the initiative or to run things now did so on a bigger scale, adapting many

[73]   *St Mary-at-the-Walls Parish Magazine*, September 1915, June 1917

[74]   *St Botolph's Parish Magazine*, March 1917

[75]   *St Botolph's Parish Magazine*, October 1918

[76]   Hunt, *Souvenir*, p. 67

[77]   A. Marwick, *The Deluge: British Society and the First World War* (Macmillan, London, 1991), pp. 240ff

pre-war patterns to meet the needs of the troops and the wounded, and involving larger numbers of the townsfolk as assistants.

The parishes were able to call upon significant resources during the First World War in the form of active laypeople of both sexes, well-organised parochial clubs and societies, and effective systems of district visitors. The war led the laity to take the initiative in many areas and gave an important boost to lay work. It is perhaps unfair to draw too strong a distinction between lay work and clerical work: clergy and laity saw themselves as working together to help their country in the war, and it is certainly possible that the laity were enabled to do as much as they did because of good leadership, pastoral care and encouragement from their clergy. Many of the clergy seem to have been anxious to facilitate lay work. Bishop Watts-Ditchfield sought to encourage lay work in his sermons and speeches in the diocese, and in December 1915 at his own suggestion he led a quiet day for the laity of Colchester at Holy Trinity Church, during which he delivered addresses on 'The Layman and his Church' and 'The Layman and his Life'.[78] Brunwin-Hales wrote in 1917 that due to the war there were encouraging signs of 'the fullness of lay work' which was 'a consummation devoutly to be wished'.[79]

The war led to an increase in the ministry of Readers in the Church of England, and in July 1917 Bishop Whitcombe admitted a number of local men to serve as Readers in Colchester and the surrounding parishes.[80] The National Mission of Repentance and Hope (see below) boosted lay work, as did conscription, because it forced men and women to take over tasks previously performed by other members of their congregations, and thus to develop confidence and learn to take the initiative in new fields. If the *Colchester War Memorial Souvenir* book (1923) can be taken as a reasonably accurate indication of popular reflection upon wartime experiences in the years immediately after the Armistice, many laypeople – or at least middle-class laypeople – seem to have felt that on the whole they had not been found wanting, but had successfully risen to meet the unparalleled demands of wartime.[81]

---

[78]   ERO, Colchester Ruri-decanal Chapter Minutes, 15 November 1915
[79]   *St Mary-at-the-Walls Parish Magazine*, March 1917
[80]   *St Peter's Parish Magazine*, August 1917
[81]   Hunt, *Souvenir*, p. 69

6

Prayer and Worship

The Church of England can sometimes appear a very complicated and indeed contradictory organisation. Since the Elizabethan Settlement in the sixteenth century, the Church has aspired to be the Church of the English nation, providing a broad religious home for English men and women of a variety of theological outlooks and spiritualities. The Church of England has long contained different churchmanships, and at times it feels like at least three Churches rolled into one.[1] This has been aided by a certain studied ambiguity: the Communion rite in the Book of Common Prayer after 1559, to take one example, was patent of several different interpretations.

The late eighteenth and early nineteenth centuries saw the Evangelical Revival amongst evangelicals in the Church of England and Nonconformist churches. This deepened the spiritual vision and commitment of individual evangelicals, renewed the life of some churches, led to greater expectations amongst the clergy and inspired missions at home and overseas. It was emphatically Protestant in character.

Renewal of a quite different sort began in 1833 with the Oxford Movement and subsequent Catholic Revival. This startled many in the Church of England by claiming that their Church was not Protestant, as many had long believed, but that its formularies might be interpreted to show that it was a part of Catholic Christendom. The Catholic Revival led to a renewal of liturgical worship and sacramental spirituality amongst its followers, and to the revival of the religious life.[2] One result of the Catholic Revival, however, was an increase in conflict as Protestant-minded members of the Church of England came to believe that their

---

[1] D. MacCulloch, 'The Myth of the English Reformation', *Journal of British Studies* 30 (1991), 1–19

[2] A. Hughes, *The Rivers of the Flood: A Personal Account of the Catholic Revival in England in the Twentieth Century* (Faith Press, London, 1961), pp. 15–16, 23–6, 113, 121, 128

Reformation identity was being undermined and erroneous doctrines were being reintroduced by Anglo-Catholics.

The Church of England in 1914–18 might perhaps be pictured as a dynamic and moving triangle, with Anglo-Catholics, evangelicals and liberals in the three corners, and the various intermediate churchmanships – what were usually known as 'middle-of-the road' or 'central' – ranged along the three sides of the triangle. Each corner of the Anglican triangle tugged in a different direction and tussled for the identity of the Church of England. The Anglo-Catholics stressed the Church of England's Catholic heritage, and sought to enrich their worship in a more Catholic and sometimes Roman direction. The evangelicals saw themselves as children of the Reformation, the influence of which they sought both to promote and also to protect from Anglo-Catholic or liberal incursion. Liturgically speaking, they wanted nothing other than the 1662 Prayer Book, which they interpreted in a Protestant manner. The liberals – also sometimes known as modernists – wished to remodel or 'modernise' Christianity to accommodate their understanding of contemporary thought and needs. In the early years of the twentieth century, several modernist theologians controversially advocated the revision of the liturgy in a liberal direction, by, for example, abolishing the Athanasian Creed.[3] At times, this diversity amongst Anglicans led to a beneficial mutual enrichment; though it also sometimes resulted in bitter disagreement and controversy.

Public Worship in Colchester in 1914

The pattern of Sunday services in the parish churches of Colchester in 1914 bore a remarkable degree of uniformity. In all churches, Sunday began with Holy Communion, also sometimes known as the Eucharist, at 8.00 a.m. This was followed at 11.00 a.m. by Morning Prayer, also known as Mattins, and a sermon, which was the principal service of the day. Mattins was sometimes preceded by the Litany, and occasionally followed by Holy Communion. A children's service was held in all

---

[3] L. Pullan, 'Prayer Book Revision: The Absurdities and Dangers of the Convocation Proposals', *All Saints' Margaret Street Church and Parish Paper* 25/329 (March 1911), 53–7

parishes on most Sundays at 2.00 p.m. or 2.30 p.m., and the day ended with Evening Prayer, also known as Evensong, and a sermon at 6.30 p.m. or 7.00 p.m. In the Anglo-Catholic parishes, Mattins was said at 10.00 a.m. and the principal service at 11.00 a.m. was a Sung Eucharist, or High Mass if the three sacred ministers of priest, deacon and subdeacon were available.

Three of the Anglo-Catholic parishes, St Leonard's-at-the-Hythe, St Paul's and St James's, had a daily celebration of Holy Communion.[4] The majority of the other parishes had celebrations on major holy days, and some had a regular weekly celebration. The daily offices of Mattins and Evensong appear to have been recited publicly in many churches, and all parishes had extra-liturgical acts of worship on weekdays for parish organisations, devotional guilds and religious confraternities.

Although the pattern of Sunday worship was broadly the same in all the parishes, there was a wide diversity of liturgical practice in Colchester. All parishes used the 1662 Book of Common Prayer, but this was frequently interpreted in a variety of ways and supplemented or diluted according to taste. In the Anglo-Catholic parishes, the priest celebrated Holy Communion facing eastwards across the altar – *ad orientem* – symbolically looking east towards Jerusalem. He wore eucharistic vestments, which symbolised the eucharistic sacrifice, and sometimes used incense. In two of the evangelical parishes, St Peter's and St Mary Magdalen's, the priest stood at the north end of the holy table, wore a surplice, black scarf and academic hood, and celebrated Holy Communion in a very plain manner.[5] In many of the middle-of-the-road churches such as St Mary-at-the-Walls, the clergy celebrated *ad orientem* and wore surplices and coloured stoles or black scarves for Holy Communion.[6] In Anglo-Catholic parishes, the 1662 Book of Common Prayer was sometimes

---

4   ERO, Diocese of Chelmsford, Annual Statistical Returns, 1914–15
5   Canon Robin Wilson, interview, 17 December 1998. Parishioners at St Peter's, which is in the patronage of the Simeon Trust, were shocked in the 1940s when an incumbent enlarged the sanctuary, adopted the eastward position and introduced the use of coloured stoles. Information about St Mary Magdalen's from the Rev. Paul Davis (interview, 20 December 1998), who also mentioned that the third evangelical parish, St Nicholas's, was 'very Anglican', with the celebrant facing east and flowers on the altar
6   Mrs Dolly Thimblethorpe, interview, 7 January 1999. Christopher J. Whitcombe, letter to the author, 22 December 1998

supplemented with material from the Roman Missal or with plainchant propers from books such as the *English Hymnal*.[7]

The worship in all of Colchester's churches in 1914, when compared with what might have been experienced in 1850, had been influenced to one degree or another by the Catholic Revival, even if it was only to the extent of robed choirs or the use of the surplice by the clergy in every parish. The centrality of Mattins as the principal Sunday morning service should not be misunderstood to mean that Holy Communion was not highly esteemed, nor should a simple mode of celebrating the sacrament in an evangelical or middle-of-the-road parish be equated with a simplistic understanding of the Eucharist.[8] During the nineteenth century there was a revival of the practice of fasting-communion, which meant that in many parishes, communicants fasted from midnight and received Holy Communion at 8.00 a.m., before going home to breakfast, after which they would often return to church for Mattins and the sermon.

Having said all of this, it is important to note that the differences of churchmanship between parishes were not as great as might have been expected, because the principal service was Mattins rather than Holy Communion. At the middle-of-the-road St Mary-at-the-Walls, Colchester's wealthiest parish with a strong musical tradition, Mattins was sung by a large and well-trained choir, and the service was reminiscent of that in a cathedral. At the evangelical and poorer St Mary Magdalen's, the same service would have been much simpler. Most other parishes in Colchester were somewhere between the two. The format of Mattins, however, was the same in all of Colchester's parish churches, and the 1611 Authorized Version of the Bible and the 1662 Book of Common Prayer provided a common and rich language for worship.

---

[7]   At St Stephen's, Behr kept Corpus Christi and All Souls' Day (*St Botolph's Parish Magazine*, July and November 1914), which indicates that he supplemented the 1662 Book of Common Prayer with material from an additional source. The Rev. Paul Davis (interview, 20 December 1998), who was a curate at St James's in the 1950s, believes that during the First World War a Missal produced by the Society of St John the Evangelist was used at both St James's and St Paul's

[8]   P.B. Nockles, *The Oxford Movement in Context* (Cambridge University Press, Cambridge, 1994), pp. 212–17

Support for the State in the Liturgy

The Church of England is an Established Church and has a long tradition of praying for the state in its public worship. The 1662 Book of Common Prayer includes intercessions for the monarch, the Royal Family, the Privy Council and Parliament during Morning and Evening Prayer, the Litany, the Holy Communion and in several other places.[9]

During the nineteenth century, the custom arose in Colchester, as in many other towns, of holding special 'civic services' attended by the mayor and corporation.[10] In Colchester, these were usually held near St George's Day, 23 April.[11] The army was sometimes involved in civic services, for instance in 1897, when the garrison commander invited the mayor and town councillors to wear their robes and walk in the military procession to the Abbey Fields for an open-air service to celebrate Queen Victoria's diamond jubilee.[12] In 1910, a civic memorial service for Edward VII was attended by the 'Mayor, Alderman, Councillors and Corporate officers, also Borough Justices, Council Committees, Governors of the Grammar

---

[9] At Morning and Evening Prayer in the 1662 Book of Common Prayer, intercessions are offered for the monarch in the suffrages, and also after the third collect in the so-called 'State Prayers', where there is additionally a prayer for the Royal Family. The monarch and Royal Family are mentioned in the Litany. The Prayer Book contains prayers 'In Time of Wars and Tumults', 'A Prayer for the High Court of Parliament, to be read during their Session', and thanksgivings 'For Peace and Deliverance from our Enemies', and 'For Restoring Publick Peace at Home'. During Holy Communion, the priest must say one of two collects for the monarch, before saying the collect for the day. The monarch and Privy Council are also mentioned in the Prayer for the Church Militant. The Prayer Book contains 'Forms of Prayer to be used at Sea' for the Royal Navy. During the consecration of bishops, there is a place where the monarch's mandate for the consecration is appointed to be read. There are three 'Forms of Prayer with Thanksgiving to Almighty God' appointed for use in all churches and chapels in the realm upon the anniversary of the accession of the reigning sovereign. The Prayer Book is also bound with the Thirty-Nine Articles of Religion (although, strictly speaking, they are not a part of it) which contains Article XXXVII, 'The King's Majesty hath the chief power in this Realm of England,' etc.

[10] ERO, Borough of Colchester Council-in-Committee Minutes, 29 March 1900. These services were usually in Anglican churches, though the council were occasionally invited by Nonconformist chapels, e.g., 29 August 1902, when they were invited to attend Lion Walk Congregational Church – the minutes do not make it clear whether or not they accepted

[11] ERO, Borough of Colchester, Council-in-Committee Minutes, 29 March 1900

[12] ERO, Borough of Colchester, Council-in-Committee Minutes, 2 June 1897

School and Scholars, Customs, Excise, Inland Revenue Staff, Post Office Staff and others'.[13]

Individual parish churches also held special services to mark the death of Queen Victoria in 1901, the coronation of Edward VII in 1902, his death in 1910 and the coronation of George V in 1911.[14] A number of parishes held special services during the 1899–1902 South African War. At the evangelical St Peter's, for instance, there was a special collection for the war fund in 1900, and thanksgiving services were held to mark the return of volunteers from South Africa in 1901, and for the conclusion of the war in 1902.[15] All parishes seem, on their own initiative, to have had special prayers and sermons on Sunday 9 August 1914, the first Sunday after the declaration of war.

National Days of Prayer

The Church of England had a long tradition, dating from 1533, of organising national days of prayer, at the request of the state, on occasions of national or royal thanksgiving, and in times of national emergency, such as wars, unseasonable weather and epidemics. The usual method of arranging for national days of prayer was an instruction from the Privy Council to the archbishop of Canterbury.

On 11 August 1914 the archbishops of Canterbury and York issued a circular letter entitled 'A Call to Prayer', appointing Friday 21 August as a national day of prayer. The archbishops communicated with the authorities of the Roman Catholic Church and the Free Church Council and expressed the hope that, 'as far as is practicable, the observance should have a national character. The needs, the anxieties, the hopes, are common to all: it is fitting that they should be laid in common prayer before Almighty God.'[16]

The parishes of Colchester responded with enthusiasm. Many churches held special morning and evening services on 21 August, and some also at midday. St Botolph's organised a united service for the townsfolk at 3.00

[13]   ERO, St Peter's Register of Services, 20 May 1910
[14]   St Peter's Registers of Services, 2 February 1901, 9 August 1902, 20 May 1910
[15]   St Peter's Registers of Services, 7 January 1900, 9 June 1901, 8 June 1902
[16]   LPL, Davidson Papers, vol. 367, p. 81

p.m. and Bishop Watts-Ditchfield came unexpectedly from Harwich and preached the sermon.[17] Half a mile away, the mayor and corporation, the guardians of the poor, and borough officials processed in state to St Peter's for a civic service of intercession for victory.[18] The church was packed to capacity, and the names of those who attended in the local press read like a 'Who's Who' of Colchester's social elite. Ward officiated, and Bishop Whitcombe preached a stirring address on the importance of intercessory prayer, which was reproduced in the *Essex County Standard*. At the end of the service, the organist played 'God Save the King', and the national anthems of Great Britain's principal allies, 'God Save the Tsar', and the 'Marseillaise'.[19]

Following the success of the national day of prayer on 21 August 1914, it was decided to hold another on the first Sunday of 1915, 3 January. This was held on a Sunday because Archbishop Davidson realised that the government would not countenance suspension of war work on a weekday. Davidson worked hard to ensure the 1915 national day of prayer was a success: he persuaded the Lord Mayor of London to appeal to provincial mayors to organise formal civic attendance at the national day of prayer in their towns and cities, and 'to urge their fellow-citizens to a right and worthy observance of the day'.[20] Davidson also contacted Cardinal Francis Bourne, the Roman Catholic archbishop of Westminster, and successfully arranged through him for services to be held in Roman Catholic churches in France and Belgium. It is believed that the archbishop also arranged for intercessions to be offered by the Orthodox Church in Russia.[21]

In the event, the national day of prayer on 3 January 1915 generated widespread interest, and nearly 3 million copies of the order of service produced by the Church of England were sold.[22] In Colchester, the bishop of Chelmsford preached before the mayor and corporation in St

---

[17]   *St Botolph's Parish Magazine*, September 1914
[18]   *St Peter's Parish Magazine*, September 1914
[19]   *Essex County Standard*, 22 August 1914
[20]   P. Williamson, 'National Days of Prayer: The Churches, the State and Public Worship in Britain, 1899–1957', *English Historical Review* 128/531 (April 2013), 323–66, 333
[21]   Williamson, 'National Days of Prayer', 332. *St Mary-at-the-Walls Parish Magazine*, January 1915
[22]   Williamson, 'National Days of Prayer', 326

Peter's, and all parishes held special services or intercessions.[23] Behr was especially busy at the Anglo-Catholic St Stephen's:

> We kept the day as a whole 'Day of Watching' as far as we could. The day began as it should with a Celebration of the Holy Eucharist at 6 a.m., followed by another at 9 o'clock. A Litany of Intercession was said. At 10 the Infants met, and at 10.30 the Children of the Catechism, when Matins was said, and at 11 there was a Sung Celebration of the Holy Eucharist, at which there were 22 Communicants, a large number for a late Celebration at S. Stephen's.
>
> At the close a short Intercession was made for those who had fallen in the war, when we especially remembered our own beloved ones. At the conclusion a beautiful new hymn composed by Mr E. Skeffington, words by Mr Arkwright, 'Father we bring our dead to Thee,' was sung. At 3 o'clock the Children of the Catechism had their Service of Intercession, and at 4 the Rev. C.V. Boddington conducted an hour with intercessions for those who had fallen, and there was a large congregation; at 5 the Intercession of the SPCK, and at 6 another Intercession for the fallen; 6.30 Evensong and a short Address and Intercession according to form prescribed, conducted from the pulpit; at 9.30 the Ancient Service of Compline was said and special Intercession was made; at Midnight there was another Celebration of the Holy Communion and the day concluded with a final Celebration at 6 a.m. on Monday morning. The bell was tolled for 5 minutes at each hour of the day up to Evensong, when, unfortunately, the rope broke and the remaining hours were unable to be rung.[24]

This national day of prayer at the turn of the New Year proved successful and was repeated in future years. In late 1915, Bishop Watts-Ditchfield asked that everyone in the diocese of Chelmsford should not merely observe the first Sunday of 1916, 2 January, as a day of intercession, but should additionally keep the two preceding days as days of prayer and fasting.[25] At St Botolph's, St Mary-at-the-Walls and St Nicholas's, Saturday 1 January 1916 was kept as a day of unceasing public prayer for victory and for those serving in the army and navy, with volunteers pray-

23   *St Peter's Parish Magazine*, January 1915
24   *St Botolph's Parish Magazine*, February 1915
25   *St Botolph's Parish Magazine*, February 1916

ing in thirty-minute relays throughout the twenty-four hours. Services on Sunday 2 January 1916 were well attended.[26]

There was no national day of prayer on 1 January 1917 because the Church of England was concluding the National Mission of Repentance and Hope, but New Year's Eve, 31 December 1916, was instead observed as a day of prayer and consecration throughout the country.[27] In 1918, the first Sunday was 6 January, the feast of the Epiphany, which King George V commanded by a royal proclamation read at church services to be observed as a day of prayer and thanksgiving throughout his dominions.

In previous centuries, some national days of prayer had been styled 'days of humiliation', although the term was employed less often during the nineteenth century, and Queen Victoria had opposed the appointment of a 'day of humiliation' in 1899 during the South African War.[28] During the First World War, some people – mostly, but not entirely, evangelical Anglicans, Nonconformists and some Scottish Presbyterians – pressed unsuccessfully for the term to be revived. This was because they saw the war as God's judgement and believed that corporate repentance of sins at the behest of the state, and an acknowledgement of the nation's dependence upon God's will, were necessary to regain Divine favour. Other Christians appear to have understood national days of prayer as occasions when God was asked to bless the British Empire and its peoples and to help them achieve victory. Some people probably held a mixture of both beliefs. In the summer of 1917, the World's Evangelical Alliance, an inter-denominational evangelical association, asked Davidson to press Lloyd George for an additional day of national humiliation and prayer, but the prime minister declined, arguing that this might be misunderstood by both Britain's allies and enemies at an anxious time in the war.[29]

[26] *St Botolph's Parish Magazine*, February 1916. *St Mary-at-the-Walls Parish Magazine*, February 1916

[27] *St Mary-at-the-Walls Parish Magazine*, December 1916

[28] G.K.A. Bell, *Randall Davidson, Archbishop of Canterbury* (Oxford University Press, Oxford, 1935), p. 313

[29] Williamson, 'National Days of Prayer' 352. Bell, *Randall Davidson*, p. 827

FORMS

OF

PRAYER and THANKSGIVING

TO

ALMIGHTY GOD

TO BE USED ON

THE FEAST OF THE EPIPHANY
SUNDAY, THE SIXTH OF JANUARY, 1918

Being the Day appointed for Intercession on Behalf of the Nation and Empire in this Time of War.

Issued under the Authority of the Archbishops of Canterbury and York.

THE KING'S PROCLAMATION

¶ *In the Order of Holy Communion after the Creed at least once in the day, and at Morning or Evening Prayer, or before the Forms of Prayer hereinafter set forth, the Minister shall read the King's Proclamation, saying as follows:*

Brethren, I bid you hear the words of His Majesty the King appointing this day to be set aside as a Day of Prayer and Thanksgiving in all the Churches throughout his Dominions.

TO MY PEOPLE.—The world-wide struggle for the triumph of right and liberty is entering upon its last and most difficult phase. The enemy is striving by desperate assault and subtle intrigue to perpetuate the wrongs already committed and stem the tide of a free civilization. We have yet to complete the great task to which, more than three years ago, we dedicated ourselves.

At such a time I would call upon you to devote a special day to prayer that we may have the clear-sightedness and strength necessary to the victory of our cause. This victory will be gained only if we steadfastly remember the responsibility which rests upon us, and in a spirit of reverent obedience ask the blessing of Almighty God upon our endeavours. With hearts grateful for the Divine guidance which has led us so far towards our goal, let us seek to be enlightened in our understanding and fortified in our courage in facing the sacrifices we may yet have to make before our work is done.

I therefore hereby appoint January 6th—the first Sunday of the year—to be set aside as a special day of prayer and thanksgiving in all the Churches throughout my dominions, and require that this Proclamation be read at the services held on that day.

GEORGE R.I.

24 King George V's proclamation appointing 6 January 1918 as a special day of prayer and thanksgiving in all churches throughout his dominions

Declaration Day, 4 August

Throughout the First World War, the Church of England and other denominations arranged special services on the anniversary of the declaration of war, 4 August, which came to be known as 'Declaration Day'.

In Colchester, the ruri-decanal chapter did not get around to planning a day of prayer on the first anniversary of the declaration of war until 30 July 1915. At short notice, many parishes arranged to hold special services on 4 August 1915, and it was hoped the daily intercession service at Holy Trinity might be specially adapted. At the last minute, the Rev. H.C. Martin, the senior military chaplain in Colchester, invited the parish clergy and their congregations to take part in an open-air parade service of intercession to be held on the Abbey Fields at midday on 4 August, which was to be attended by the general and his staff.[30]

The 1915 open-air service made a positive impression on the clergy of Colchester and their parishioners. In 1916, in addition to the services planned by parish churches for the national day of prayer on Saturday 4 August, the ruri-decanal chapter took the initiative and started to organise another open-air service. Having discovered that the chief constable was unhappy about a procession through the streets – presumably in case of an air raid or other disturbance – the Colchester clergy began to plan an open-air service in the ruins of St Botolph's Priory. They were then approached by the mayor, who suggested that that if they were willing to hold an open-air service a day earlier, the borough would make Castle Park available to them, and the mayor and corporation would like to attend. The ruri-decanal chapter happily adopted the mayor's suggestion.[31]

By the time the open-air service took place on 3 August 1916, many families in Colchester had had relatives killed or wounded in the battle of the Somme, and a steady stream of ambulance trains was bringing casualties from France to the town's hospitals. Thousands of people crowded into Castle Park for the service, which was attended by the civil and military authorities, in addition to the mayor and corporation. Colchester's Nonconformist ministers were especially invited to take part, though no one seems to have invited the Roman Catholic priest, presumably on the grounds that they knew he would be obliged to decline.

---

[30]   ERO, Colchester Ruri-decanal Chapter Minutes, 30 July 1915
[31]   ERO, Colchester Ruri-decanal Chapter Minutes, 16 April 1916, 28 July 1916

The service began with the hymn 'All People that on Earth do Dwell,' followed by prayers led by Brunwin-Hales. The Rev. J.R. Mitchell of the Eld Lane Baptist Church read passages of Scripture, and after the hymn 'Lord God of Hosts', Bishop Whitcombe preached the sermon. After the hymn 'Now Thank we All our God', the Rev. J. Day, a Wesleyan minister, led prayers of thanksgiving. The service ended after the hymn 'O God of Love', with the blessing (presumably pronounced by Bishop Whitcombe) and the national anthem. It is interesting to note that the pressure of two-and-a-half years of war finally brought together the different denominations, although this only occurred within the context of outdoor civic services, and on the neutral ground of Castle Park. No Nonconformist ministers were invited to participate in services inside Anglican parish churches during the war, and, when a civic service was held on St George's Day 1916 in Wimpole Road Methodist Church during the mayoralty of the Nonconformist A.G. Aldridge, none of the Anglican clergy was invited.[32] Anglican priests and Nonconformist ministers did not participate in services in each others' churches until the celebration of the Armistice in November 1918.[33]

In 1917, Declaration Day, 4 August, fell on a Saturday again. In Colchester, the clergy decided not to hold another large open-air service, but instead to concentrate their efforts on a combined Anglican service of intercession at Holy Trinity at 12.30 a.m. In the parish churches, the day of prayer was primarily observed on the following day, Sunday 5 August.[34]

Declaration Day in 1918 occurred after the British Army on the Western Front had withstood the German spring offensive and was beginning the counter-offensive that would lead to victory in November. Indeed, on 8 August 1918, General Ludendorff would conclude that the German Army had been beaten. It was decided to observe Declaration Day – which conveniently fell on a Sunday – as a further national day of prayer. The two Houses of Parliament joined King George V and Queen Mary at a special service of intercession in St Margaret's Church, Westminster. In Colchester, it was decided once more to hold a large open-air service in Castle Park on 4 August 1918, which was again attended by the mayor and corporation, the civil and military authorities, representatives from

[32]   *Essex County Telegraph*, 6 May 1916
[33]   CL, Jarmin Collection, fol. 120
[34]   ERO, Colchester Ruri-decanal Chapter Minutes, 24 July 1917

"Lift up your heads, for your redemption draweth nigh!"

FOURTH

ANNIVERSARY OF THE GREAT WAR.

COLCHESTER CITIZENS'

Commemoration Service

CASTLE PARK, 3 p.m., AUGUST 4th, 1918.

Hymn:

O GOD, our help in ages past,
 Our hope for years to come,
Our shelter from the stormy blast,
And our eternal home;

Beneath the shadow of Thy Throne
 Thy saints have dwelt secure;
Sufficient is Thine Arm alone,
 And our defence is sure.

Time, like an ever-rolling stream,
 Bears all its sons away;
They fly forgotten, as a dream
 Dies at the opening day.

O God, our help in ages past,
 Our hope for years to come,
Be Thou our guard while troubles last,
 And our eternal home. Amen.

Lesson: Romans viii., 31, 32, 35, 37-39.

Prayers: Our Father, &c. (*said by all*).

For the King and the British Empire.

ALMIGHTY God, the fountain of all goodness, we humbly
 beseech Thee to bless our Sovereign Lord, King GEORGE, the
Parliaments in all the dominions of the King, and all who are set in
authority under him. Grant that all, of whatever race or colour or
tongue, may, in prosperity and peace, be united in the bond of
brotherhood, and in the one fellowship of the Faith, so that we may
be found a people acceptable unto Thee; through Jesus Christ our
Lord. *Amen.*

For Sailors, Soldiers, and Airmen.

O LORD God of Hosts, stretch forth, we pray Thee, Thine almighty
 arm to strengthen and protect the sailors and soldiers and
airmen of the King in every peril, of sea and land and air; give them
victory in the day of battle, and in the time of peace keep them safe
from all evil; endue them with loyalty and courage; and grant that
in all things they may serve as seeing Thee who art invisible; through
Jesus Christ our Lord. *Amen.*

25 Order of service for the Declaration Day open-air service in Castle Park,
4 August 1918

the Nonconformist Churches – though still no Roman Catholic clergy – and by a large congregation of townsfolk.[35]

Large services of intercession for victory, bringing together the Church of England, the Nonconformist churches and chapels, the mayor, corporation, civil and military authorities, and attracting thousands of people, were very much the product of their times. These services arose from a combination of the existing tradition of national days of prayer, civic religious services, widespread habits of churchgoing in Colchester, patriotism, pastoral need and the unprecedented pressures of a world war. Nor should the support afforded to these services by the social elite be underestimated. National days of prayer during the First World War were the seedbed in which developed rituals of remembrance after the Armistice in 1918. The idea that the war should be met with corporate repentance was given further expression during the 1916 National Mission of Repentance and Hope (see below).

Parish Wartime Intercession Services

The primary purpose of the Church's liturgy is the worship of Almighty God, but liturgy also has important pastoral and teaching applications. During the First World War, church services were an important pastoral tool, whereby the clergy were enabled to minister to the needs of their congregations and provided a channel whereby both clergy and laity could focus their concerns, anxieties and grief. This principally expressed itself in the development of regular wartime intercession services.

The Church of England had a long tradition of reciting the Litany from the 1662 Book of Common Prayer on Wednesdays and Fridays; during the nineteenth century many parishes also began holding intercession services in church on weekday evenings. This widely understood pattern of prayer was adapted during the First World War to meet wartime needs. The ruri-decanal chapter discussed intercessory prayer at its emergency meeting three days after the declaration of war, and each parish in Colchester arranged to hold an evening intercession service every week.[36] These services were continued throughout the war. The chapter addition-

[35]   ERO, Colchester Ruri-decanal Chapter Minutes, 5 July 1918
[36]   ERO, Colchester Ruri-decanal Chapter Minutes, 7 August 1914

ally agreed to hold a daily intercession service for the whole town in Holy Trinity Church, which anyone could attend. At 12.30 p.m. every day a bell was rung, and later an electric siren provided by the borough and nicknamed 'Bellona' was sounded, to announce this service. The townsfolk who were unable to get to Holy Trinity for the daily intercession service were asked to pause for a moment and to offer a silent prayer for the men of Colchester serving in the armed forces.

Wartime intercession services appear to have been 'hymn sandwiches', with litanies, prayers and lists of names read aloud. Most parish churches in Colchester set up framed rolls of honour inscribed with the names of parishioners on active service, so that the congregation might pray for them. Lists were sometimes displayed of parishioners who had been killed. Some churches displayed the Union Jack, and the parishioners of St Mary-at-the-Walls paid for the flags of all the Allied nations to be displayed on the pillars, which people recalled as being most impressive.[37]

It was sometimes claimed later in the twentieth century that during the First World War an emotional and psychological gulf had arisen between soldiers in the trenches and their relatives at home.[38] More modern historical research suggests that this alienation of soldiers from civilians has been exaggerated – there is plenty of evidence that civilians in Britain had a fairly accurate idea of what was going on in France – and that soldier–civilian alienation quickly became something of a literary stereotype.[39] However, many British soldiers tended to keep quiet about the worst horrors of trench warfare, either because these were too painful, or to avoid upsetting their families: I have met a number of old soldiers who would cheerfully reminisce about their time in the army, but draw a veil over their experience of being in action. It is probable, therefore, that a large number of soldiers did undergo some degree of alienation – literary stereotypes often have some basis in fact – and that the soldiers' families came to realise that they sometimes found readjusting to civilian life and conversation difficult when they came home on leave. Services of intercession were perhaps one way in which relatives in England felt that

[37] Mrs Dolly Thimblethorpe, interview, 16 March 1998
[38] Wilkinson, *Church of England*, pp. 123–4
[39] A. Gregory, *The Last Great War: British Society and the First World War* (Cambridge University Press, Cambridge, 2008), pp. 132–6

they were able to do something to support their men at the front and to aid the nation's war effort.

From time to time articles appeared in parish magazines in Colchester reminding readers that the intercession services were still being held, and exhorting them to attend.[40] Surviving service registers do not give attendance figures, but it is reasonable to deduce that attendance at intercession services was probably patchy, and depended on the news from the front and on the amount of time parishioners had available to go to church after they had coped with the wartime dislocation of everyday life and had participated in other church activities. This should not be interpreted to mean that the intercession services were not valued; it is likely that many parishioners, whose spare time was spent helping in social clubs for the troops or working with young people or the wounded, were pleased to know that at the same time prayers were being offered in church for their loved ones at the front.

The Effect of the Army upon Worship

The presence in Colchester of many thousands of troops and wounded soldiers had an impact on worship in Colchester's parish churches during the First World War, as on many other aspects of parochial life. The most obvious change was the use by the army of five churches – All Saints', St Mary-at-the-Walls, St Nicholas's, St Leonard's, Lexden, and All Saints', Stanway – for church parades for the troops who could not be accommodated in the Garrison Church. St Nicholas's was of moderate evangelical churchmanship, and the others were of middle-of-the-road churchmanship. It may be significant that the army avoided the town's Anglo-Catholic churches – many Anglo-Catholics believed they were discriminated against by the army during the war – but this arrangement might have been simply due to considerations of distance.

Church parades were compulsory for the troops, and were usually held in the five Colchester churches at 9.30 a.m. or 10.00 a.m. on Sundays, prior to the main parochial service at 11.00 a.m. Parade services usually took the form of a highly abbreviated version of Mattins, much to the

[40]   *St Botolph's Parish Magazine*, October 1914, December 1914, October 1915, January 1917, July 1917, October 1917, January 1918, October 1918

chagrin of regular churchgoers in the army, who would have preferred the sort of service they had previously experienced in their parish churches, and to the displeasure of Anglo-Catholics, who wanted Holy Communion. In 1916 the Rev. the Hon. H.H. Courtenay, an Anglo-Catholic priest, critically described parade services:

> When I was acting Chaplain last year to a Brigade, on my taking up the duties, three forms of service which were in use were put into my hands. At first sight they seemed to have some resemblance to the daily Office, but on a nearer view they can best be described as a combination of a mongrel Mattins and a hybrid Evensong – one omitted any reference to the penitential element, and in another the recitation of the Psalter was not even hinted at. A few prayers, as many hymns as possible, always including 'Onward Christian Soldiers' and 'Fight the Good Fight,' and a short sermon seems to be the recognized public religious ministration to the soldiers here and at home, though I am told that now that here and at the front it is found that such a form of service is not suitable to the trenches, or even the rest camps and base, but that the Blessed Sacrament is the only real satisfaction of the spiritual needs of those who are facing death for their King.[41]

Parade services were usually conducted by army chaplains, but the parish clergy also often officiated and preached. Far from resenting the presence of the troops in their churches, the five Colchester congregations welcomed them with enthusiasm, and many parishioners attended the parade services in order to support the troops, and seem to have become genuinely fond of them. The Church of England Men's Society produced special hymn sheets for parade services, and CEMS members were often on hand to welcome the troops. One of the clergy of St Mary-at-the-Walls wrote in December 1914:

> S. Mary's is nearly filled every Sunday morning at 10 o'clock by the 8th Essex Cycle Corps, and the Services are inspiring to those who take part in them by reason of the singing, which is most hearty. The Rev. John Holyoak

---

[41]   English Church Union, *Religious Ministrations in the Army, Report of the Proceedings of a Meeting of the English Church Union held in the Hoare Memorial Hall at the Church House, Westminster, on Wednesday, February 23rd, 1916* (English Church Union, London, 1916), pp. 7–8

preached on his last Sunday, and the Rev. Frank Burnett on his first at the Service. The CEMS hymn sheets are distributed each Sunday by Mr Lingley, and Mr Kingdom plays the organ … We are glad to see the number of soldiers at our Churches increasing on Sundays, the new notice boards near S. Mary's and Christ Church doubtless aiding in this respect.[42]

The last sentence is probably a reference to the large numbers of soldiers who came voluntarily to Evensong in the town centre churches, especially during the winter. As early as November 1914, Ward, whose galleried church could seat 2,000, was writing in St Peter's magazine that 'it would be a great assistance to our Churchwardens and Sidesmen if our own people would kindly come as early as convenient on Sunday evenings, as it is so difficult to keep seats at liberty owing to the troops, who we are pleased to welcome to the Church in still increasing number.'[43] Such appeals appear in magazines and annual vestry minutes throughout the war.[44]

Services were regularly held by the parish clergy of Colchester for the wounded in the hospitals. Holy Communion was celebrated on weekdays, and special services on Sunday afternoons were attended by church choirs and parishioners.[45] The Sunday afternoon hospital services seem to have been simple 'hymn sandwiches', more suited to the needs of the sick, and another indication of the increasingly perceived need to supplement the provisions of the 1662 Book of Common Prayer.

Surviving service and burial registers show that army chaplains celebrated Holy Communion and preached in Colchester's parish churches from time to time, and occasionally helped the parish clergy in other ways, for example by occasionally officiating at funerals of parishioners.[46]

---

[42]   *St Mary-at-the-Walls Parish Magazine,* December 1914
[43]   *St Peter's Parish Magazine,* November 1914
[44]   *St Peter's Parish Magazine,* November 1916, October 1918. ERO, St Peter's Parochial Church Council Minutes, 21 November 1916. *St Mary-at-the-Walls Parish Magazine,* March 1916
[45]   *St Mary-at-the-Walls Parish Magazine,* November 1915
[46]   *St Mary-at-the-Walls Parish Magazine,* August 1917, June 1918, November 1918

Patterns of Wartime Church Attendance

At the start of the First World War some parishes in England experienced an increase in church attendance which proved to be of no lasting duration.[47] In Colchester, the opposite occurred: church attendance diminished slightly in the autumn of 1914, when soldiers were billeted in private houses, and their civilian occupants were reluctant to go to church, in case anything unpleasant happened during their absence.[48] Once the troops had begun to be accommodated in tents and huts instead of billets, parishioners returned to church, and attendance in Colchester remained high throughout the First World War. In December 1917 Brunwin-Hales observed, 'it is good … to note that our Churches are even fuller than they were in the first two years of the war.'[49] The high rates of church attendance in Colchester are reflected in the numbers of Easter communicants and of confirmations throughout the war (see Table 3).

The high rates of church attendance throughout the First World War were attributable to a number of factors. In part, this was a continuation of the high rates of church attendance experienced in Colchester prior to 1914. It has been estimated that at times during the second half of the nineteenth century as many as 70 per cent of Colchester's population may regularly have attended a church or chapel. Between 1914 and 1918, the parish churches doubtless reaped the benefits of their pastoral work and teaching in the years leading up to the war.[50]

Colchester also contained a stable and cohesive society, and the social elite set an example of churchgoing and of support for the Church of England throughout the war. The 1916 National Mission of Repentance and Hope renewed the spiritual life of many parishes.[51] Parish churches, with their web of activities and human contacts, offered an important means of care and support for the anxious and bereaved throughout the war. In connection with this, it may be observed that although some people turn away from God in times of pain and suffering such as wartime, other

[47] Wilkinson, *Church of England*, p. 79
[48] *St Mary-at-the-Walls Parish Magazine*, December 1914. ERO, St Leonard's, Lexden, Vestry Minutes, 1915
[49] *St Mary-at-the-Walls Parish Magazine*, January 1918
[50] A. Phillips, 'Four Colchester Elections', *An Essex Tribute*, ed. K. Neale (Leopard's Head Press, London, 1987), pp. 199–227, p. 215
[51] Wilkinson, *Church of England*, p. 79

Table 3: Numbers of Easter communicants and confirmations in Colchester,
1912–21

Year	1912	1913	1914	1915	1916	1917	1918	1919	1920	1921
Easter communicants										
	3,474	3,556	3,302	3,434	3,690	3,458	3,471	3,353	3,628	3,712
Confirmations										
Male	116	83	110	109	96	109	141	100	123	97
Female	177	147	140	157	161	137	149	145	189	174
Total	293	230	250	266	257	246	290	245	312	271

Source: Figures taken from ERO, Annual Summaries of Church Work and Finance in the Diocese of St Albans and of Chelmsford, 1912–21. The figures are taken from the annual statistical returns from Berechurch, Holy Trinity, St Botolph's (incl. St Stephen's), St Giles's (incl. St Barnabas's), St James's (incl. St Anne's), St John's, St Leonard's-at-the-Hythe, St Martin's, St Mary-at-the-Walls, St Mary Magdalen's, St Nicholas's, St Paul's, St Peter's, Greenstead, St Leonard's, Lexden, Myland and All Saints', Stanway. There is no firm evidence about the size of Colchester's population during the war. The military population increased dramatically, but the anecdotal evidence would suggest that as Colchester was in a restricted zone there was not much of an increase in the civilian population. Men of military age would have been serving in the army or navy, and it seems reasonable to surmise that the population from which these statistics were drawn was of more or less the same size or marginally smaller throughout the war

people turn to Him for comfort and support, and return to the Church as a consequence. On a more prosaic level, it should not be overlooked that, apart from going to church, there was not much else to do on Sundays in Colchester, especially during the winter months.

Liturgical Controversies: Reservation of the Blessed Sacrament

The First World War brought to the fore two liturgical controversies which had spluttered on in the Church of England for years before 1914: the reservation of the sacrament and prayers for the dead.

Reservation of the sacrament of the Eucharist is a very ancient part of Christianity and would have been familiar to the grandchildren of some of the people who knew Jesus. By the second century AD, when Christians met to celebrate the Eucharist in secrecy for fear of persecution, they were often given some of the sacramental Body of Christ to take home with them. They would spend a period of time in prayer each day and then communicate themselves with this sacrament. Following the conversion of the Emperor Constantine to Christianity in AD 315, the sacrament began to be reserved in churches for the Communion of the sick and dying.[52] In the Orthodox Churches, the sacrament was reserved very simply and only at certain times of the year, for example in Great Lent.

In the Roman Catholic Church, from the thirteenth century onwards, the reserved sacrament began to be used as an aid to prayer and a focus of devotion. This was a spiritual movement, generated from the bottom up, which grew out of the desire of medieval Catholics to draw closer to Jesus in his sacramental presence. It was based upon the doctrine of the Real Presence, which was shared by both Orthodox and Roman Catholic Christians. But whereas the Orthodox Churches simply taught the Real Presence as a Divine Mystery, without seeking to describe how this occurs in the Eucharist, Roman Catholics sought to understand the Real Presence through the doctrine of transubstantiation. This spiritual development found expression in the elevation of the host and chalice by the priest immediately after their consecration, so that the sacramental Body and Blood of Christ might be adored by the congregation; in genuflection as a sign of reverence towards the Real Presence of Christ; in the feast of Corpus Christi; and in extra-liturgical devotions such as Benediction of the Blessed Sacrament.

During the English Reformation, the 1549 Book of Common Prayer made provision for the temporary reservation of the sacrament for the Communion of the sick, but its use as an aid to devotion was suppressed. Subsequent editions of the Book of Common Prayer in 1552, 1559 and 1662 made no provision for the reservation of the sacrament, and by the second half of the sixteenth century the practice had largely died out. In Scotland, however, the Scottish Episcopal Church came to appreciate the value of reservation for the Communion of the sick and dying, and from the eighteenth century the sacrament was reserved in Episcopal churches. The Oxford Movement in the Church of England in the nineteenth century led to a greater appreciation of the Eucharist, as well as to higher pastoral expectations and better care of the sick and dying. Once again,

---

[52]   C. Harris, 'The Communion of the Sick', *Liturgy and Worship: A Companion to the Prayer Books of the Anglican Communion*, ed. W.K. Lowther Clarke and C. Harris (SPCK, London, 1936), pp. 541–615, pp. 546–610

in a movement generated from the bottom up, the sacrament began to be reserved in Anglo-Catholic churches in England and in parts of the Anglican Communion overseas, in order to communicate the sick and dying. With reservation sometimes came the revival of the use of the sacrament as an aid to devotion.[53]

Not surprisingly, many evangelicals, such as Bishop Watts-Ditchfield, were unhappy about the permanent reservation of the sacrament. From the Elizabethan Settlement onwards, the Church of England had contained a diversity of beliefs about the relationship of God's gift to the elements of bread and wine of the Eucharist.[54] Some Anglicans held a *virtualist* view of the sacrament and believed that bread and wine were solemnly set apart in the prayer of consecration, and whilst not changed physically into Christ's body and blood, became so in virtue, power and effect. Other Anglicans held a *receptionist* view, and believed that when the congregation received the consecrated bread and wine with faith, they received the body and blood of Christ in their hearts.[55] A minority of Anglicans between the seventeenth and nineteenth centuries maintained a traditional belief in the Real Presence.[56] After 1833, the Oxford Movement altered the balance of eucharistic beliefs in the Church of England. Anglo-Catholics believed and taught the Real Presence – indeed, the Confraternity of the Blessed Sacrament was founded in 1862 to propagate this doctrine and its concomitant spirituality – and the number of Anglicans believing in the Real Presence grew considerably in the nineteenth and early twentieth centuries.

Reservation of the sacrament made little sense – and the use of the sacrament as an aid to prayer and devotion made even less – to those whose eucharistic theology was virtualist or receptionist. Many evangelicals opposed Anglo-Catholic belief in the Real Presence and associated liturgical practices, fearing that they were a betrayal of the Thirty-Nine Articles and tending towards an idolatrous view of the sacrament and

[53] R.W.F. Beaken, *God's Gifts for God's People: Reservation of the Blessed Sacrament* (The Fitzwalter Press, East Harling, 2009), pp. 6–7

[54] J.R.H. Moorman, *The Anglican Spiritual Tradition* (Darton, Longman and Todd, London 1983), pp. 60–4, 94, 103, 131. Nockles, *The Oxford Movement in Context*, pp. 209–27

[55] Nockles, *The Oxford Movement in Context*, pp. 236–37

[56] J. Pinnington, *Anglicans and Orthodox, Unity and Subversion, 1559–1725* (Gracewing, Leominster, 2003), pp. 22, 27, 29

the reintroduction of Popery via the vestry door.[57] In 1911, the bishops of the Church of England gave guarded permission for the sacrament to be reserved solely for Communion – and not as an aid to devotion – in parts of parish churches inaccessible to the public. The controversy over reservation simmered on. In 1913 the – admittedly rather exotic – Anglican Benedictine monks of Caldey were received into the Roman Catholic Church in a welter of publicity, in part because they had been instructed by Bishop Charles Gore, their new visitor, to discontinue using the reserved sacrament as an aid to prayer and devotion.[58]

During the First World War, increasing numbers of Anglo-Catholic parish priests and some military chaplains sought to reserve the sacrament in order to administer Holy Communion in a hurry to the wounded, to troops returning to the front, to civilians injured in air raids and possibly to grieving parishioners.[59] Under the pressure of wartime pastoral needs, some parishes started using the reserved sacrament as a focus for prayer and for devotional purposes. In 1917, Bishop Winnington-Ingram of London 'frankly admitted' to Convocation that the 1911 bishops' regulations had broken down in his diocese, because 'the tide of human grief and anxiety had been too great, the longing to get to the Sacramental Presence of our Lord had been too urgent'.[60]

It is unclear whether the sacrament was permanently reserved in any of Colchester's Anglo-Catholic churches during the First World War. I have found one reference to Benediction of the Blessed Sacrament in Colchester, in a letter written by Private Walter Deasy of the Manchester Regiment, but it is not apparent whether he was an Anglo-Catholic or

[57] See, for example, F. Close, *The Restoration of the Churches is the Restoration of Popery: Proved and Illustrated from the Authenticated Publications of the 'Cambridge Camden Society': A Sermon Preached in the Parish Church, Cheltenham, on Tuesday, 5 November, 1844* (J. Hatchard and Son, London, 1844), F. Close, *The Roman Anti-Christ, a 'Lying Spirit': Being the Substance of a Sermon Preached in the Parish Church, Cheltenham, November the 5th, 1845* (J. Hatchard and Son, London, 1845), F. Close, *The Catholic Revival', or, Ritualism and Romanism in the Church of England* (Hatchard and Co, London, 1866) and also parts of F. Close, *Semper Idem; or Popery Everywhere and Always the Same: A Sermon Preached in the Parish Church, Cheltenham, November 5th, 1851* (J. Hatchard and Son, London, 1851)
[58] Anson, *The Call of the Cloister*, pp. 178–81
[59] Wilkinson, *Church of England*, pp. 147–8
[60] Wilkinson, *Church of England*, p. 178

a Roman Catholic.[61] Behr kept the feast of Corpus Christi at St Stephen's.[62] This may mean either that the Anglo-Catholics in Colchester had not yet got around to introducing reservation, or that they did so very quietly in order to avoid attracting adverse attention. Watts-Ditchfield's unsuccessful attempts to stamp out reservation at Little Bardfield in 1914 would have been well known in Essex Anglo-Catholic circles.

In October 1915 Watts-Ditchfield visited Bishop Charles Gore at Oxford to discuss reservation. Gore urged that the sacrament should only be reserved for the Communion of the sick.[63] We know from Watts-Ditchfield's diary that in 1915 he regarded the 'Adoration of the Sacred Elements' as dangerous, and there is no reason to think he later modified his views.[64] On 12 April 1917, Watts-Ditchfield convoked a diocesan synod of clergy to discuss reservation and invited Gore to be the principal speaker (not, perhaps, the happiest of choices, given the part he had played in the secession of the monks of Caldey four years earlier). Gore attacked the Roman doctrine of transubstantiation as erroneous and asserted that the sacrament ought to be reserved solely for Communion of the sick. Watts-Ditchfield said that he had sought to be fair, but he was critical of 'Romanists in our very midst who practise and teach many things with which the Primitive Church had not to contend', and he asked all clergy reserving the Sacrament 'in any shape or form' to write to him with full details 'in the next two or three days.'[65] The next year Watts-Ditchfield informed the Servants of Christ, an enclosed community of twenty-three Anglican Cistercian nuns at Pleshey, that he could no longer allow them to reserve the sacrament in their chapel, although they had previously done so without controversy for ten years. The community presumably had a daily Eucharist, from which Communion might be taken to a sick sister; and so it may be inferred that they reserved the sacrament, at least in part, as an aid to their lives of prayer and contemplation. After much agonising, the Servants of Christ decided to leave the diocese of Chelms-

61   IWM, Papers of W. Deasy, undated letter marked 'Monday', probably from 1917
62   *St Botolph's Parish Magazine*, July 1914
63   ERO, Watts-Ditchfield diaries, 16 October 1915
64   ERO, Watts-Ditchfield diaries, 17 September 1915
65   J.E. Watts-Ditchfield, *Reservation: Addresses by the Bishop of Oxford, the Right Rev. Charles Gore, DD, and the Bishop of the Diocese, the Right Rev. J.E. Watts-Ditchfield, DD, to the Clergy of the Diocese of Chelmsford, together with a Series of Questions and Answers* (Robert Scott, London, 1917), pp. 31–2, 96, 104–5

ford, and eventually settled in Buckinghamshire in order to continue reservation in their chapel.[66]

Liturgical Controversies: Prayers for the Dead

Although reservation of the sacrament led to a great deal of controversy, overall comparatively few parishes were affected. Prayers for the dead was an altogether larger issue. Prayers for the dead could be found in the Church of England before the First World War, but were not common. The tradition of commending the dead to God in prayer is very ancient in Christianity, but, by the time of the Reformation, it was surrounded by widespread abuses, centring upon the sale of indulgences and a system of chantry priests, perpetually offering Requiem Masses for the repose of the souls of the dead in return for stipends. Although the 1549 Book of Common Prayer had contained intercessions for the dead, later revisions omitted such prayers. The only reference to the departed which could be interpreted as a prayer for them in the 1662 Book of Common Prayer came in the prayer for the church militant in the Holy Communion: 'And we also bless thy holy Name for all thy servants departed this life in thy faith and fear; beseeching thee to give us grace so to follow their good examples, that with them we may be partakers of thy heavenly kingdom.'[67]

Since the English Reformation, the practice of deliberately not praying for the dead had long been part of the self-identity of most – but, by the early twentieth century, not quite all – Anglican evangelicals.[68] Most evangelicals had little if any direct experience of prayer for the dead and may have thought of it as an attempt to persuade God with

[66] Anson, *The Call of the Cloister*, p. 474. The former convent at Pleshey is today the Chelmsford Diocesan House of Retreat. The sacrament is reserved in the chapel

[67] E.J. Bicknell, *A Theological Introduction to the Thirty-Nine Articles of the Church of England* (Longmans, Green, London, 1955), p. 351, suggested that the departed were also supposed to be included in the sentence from the prayer of oblation, 'that we and all thy whole church may obtain remission of our sins'. One 'W.C.B.', writing anonymously in the *Chelmsford Diocesan Chronicle* in December 1918, also suggested that the first prayer in the Burial Service in the Book of Common Prayer is a prayer for the departed

[68] Bell, *Randall Davidson*, p. 830

prayers and Requiem Masses to modify His judgement upon a soul. Charles Neil and J.M. Willoughby, writing in 1912 in *The Tutorial Prayer Book*, a classic evangelical study of the Book of Common Prayer, commented:

> There is no passage in the Old or New Testaments which enjoins, sanctions, or recommends prayers for the dead, believing or unbelieving. The righteous enters 'Paradise' at death, and are 'in joy and felicity' (Phil. i. 21–23); they are therefore in no want of our prayers or intercessions. If the unrighteous can be helped by our prayers, it is incredible that the many directions for prayer in the Bible should contain no reference whatever to this all-important matter.[69]

To many evangelicals, prayer for the dead seemed unscriptural and unnecessary and appeared contrary to the doctrine of justification by faith alone. It was also a practice they associated with Roman Catholicism. In most evangelical and middle-of-the-road parishes before 1914, intercession would be offered for a parishioner whilst he was ill, but not once he had died.

The tradition of prayer for the dead was never entirely forgotten in the Church of England, and, following the Oxford Movement in the nineteenth century, it enjoyed a certain revival. Anglo-Catholics saw prayer for the dead as a loving and devout way of supporting the soul of a fellow Christian believer as it underwent purification and healing after death. Such purification and healing was held to be an aspect of God's judgement, in preparation for the Beatific Vision. In 1898 the archbishop of Canterbury, Frederick Temple, ruled that prayers for the dead were legal in the Church of England, but not compulsory. Prayers for the dead were included in a 'form of intercession' issued in 1900 during the South African War, and in the 'form of service' issued in 1902 to commemorate Queen Victoria. The proposals for Prayer Book revision produced by the Committee on the Royal Letters of Business in 1911 contained restrained prayers for the dead in the burial service.[70]

[69] C. Neil and J.M. Willoughby, eds, *The Tutorial Prayer Book, for the Teacher, the Student, and the General Reader* (Harrison Trust, London, 1912), p. 481

[70] Chadwick, *The Victorian Church, Part 2*, p. 356. Wilkinson, *Church of England*, p. 176. Pullan, 'Prayer Book Revision'

Many evangelicals, including Bishop Watts-Ditchfield, continued to reject prayers for the dead. The bishop was dismayed to learn that such prayers might be included in the forms of prayer authorised for the national day of intercession on 21 August 1914. He interrupted his holiday in Llandudno to send a telegram to Archbishop Davidson conveying his opposition to prayer for the dead on 10 August.[71] He followed it up with a letter to Davidson, written later the same day:

> You would receive my telegram stating that I would gladly authorise the prayers drawn up by the Bishop of Ely and the Dean of Wells provided there were no prayers for the Dead such as were in the collect proposed by the Bishop of Oxford and defeated in Convocation. I think that if such were inserted they would cause strife and division when there ought to be unity and peace. It would also once more show the divided counsels among the Bishops if one sanctioned them and another did not. Correspondence would ensue in the Press and united Services in many districts would become impossible if such prayers were inserted. I am venturing then to urge that any prayers of this kind which a very considerable section of the Church would not and could not use, should not be inserted. I am quite aware that some Churchmen desire such but the question to be decided is whether any such collect should be authorised to be said in Church if it differs in teaching to those already in the Prayer Book. I am sure you will forgive my writing [to] you but I am anxious that the Church should be united in this time of stress and strain. As I said in Convocation I have my own personal views on the question but I am very zealous concerning the Services in Church that they should not contain anything but what is definitely taught by and can be proved by Holy Scripture.[72]

Archbishop Davidson replied the following day in his customary measured tones:

> I do not think that in the Form now to be issued the words relating to the departed are such as ought to cause difficulty to any reasonable man; but it is delicate ground and I cannot be quite sure whether you would agree with me or not. The pressure that we should go very much further than we think

---

[71]   LPL, Davidson Papers, vol. 367, p. 85
[72]   LPL, Davidson Papers, vol. 367, p. 79

of going in that direction is great, and I know what was felt at the time of
the South African War when [Anglican] people went to Roman Catholic
Churches because they failed to find in ours any prayer for the Dead. I
draw a great distinction between what we can put in the Prayer Book and
what we can draw up for use in an emergency like this when the hearts of
people are greatly moved. I have, however, with the Bishop of Ely taken
the greatest care to say no word which so far as I can judge teaches false
doctrine. In view of the possible question that some Bishops may entertain
– e.g. Liverpool, Manchester, and I think one or two besides yourself – I
have simply arranged for an imprimatur to the effect that 'Authority has
already been obtained from the Bishops of the following Dioceses' and
have omitted the names of those who have raised any question. It will be
quite easy for them to authorise the Form afterwards if they approve it
when they see it.[73]

Watts-Ditchfield let the subject drop for a while, but returned to the
offensive in April 1915 with a prominent article, printed entirely in bold
font, in the *Chelmsford Diocesan Chronicle*:

MEMORIAL SERVICES. The Bishop once more draws attention to the
fact that under no circumstances should such Services be held unless they
have his sanction. The oath taken by each Clergyman makes this incumbent upon him and he cannot expect the Blessing of God on Services held
in violation of his most solemn word. The Bishop has already sanctioned
the most excellent Form drawn up by the Bishop of Stepney. He has also
approved of the Form of the Bishop of Chichester, published by the SPCK,
and will do his utmost to meet the wishes of the Clergy who submit other
Forms to him.[74]

In 1916, Watts-Ditchfield further asked that all forms of prayer to
be used in the diocese of Chelmsford on the national day of prayer on
4 August should first be submitted to him for his sanction, but he was
fighting a losing battle.[75] Many Anglicans began to re-examine their
attitudes towards prayer for the dead, led by Archbishop Davidson, who

[73]   LPL, Davidson Papers, vol. 367, p. 88
[74]   *Chelmsford Diocesan Chronicle*, April 1915
[75]   *Chelmsford Diocesan Chronicle*, July 1916

personally had come to believe in praying for the departed.[76] A sermon preached on the subject by Davidson on All Souls' Day 1914 was widely circulated. After recognising the abuses of the medieval system, Davidson continued:

> But surely now there is a place for a gentler recognition of the instinctive, the natural, the loyal craving of the bereaved, and the abuses of the chantry system and the extavangances of Tetzel need not now, nearly four centuries afterwards, thwart or hinder the reverent, the absolutely trustful prayer of a wounded spirit who feels it natural and helpful to pray for him whom we shall not greet on earth again, but who, in his Father's loving keeping, still lives, and, as we may surely believe, still grows from strength to strength in truer purity and in deepened reverence and love.[77]

In 1917 official forms of prayer were issued containing explicit prayers for the dead for the first time:

> Almighty and Everlasting God, unto whom no prayer is ever made without hope of thy compassion: We remember before thee our brethren who have laid down their lives in the cause wherein their King and country sent them. Grant that they, who have readily obeyed the call of those to whom thou hast given authority on earth, may be accounted worthy of a place among thy faithful servants in the kingdom of heaven; and give both to them and to us forgiveness of all our sins, and an ever increasing understanding of thy will; for his sake who loved us and gave himself for us, thy Son our Saviour Jesus Christ. Amen.[78]

Some evangelicals continued to object, but Davidson pointed out that the prayers were to be said at the discretion of the minister, 'where the Ordinary [usually, the diocesan bishop] permits'. They were widely used.[79]

---

[76]   LPL, Davidson Papers, vol. 195, p. 263
[77]   Bell, *Randall Davidson*, pp. 830ff
[78]   Bell, *Randall Davidson*, pp. 828–9
[79]   Bell, *Randall Davidson*, pp. 829–30

Prayers for the Dead in the Parish Churches of Colchester

Colchester suffered the highest casualty rate of any town in East Anglia during the First World War. Jack Ashton recalled that many of the townsfolk grieved in private and tried to put on a brave front in public.[80] In the face of such widespread bereavement and sorrow, the post-Reformation custom of not praying for the dead was often found to be inadequate to meet pastoral and spiritual needs. In 1915, Bishop Whitcombe presented a paper entitled 'Prayers for the Dead' at the Colchester Clerical Society and chaired a discussion afterwards.[81] Prayers for the dead began to be heard in more of Colchester's parish churches. This was a gradual development, but it would seem to have gathered pace in the years 1916–17, which saw the introduction of conscription and high casualties during the battles of the Somme and Passchendaele. In the autumn of 1916, street war shrines in memory of the dead were erected by some townsfolk on East Hill, Harwich Road and Ipswich Road, which would indicate that in the face of so much grief, new patterns of mourning the dead were evolving.[82]

An article in *St Mary-at-the-Walls Parish Magazine* in November 1916 indicates how attitudes towards prayers for the dead were changing in one middle-of-the-road parish, where there is no evidence that prayers for the dead were used before the war:

All Saints' Day grows dearer to us as we realise how our friends multiply in Paradise. This is especially true as the scythe of war cuts down the flower of our youth and leaves us desolate … In the Holy Communion we can best realise the Communion of Saints in worship, and understand that with the whole company of Heaven we are praising God. So we trust many will gather to the Altar on November 1. On that day also there will be a choral Memorial Service at 6.30 at S. Mary's, when the gratitude we all feel for those who have laid down their lives for us may be expressed in the worship of God, who raised these heroes up to fall for our country. Let us pray Him that He who began a good work in them will continue it within the veil, until Christ comes again.[83]

---

[80]   Mr Jack Ashton, interview, 10 February 1998
[81]   ERO, Colchester and District Clerical Society Annual Reports, 1914–1915
[82]   *Essex County Standard*, 16 December 1916
[83]   *St Mary-at-the-Walls Parish Magazine*, November 1916

The three evangelical parishes in Colchester seem to have remained unaffected by the revival of prayers for the dead. Evangelical Anglicans grieved as deeply as those of other churchmanships, and yet the belief that prayers for the dead were wrong was an explicit part of their theological identity and outlook. Consequently, however much they mourned their relatives and friends killed in the war, most evangelicals simply would not have thought to pray for them. Middle-of-the-road Anglicans did not have such a strong antagonism towards prayers for the dead, and it was easier for them to adopt this practice.

Requiem Masses

The revival of prayer for the dead in the Church of England affected parishes of different churchmanship in different ways. In Anglo-Catholic folklore, the First World War has been believed to be responsible for the revival of Requiem Masses. The evidence from Colchester is that the parishes which celebrated Requiem Masses during the war were the four Anglo-Catholic ones, which were accustomed to do so anyway. The principal difference was that during the war, they celebrated Requiems more frequently: at St Stephen's, for instance, in October 1914, Behr introduced a weekly Requiem at 7.00 a.m. on Saturdays.[84] The bulk of middle-of-the-road parishes in Colchester would have shied away from referring to a service of Holy Communion as a 'Requiem', but it would seem that in a number of churches, parishioners killed in the war were prayed for by name during Sunday services or during weekly intercession services.[85]

Most parishes in Colchester, with the exception of St Leonard's, Lexden, Holy Trinity and St Nicholas's, declined to hold memorial services for individuals killed in the war. Brunwin-Hales wrote in the autumn of 1916: 'we have had no Memorial Services for individuals in our Parish, and it is, in our opinion, better so. All who have fallen should be equally honoured, so far as can be, "high and low, rich and poor, one with another."'[86] Some parishes, instead, organised annual memorial services for all of their parishioners killed in the war. These were often

---

[84] *St Botolph's Parish Magazine*, October 1914
[85] Mr Jack Ashton, interview, 10 February 1998
[86] *St Mary-at-the-Walls Parish Magazine*, November 1916

held on All Saints' Day, 1 November, though some churches in Colchester arranged their memorial services instead for All Souls' Day, 2 November, the traditional liturgical day for praying for the dead, despite the absence of provision for All Souls' Day from the 1662 Prayer Book calendar.

'The Place of Meeting'

One surprising phenomenon of the First World War was the success of a card published by A.R. Mowbray and Company, entitled 'The Place of Meeting', which reproduced a painting by the Anglo-Catholic artist Thomas Noyes-Lewis of a High Mass of Requiem for troops killed in the war. Behind the altar was a triptych reredos, with St George and other martial saints depicted on the right panel. Behind the altar, Noyes-Lewis showed the ranks of departed soldiers and sailors for whom the Requiem is being offered. The picture's significance lies in its confident message. There is no doubt in the artist's mind that the Requiem Mass is helping the dead soldiers and sailors, who are depicted in their resurrection bodies, with scarcely a touch of Flanders mud on their immaculate uniforms, gazing down reverently towards the consecration upon the altar. Amongst their number may be observed both officers and men, an army chaplain, and, towards the back of the picture, the dead of previous wars, including a couple of crusader knights – a popular image amongst the public for British soldiers during the First World War.[87] 'The Place of Meeting' sold in such large numbers that they cannot all have been bought by Anglo-Catholics; some at least must have found their way into the hands of middle-of-the-road Anglicans.[88]

[87]   See, for example, the line from the hymn 'O Valiant Hearts': 'Tranquil you lie, your knightly virtue proved'. At the burial of the Unknown Warrior in Westminster Abbey in 1920, a Crusader knight's sword was donated by King George V from the Royal Collection at Windsor Castle and was laid upon the coffin before its burial

[88]   Information gathered by the author when working for A.R. Mowbray and Company, 1983–4. Conversation with the Rev. Philip Ursell, principal of Pusey House, 30 May 1999. 'The Place of Meeting' seems to have been printed in two sizes: a small version for use as a bookmark and a larger version for framing. Examples can still occasionally be found hanging in undisturbed corners of old parish churches

Churchmanship

In December 1918, a lengthy article appeared in the *Chelmsford Dioc-esan Chronicle* arguing, on the basis of New Testament principles, that 'some prayer for the dead is according to the best and purest form of Christianity'.[89] Such an article would have been inconceivable before the First World War. In his biography of Randall Davidson, G.K.A. Bell asserts that before the war, prayers for the dead were not common in the Church of England, but that afterwards they were widespread. This is perhaps a slight exaggeration – a century later, there are still parishes where prayers are not said for the departed[90] – but the difference was that whereas before 1914 prayers for the dead were seen as something done by a small number of Anglo-Catholic extremists, by 1918 they had become respectable in the mainstream Church of England and were to be found in increasing numbers of parishes in the 1920s and 1930s.

One noteworthy feature of the growth of prayers for the dead and of the reservation of the Sacrament during the First World War is that, although these developments exacerbated differences of churchmanship, they do not appear to have led to any antagonism between the parishes and clergy of Colchester. There is no evidence to suggest that the clergy of the evangelical parishes complained that their neighbouring Anglo-Catholic parishes were celebrating Requiem Masses and reserving the sacrament, or that other parishes had introduced prayers for the departed. They may privately have had qualms, but it is as though a gentlemen's agreement existed amongst the clergy not to interfere or criticise their neighbours' parishes. This reflects the mutual support and understanding which existed amongst the Colchester clergy before 1914, and which was further strengthened through wartime cooperation and common suf-fering. A generation earlier, a more assertive evangelicalism might have acted differently.

---

[89] *Chelmsford Diocesan Chronicle*, December 1918, by one 'W.C.B.'

[90] It is entirely possible that the growth of evangelicalism and of low church liberalism (which are not quite the same thing) in the Church of England in the late twentieth and early twenty-first centuries may mean that in some parish churches where prayers were once routinely said for the dead in the decades after the First World War, they are no longer, there having been a change of churchmanship, or at least the appoint-ment of a different kind of vicar

Liturgical Developments and Changes

Reservation of the sacrament and the use of prayers for the dead were not the only liturgical changes to have grown in the Church of England during the First World War. The experience of trying to meet wartime pastoral needs and minister to the troops using the 1662 Book of Common Prayer led to a wider appreciation of the need for Prayer Book revision. A number of priests, having conducted short parade services for the troops, began to wish they might sometimes be allowed to abbreviate or augment their regular parochial Sunday services.[91]

Several parishes in Colchester began to experiment with their Sunday services during the war. At St Botolph's, Evensong was held in the open air in the ruins of St Botolph's Priory during the summer of 1916, and services were shortened with Bishop Watts-Ditchfield's approval as part of the parish's programme for the National Mission of Repentance and Hope.[92] Some clergy wished to abandon Evensong altogether in the winter months, or to move the service to an earlier hour, because of the restrictions on lighting during wartime, but Watts-Ditchfield completely refused to allow Evensong to be dropped – at least until 1918, when the shortage of clerical manpower led to the rearrangement of services in many parishes – and he put obstacles in the way of changing the time of Evensong, on the grounds that once the habit of attending church at a certain hour had been lost, it would be very difficult to re-establish it later.[93]

The necessity of ministering to anxious or grieving parishioners under the unprecedented conditions of wartime led some clergy to enrich the 1662 Book of Common Prayer with material from other liturgical sources, especially for weekly intercession services. Litanies were very popular: at St Mary-at-the-Walls, for instance, an interest amongst the congregation in Britain's ally Russia led to the frequent use of a Russian Orthodox litany. A litany devised by Bishop Winnington-Ingram was also used, and there are references to a 'Bishop's litany'. Use was also made of something called the 'Moot Hall litany', which was probably compiled locally for use at a patriotic meeting in the Moot Hall, the principal room of Colchester

---

[91]   Munson, *Echoes of the Great War*, diary entry for 13 August 1916
[92]   *St Botolph's Parish Magazine*, July 1916
[93]   *Chelmsford Diocesan Chronicle*, 1915, p. 191

town hall.[94] Hymn singing was an important and popular part of worship, and many hymns were composed for use in wartime, such as J.S. Arkwright's 'Father, we Bring our Dead to Thee', which largely disappeared from use after the Armistice.[95]

The attitude of Bishop Watts-Ditchfield towards liturgical experimentation was complex and generally not very encouraging, although he fully realised the importance of liturgy in wartime. At the start of the war, he asked that all churches in his diocese should be open every day, that parishes should arrange more frequent celebrations of Holy Communion, and that daily intercession in churches and continuous intercession at home by groups of laypeople should be arranged whenever possible.[96] With his concern for evangelism, Watts-Ditchfield was not dismissive of all change. On occasion he took the initiative, such as Good Friday 1917, when, at his own suggestion, the bishop led a large procession of witness through Colchester.[97] Changes and augmentation of the 1662 Book of Common Prayer, however, were altogether another issue. Watts-Ditchfield was determined to control liturgical change in his diocese and to prevent what he saw as errors creeping into the Church of England through its worship. He would countenance only the most limited interpretation of the text and rubrics of the Prayer Book, as is demonstrated by the following article from the *S. Albans and Chelmsford Diocesan Gazette* shortly after the outbreak of war:

> The Bishop earnestly hopes that Incumbents will, in all cases, submit for his sanction as Ordinary, all forms of Services or Special Collects which are not found in the Prayer Book or in the Forms named above. He is quite prepared to sanction large variations in Service at the present time so long as they are in the spirit of those already sanctioned. He emphasizes this point as he has seen some Forms which are being used without his sanction. This will no doubt be by inadvertance but he believes that all

---

[94] ERO, St Mary-at-the-Walls Registers of Services, 1907–17. The Russian litany was first used on 23 June 1915. There is a reference to the 'Bishop's War Liturgy' on 1 December 1915, which had become 'Bishop's Litany' by 24 May 1916. The 'Bishop of London's Litany' appears on 3 May 1916; these are probably all references to the same litany. The 'Moot Hall Litany' appears first on 19 January 1916

[95] *St Botolph's Parish Magazine*, February 1915

[96] *St Albans and Chelmsford Diocesan Gazette*, 1914, p. 172

[97] ERO, Colchester Ruri-decanal Chapter Minutes, 9 February 1917

Incumbents will see the advisability of the Bishop being consulted in such matters. He does not wish this direction to be so interpreted as to preclude suggestions for silent prayer or even a short extemporary prayer but simply to apply to any Collect or Service which is formally used from time to time.[98]

Upon closer examination, the 'large variations in the Service' authorised by the bishop turn out to have been mainly limited to modest abbreviations of Mattins and Evensong.[99]

The Church of England's experience during the First World War permanently changed its patterns of prayer and worship over the next few decades. On the surface, at least, much remained the same: in many parishes, the pattern of Sunday worship – 8.00 a.m. Holy Communion, 11.00 a.m. Mattins, 6.30 p.m. Evensong – remained unchanged until well after the Second World War. The First World War, though, may be said to have loosened things up. Between 1914 and 1918, parish priests and army chaplains had frequently conducted alternative and frequently simpler forms of service than those provided in the 1662 Book of Common Prayer, whether parade services, litanies or 'hymn sandwiches'. The war had also reinforced their perception that large numbers of men and

---

[98]   *St Albans and Chelmsford Diocesan Gazette*, 1914, p. 172, printed in bold type for emphasis in the original

[99]   The bishop seemed more concerned about the use of additional material than with abbreviations. The order for the intercession service held at St Botolph's on 2 January 1916, for example, says prominently 'Authorised by the Lord Bishop of Chelmsford' but it is merely Mattins with some special prayers at the end. It is mentioned in *St Botolph's Parish Magazine* in July 1916 that Watts-Ditchfield had permitted a shorter form of Evensong, but, knowing the bishop's mind, this probably meant that he permitted the use on Sundays of the slightly shortened form of Mattins and Evensong which was allowed on weekdays by the Act of Uniformity Amendment Act of 1872. The Rev. Andrew Clark, Rector of Great Leighs (in his diaries in Munson, *Echoes of the Great War*), complained from time to time that he was not allowed to shorten the services; for example, the following entry from Sunday 13 August 1916: 'The old women on the Episcopal Bench are devising old-womanish National Missions, and relays of women preachers, but will not move a finger to lighten the church service of dreary incrustations of a by-gone age, or of allowing reasonable liberty of substituting reasonable alternatives for intolerably long psalms and lessons for the day. The consequence of this episcopal stick-in-the-mud policy is that the English people are being driven away from the Anglican Church.' Evidently Clark was not impressed by Watts-Ditchfield's readiness to sanction 'large variations in the service'

women were untouched by the Church's message. Clergy in the 1920s and 1930s were, as a result, more inclined to augment the material found in the Prayer Book than they had been before 1914. Prayer for the dead, and even memorial services, became more common after 1918.

The First World War brought about a wider appreciation of the importance of Holy Communion in the spiritual life. This was the result of many factors, principally of more frequent celebrations of Holy Communion in all parishes during the war, which coincided with more widespread belief in the Real Presence amongst Anglicans. The National Mission of Repentance and Hope (see below) also played a part, by recalling the lapsed to the sacraments.[100] The Eucharist came to be more widely understood as a channel of intercession, for example in 1916, when the Colchester chapter agreed to hold 'a Celebration of the Holy Communion every Thursday with "special intention" for the [National] Mission'.[101]

Renewed appreciation of Holy Communion in the parishes was paralleled by a similar experience amongst many troops at the front and their chaplains.[102] It is probable that soldiers who had derived strength and comfort from receiving Holy Communion in France brought this spiritual insight back with them to their parish churches after the war. The Parish Communion movement, which slowly changed the face of Sunday worship in the Church of England later in the twentieth century by encouraging a Parish Communion service in parish churches at about 9.30 a.m., gradually displacing Mattins as the principal Sunday morning service, owed much to wartime experiences of Holy Communion and of liturgical experiment and augmentation in 1914–18.[103]

An increasing number of parishes began to reserve the sacrament in the 1920s and 1930s. During the war, more clergy had experienced using the reserved sacrament to administer Holy Communion in a hurry to the sick and dying, as well as to troops on leave, and they had found it a great help in their ministry. Amongst some clergy and laity, the use of the reserved sacrament as an aid to prayer had also been experienced for the first time during the war. The growth of Anglo-Catholicism in the Church of England in the inter-war years was a result of many factors, but

---

[100] *St Mary-at-the-Walls Parish Magazine*, August 1916
[101] ERO, Colchester Ruri-decanal Chapter Minutes, 16 June 1916
[102] Wilkinson, *Church of England*, p. 83
[103] D. Gray, *Earth and Altar* (Canterbury Press, Norwich, 1986), pp. 45–50, 181–3

one of them must surely have been a greater appreciation of the Eucharist during the war.

Just as rolls of honour and street shrines were the seedbed from which later sprang many parish war memorials, so wartime services of intercession and national days of prayer, with ecclesiastical, civic and military involvement, likewise prepared the way for the evolution after the war of special rites and ceremonies to mark Armistice Day in communities across the country. Not for nothing was the Remembrance service at the Cenotaph in Whitehall once described as being, for many people on the fringes of church life, the 'shop-window' of the Church of England.

Before 1914, the Church of England had realised that the 1662 Prayer Book needed revising to meet altered needs and conditions. In 1906 a Royal Commission on Ritual had recommended that the Convocations should revise the law relating to worship to gain greater 'elasticity', and work to revise the Church's liturgy had begun. By 1922, however, largely as a result of experience during the First World War, it had become evident that tinkering with the 1662 Prayer Book would be inadequate, and that what was needed was an entirely revised Book of Common Prayer. The way was prepared that would lead to the debacle of the 1928 Revised Prayer Book.

7

The National Mission of Repentance and Hope

In the autumn of 1916 – as the effects of conscription were starting to be felt in communities across Britain, and as the battle of the Somme was drawing to its bloody conclusion in France – the Church of England held a simultaneous mission across every diocese and parish in England, something it had never attempted before. The 1916 National Mission of Repentance and Hope, as it was officially known, was at times muddled, ambiguous and controversial. The national mission has received little serious attention from historians, who, when they have written about it, have often been largely critical or dismissive. As a priest who conducts parish missions, I approach the 1916 national mission from a slightly different angle to many other historical writers. A great deal of the criticism levelled at the mission was richly deserved, but its undoubted successes and achievements – perhaps because they were not immediately obvious – have often been unfairly overlooked. Not the least of these was the very fact that, at the height of the First World War, the Church of England collectively devoted much of its time, energy and money to an attempt to bring anew the message of the Gospel to the nation. In Colchester, there are grounds for concluding that the 1916 national mission was, at least, moderately successful.

The Origins of the 1916 National Mission of Repentance and Hope

Wartime Religious Revival, 1914–15

In the autumn of 1914, there was a noticeable increase in the number of people attending church services. This phenomenon was patchy, and varied a good deal across the country, but it was widely believed at the time that this was the beginning of a religious revival.[1] Theodore Woods, the vicar of Bradford and bishop of Peterborough from 1916, wrote in October 1914: 'I believe that the Church is about to have the chance of its life … The churches are crowded with worshippers, and people seem to be up against the realities in a way which three months ago would have seemed impossible.'[2]

Something similar was observable in the army in 1914–15. The men who volunteered to join Kitchener's New Army did so for a variety of reasons: some went to escape from dull jobs, or to be with their pals who had joined up, or for three square meals a day. Other volunteers, however, were idealists, inspired by high and noble motives, seeking to help the people of Belgium and combat German militarism. A great many volunteers – both officers and ordinary soldiers – were regular and devout churchgoers, including a high proportion of sons of clergymen, and ordinands who had interrupted their theological training in order to serve in the army. The experience of being sent to France, with the daily possibility of death or disfigurement, focused and crystallised the religious faith of many volunteers. Across the denominations, there were signs of a religious revival amongst the British troops in France in 1914–15. In the absence of an army chaplain, it was not uncommon for officers to conduct acts of worship, and for non-commissioned officers to lead small prayer groups in the trenches or behind the lines. The London Regiment was noted for containing a higher than average proportion of communicants in its ranks, reflecting the large numbers of Anglo-Catholic parishes in London.[3] The Rev. C.E. Doudney, a parish priest who had volunteered to become a chaplain and who served with the 18th Brigade on the Western Front in 1915, observed of the troops he met:

> [R]eligion [has been] put to the severest test which any system could possibly be put to; and we have seen it come out absolutely triumphant … instead of the faith of me [sic] being shaken, we have seen it getting stronger and stronger … Tens of thousands of men, hard, rough, working men, who perhaps never attended church at home, and never thought of it are finding definitely that God is their close Friend … I am talking abso-

[1]   Wilkinson, *Church of England*, pp. 71, 79
[2]   Quoted in Wilkinson, *Church of England*, pp. 71–2
[3]   Snape, *God and the British Soldier*, pp. 148, 154–5, 164

lute bedrock truth when I say that a miracle has happened in the hearts of these lads.[4]

It is not improbable that the increase in civilian church attendance in England and the religious revival in the army informed and reinforced each other: some soldiers may have mentioned their religious experiences and church attendance whilst in the army in their letters home or when on leave; and, for their part, their relatives may have gone to church to pray for them. Prayer and churchgoing may have been viewed as a spiritual link between families in England and their menfolk serving in the army in France.

A Sense of Guilt and Failure

In the first shocked weeks of the war in 1914, as preachers and religious writers cast around to try to understand the calamity that had befallen Europe, the idea arose that, although the war was in the first instance the result of German militarism, it might also be seen, in some sense, as a consequence of corporate and individual sin, to which the appropriate response was repentance and increased Christian devotion. Such a theme can be found in the sermon preached by Bishop Whitcombe at the borough intercession service in Colchester on 19 August 1914.[5] The 1916 National Mission of Repentance and Hope sought to address these concerns.

There were several other factors behind the national mission, such as the need to respond to criticism from the journalist Horatio Bottomley that the Church of England was not doing enough in the war, and, conversely, to respond to other criticism that some clergy were preaching unbalanced and bloodthirsty sermons.[6] Stuart Mews has suggested that by 1916 there were signs of a backlash amongst some religious leaders to the passionate emotions of the first year of the war. He contends that Church of England had helped the national cause but had reaped no religious dividend, and the resultant depression, disillusionment and

---

[4]   Snape, *God and the British Soldier*, p. 166
[5]   *Essex County Standard*, 20 August 1914
[6]   Wilkinson, *Church of England*, p. 70

division had reached such a stage that something had to be done.[7] I have found no evidence of depression, disillusionment and division in Colchester, where the war had, in fact, resulted in a positive dividend in the shape of increased congregations and greater lay activity.

The Background to the National Mission: Missions and Revivals

The idea of holding a national mission in 1916 did not arise from nowhere, but grew out of a tradition of Christian missions that had been firmly established in Great Britain during the nineteenth century. Two main strands may be identified: the American Protestant revivalist tradition and the French Roman Catholic missionary tradition.[8]

The Protestant revivalist tradition had its origins in the experience of the Protestant Churches of continental Europe, Great Britain and subsequently its American colonies. Such 'revivals' were originally seen as spontaneous events resulting from the direct intervention of God, but during the late eighteenth century, the idea developed that conversion experiences could be stimulated.[9] The early nineteenth century saw the spread of revivalism to Britain, where it made an impression amongst Nonconformists. The two best-known American revivalists were Dwight L. Moody and Ira D. Sankey, who visited England in 1862 and in 1872–75. The Church of England's parochial system did not easily lend itself to revivals of the American type, though there was limited support from some Anglican evangelicals.[10] The bulk of Anglicans were probably unaffected by such revivals, but the significance of revivalism is that, for many people, it seems to have established the idea that the purpose of missions was to convert people to Christianity, and to provide opportunities for them to make a personal commitment.

---

[7]   S. Mews, 'Religion and English Society in the First World War' (Cambridge University PhD thesis, 1973), pp. 217–20

[8]   This section is heavily dependent upon the work of Dieter Voll in *Catholic Evangelicalism* (Faith Press, London, 1963), and of John Kent in *Holding the Fort: Studies in Victorian Revivalism* (Epworth Press, London, 1978), to which works the reader is directed for more detailed treatment

[9]   See, for example, Calvin Colton, *The History and Character of American Revivals of Religion* (1832), quoted by Kent, *Holding the Fort*, particularly pp. 19–20

[10]   Voll, *Catholic Evangelicalism*, p. 43

The French Roman Catholic missionary tradition began with the work of St Vincent de Paul, who in 1617 conceived the idea of a congregation of priests who would travel the countryside preaching 'missions' to undo the damage wrought by the wars of religion and to deepen faith and spirituality in rural parishes. St Vincent's aim was not to bring about conversion experiences amongst his listeners, but to remind them of the importance of their Baptism, to bring them back to the sacraments and to help them to renew their commitment to Roman Catholicism. Missions along these lines were held again after 1815, when the French Roman Catholic Church sought to overcome the problems caused by the Revolution and to renew rural Roman Catholicism. Common features were emotional preaching, day-long processions of the Blessed Sacrament, the consecration of whole parishes to the Blessed Virgin Mary and the renewal of baptismal vows.[11]

The pattern of the French Roman Catholic missions was known in England and commended itself to the second generation of Tractarians, who were more liturgically minded than their predecessors, and also more conscious of the need to reach out to the growing numbers of urban dwellers who knew little of Christianity.[12] During the 1850s and 1860s, some Anglo-Catholic parishes started holding missions along French lines. Between 14 and 25 November 1869, the Society of St John the Evangelist (the Cowley Fathers) and the priestly Society of the Holy Cross organised a mission to London, involving 112 parishes across the city. At St Paul's, Knightsbridge, for example, the daily programme began early each morning with three celebrations of Holy Communion. Mattins was said at 8.00 a.m., followed by a penitential litany, and children were taught the Church catechism at 11.00 a.m. Evensong was said at 5.00 p.m., and a special mission service with sermon was held daily at 8.00 p.m. There were separate morning and evening instruction classes for men and women. Priests were also available twice a day to hear confessions. It was

---

[11] Kent, *Holding the Fort*, pp. 243, 254, 256, 263
[12] O. Shipley, *The Church and the World* (Longmans, Green, Reader and Dyer, London, 1867 and 1868), pp. 161–2. Another tradition existed in the Roman Catholic Church of using parish missions to convert people to Christianity from scratch, for example amongst the Passionists, which was in some ways more akin to the tradition of the Protestant revivalists, but this seems to have had less impact upon Anglicans than the French tradition of parish missions

reported in *The Times* that at the halfway stage the mission was attracting about 35,000 people per day.[13]

A second mission to London was held in February 1874, on the initiative of the bishops of London, Winchester and Rochester, who, this time, sought to involve Anglicans of all shades of churchmanship.[14] The mission took much the same form as that of 1869, except that it began and ended with special services in St Paul's Cathedral. In the next few decades, town missions were held in Leeds, Manchester, Doncaster, Hull, Lincoln, Nottingham and Sheffield. Many missions were held in individual parishes, including St James's, Colchester, in 1897.[15]

Members of Anglican religious communities began to be in demand as preachers of missions. The Community of the Resurrection, for example, had ten members engaged in missions by 1906. The following year they published the *Mirfield Mission Hymnbook*, a collection of Catholic and evangelical hymns with popular tunes for use in missions. Anglican missions appear to have been a conflation of the French Roman Catholic and American Protestant traditions: they sought to renew existing congregations, but they also hoped to reach some non-churchgoers.[16]

The Idea of a National Mission

It is difficult to be certain where the idea of holding a national mission during the First World War originated. In his biography of William Temple, F.A. Iremonger suggested that the first stirrings came from a group of laymen who wrote to Archbishop Davidson, but I have not managed to trace any correspondence at Lambeth Palace Library.[17] Two evangelical newspapers, the *Record* and the *Church Family Newspaper*,

---

[13]   A.J. Mason, *Memoir of George Howard Wilkinson, Bishop of St Andrews* (Longmans and Co., London, 1909), pp. 125–37. Kent, *Holding the Fort*, pp. 255–60

[14]   C.M. Davis, *Orthodox London: Or, Phases of Religious Life in the Church of England* (Tinsley Brothers, London, 1876), p. 374

[15]   ERO, St James's Register of Services, 1895–1905. Mission programme pasted in rear of register

[16]   A. Wilkinson, *The Community of the Resurrection* (SCM Press, London, 1992), pp. 56–7, 85. Kent, *Holding the Fort*, p. 282

[17]   Iremonger, *William Temple*, p. 206

claimed afterwards to have had a hand in promoting the national mission.[18]

The bishop of Worcester, Huyshe Yeatman-Biggs, wrote to Davidson on 19 March 1915 to express the view that the Church of England 'should make a definite attempt to recall the nation to God'.[19] After careful reflection, Davidson decided to set up a small committee of priests to examine the suggestion. The committee comprised A.W. Robinson, warden of the College of All Hallows, Barking, who acted as the chairman; Canon G.K. Joyce, warden of St Deiniol's Library, Hawarden; W.H. Frere, of the Community of the Resurrection, Mirfield; E.A. Burroughs, fellow of Hertford College, Oxford; B.K. Cunningham, warden of Bishop's Hostel, Farnham; William Temple, rector of St James's, Piccadilly, London; Ernest Holmes, archdeacon of London; Vernon Storr, canon of Winchester; Peter Green, rector of St Philip's, Salford, lecturer in pastoral theology at Cambridge and King's College, London, author of *How to Deal with the Lads* (1910) and *How to Deal with Men* (1911), an experienced leader of parish missions; and J.G. McCormick, vicar of St Michael's, Ebury Square, London. John Murray, master of Selwyn College, Cambridge, and W.B. Trevelyan, warden of the retreat house, Beaconsfield, later joined the committee. Davidson wrote to each on 29 July 1915:

> For some time past I and others have been feeling that it would be desirable in the interests of the deeper religious life of the country that a few men with special qualifications and experience should prayerfully give their minds to the consideration of ways in which we can effectively 'buy up the opportunity' which the War affords, and by the help of God bring good out of its manifold evil. We want thought to be given to our sins and shortcomings and to the best mode of overcoming them: we want fresh modes of prayerfulness, both public and private: and there are many other things in which a little spiritual counsel on the part of capable men would be, we believe, abundantly fruitful of good.[20]

[18] D.M. Thompson, 'War, the Nation, and the Kingdom of God: The Origins of the National Mission of Repentance and Hope, 1915–16', *The Church and War*, ed. W.J. Shiels, Studies in Church History 20 (Ecclesiastical History Society, London, 1983), pp. 337–50, p. 338
[19] LPL, Davidson Papers, vol. 359, fol. 1
[20] LPL, Davidson Papers, vol. 359, fol. 32

Robinson arranged for the committee to meet at Beaconsfield on 4–6 October 1915.[21] He used much military imagery when he wrote to convey the committee's views to Davidson:

> We feel that after the War a great movement should take effect having as its aim the spiritual uplift of the Nation. It should be no Neuve Chapelle but a bombardment all along the line. For this inward preparation and much organization will be needed. A Minister of Spiritual Munitions should be appointed (e.g. the Bishop of London or Oxford!). A great force of missioners should be enrolled – clerical and lay (men who have been at the Front by preference). These should be pledged to abandon all other engagements when the call to mobilise is given.
>
> Masses of workers should be trained to go through the towns and villages hereafter and great prayer should be made.
>
> The response of the people to a Call, big enough and hard enough, when made by the State, has been evidently wonderful. We feel the need of such a call from the Church, on behalf of the kingdom of Our Lord.
>
> The nation will welcome leadership – personal and unhesitating. We [*indeciph.*] an Appeal should be issued soon to the Nation and another to the clergy.
>
> All other suggested efforts would take their place in the preparation: and informal arrangements might be made to secure the sympathy and co-operation of other bodies of Christians. All other ends, moral and social, would be reached if only the great spiritual revival could be brought about. And even the expectation of this would bring new life and vigour to our existing organization.[22]

The committee expected the mission to take place after the war, and Davidson appears to have shared this view, but as the months passed, with no sign of an end to the war, the idea arose that the mission might have to be held whilst the war continued.[23]

On 3 November 1915, Davidson established an episcopal committee to 'take counsel about the contemplated general movement or Mission', consisting of the bishops of London, Chelmsford, Salisbury, St Davids,

[21]   LPL, Davidson Papers, vol. 359, fols 44–6
[22]   LPL, Davidson Papers, vol. 359, fol. 44
[23]   LPL, Davidson Papers, vol. 359, fol. 45

Sheffield and Oxford. When the committee met three weeks later, the bishops agreed on the need for definite action but were undecided whether this should take the form of an evangelistic campaign addressed to the whole nation, or a spiritual renewal of the Church from within. This was never entirely resolved, and the resulting ambiguity was evident throughout the national mission.[24]

The bishops took soundings in their dioceses about the mission, and correspondence poured into Lambeth Palace. Meanwhile one of the original committee, Peter Green, writing as the columnist 'Artifex' in the *Manchester Guardian* on 11 November 1915, leaked the proposals to hold a great national mission. The bishops of both provinces of Canterbury and York met for further discussion at Lambeth Palace on 27–28 January 1916. Finally, the archbishops of Canterbury and York announced on 4 February 1916 that the title chosen for the mission was the 'National Mission of Repentance and Hope', and that the main time for concentrated effort would be October and November 1916 It was planned that this would be led by a central council of seventy members, chaired by Bishop Winnington-Ingram, with William Temple as the secretary; it was expected that each diocese would establish its own councils to arrange and coordinate the mission.[25]

Promoting the National Mission of Repentance and Hope

The announcement of the National Mission of Repentance and Hope received a lukewarm welcome from many clergy and laity in the Church of England.[26] The *Chelmsford Diocesan Chronicle* reflected this in March 1916, and noted that many questions had been raised about the mission:

> whether it would not have been better to wait till after the war; whether an inter-denominational scheme might not have promised larger results; whether social problems must not be solved, or at least tackled, before we

[24]   LPL, Davidson Papers, vol. 359, fols 58, 99–106
[25]   LPL, Davidson Papers, vol. 359, fols 70, 107–263, 265
[26]   Matthews, *Memories and Meanings*, p. 88. Munson, *Echoes of the Great War*, diary entries for 6 March 1916, 26 May 1916, 13 August 1916, 27 September 1916. Wilkinson, *Community of the Resurrection*, p. 147

speak of spiritual ideals; whether a more general response would not be given for an appeal for service than to one for repentance, and the like.[27]

If the national mission was to be a success, it needed skilful and careful promotion. Watts-Ditchfield threw himself into this task with enthusiasm; he was soon appointed to the central committee of the national mission and had to abandon much diocesan work. The bishop wrote about evangelism or the national mission in every edition of the *Chelmsford Diocesan Chronicle* in 1916, and he travelled extensively around the diocese, promoting the national mission at ruri-decanal conferences and special meetings. A small committee of clergy and laity met in February 1916 to help formulate the diocesan programme. In the absence of a diocesan office, much of the detailed work of organising the national mission in the diocese of Chelmsford fell to Watts-Ditchfield and his chaplain, the Rev. Ellis Gowing.[28]

Diversity of Views about the National Mission

There was no single understanding or uniform interpretation of the national mission, even amongst the members of the central committee, and different aspects of the mission evidently appealed to different people.[29] Each diocese was left to arrange its own programme. This aided flexibility, but it also lead to inconsistency. All stressed the importance of Christian witness, but many evangelicals seemed primarily concerned with individual repentance, whilst Christian Socialists stressed corporate repentance: one writer to *Commonwealth* observed that no one seemed to know whether the aim of the national mission was to convert the individual or to Christianise the social order.[30] Watts-Ditchfield and Whitcombe stressed both, though Whitcombe seems to have placed slightly greater emphasis on transforming the social order.

[27]　*Chelmsford Diocesan Chronicle*, March 1916
[28]　*Chelmsford Diocesan Chronicle*, March 1916, June 1916, August 1916. Gowing, *Watts-Ditchfield*, p. 184
[29]　Thompson, 'War, the Nation, and the Kingdom of God', pp. 342, 346–9
[30]　Wilkinson, *Church of England*, p. 77

Promoting the National Mission in Colchester

Three meetings were held in Colchester during May 1916 to promote the national mission, during which the diversity of views and understandings of the national mission became apparent. On the morning of 16 May 1916, Bishop Whitcombe spoke enthusiastically about the forthcoming mission during his archidiaconal visitation, held in St Peter's church.[31] Later the same day, Bishop Watts-Ditchfield sought to generate support for the mission during a special meeting, also held in St Peter's. He admitted that the title, the 'National Mission of Repentance and Hope', was cumbersome, adding that 'it was the best they could think of'.[32] Eleven days later Bishop Winnington-Ingram, the chairman of the central committee of the national mission, addressed a well-attended meeting at the Moot Hall.[33]

The bishops' speeches at all three meetings reveal much about their understanding of the mission at an early stage in its preparation. All three spoke about the importance of repentance and suggested that if the war was not exactly a judgement from God upon the sins of the Church and the nation, it had at least enabled Christians to see those sins and failings with greater clarity.

Bishop Whitcombe expressed the hope that the mission would promote the vision of a more just and Christian society in the future:

[The Mission] is to be the beginning of a life lived on a higher plane. Christ had to be established as the Lord of all our activities, of our politics, international and national, of our commercial life, of our labour laws, of our domestic legislation, of our social relationships. That was the hope with which they went forward. And with that hope there came a vision of a future which was worth all their trials and sacrifice to attain, a vision of the establishment of that Kingdom of Heaven upon earth … It was a vision of a ransomed and purified race of men amongst whom war had ceased, and crime had ceased, and labour troubles had ceased, because slavery was at an end, not only nominally but actually, where there were no burdens of

---

[31] *St Mary-at-the-Walls Parish Magazine*, June 1916
[32] *Essex County Standard*, 20 May 1916
[33] *Essex County Standard*, 3 June 1916

injustice, no self-aggrandisement at the expense of others, no mad struggles for wealth and pleasure, because the law of Christ was supreme.[34]

Bishop Winnington-Ingram listed what he believed to be four areas of failure by the Church of England: it had absolutely failed

to permeate the manhood of the nation as gathered on their battleships and in their great camps – at any rate at home – with the sacramental religion taught in the Prayer Book. Seventy per cent of the New Army were reported to be churchmen … yet the Church had manifestly failed to make the bulk of men communicants.

Secondly, the working classes had become alienated from the Church of England: 'the Church of the Carpenter was not looked to with confidence by the carpenters of to-day.' Thirdly, some parts of the Church were troubled by sloth. Fourthly, many church services were dull: 'if they had got tired of the glorious gospel they preached, they must repent of it.' He added that there was also much in daily life which required repentance, such as industrial strife, the neglect of God, the national drinks bill, sexual immorality and failure adequately to support overseas mission.[35]

All three bishops stressed that the mission was that of the English national Church to the English nation. Watts-Ditchfield and Winnington-Ingram mentioned the British Empire and suggested that the national mission would help it fulfil its role in the world. Winnington-Ingram expressed the view that the war was a 'purifying trial' – which Watts-Ditchfield and Whitcombe did not seem to share, or at least omitted to mention – and that one of its aims was to 'breathe into the nation the spirit of fortitude and courage which their boys were showing in the trenches'.[36]

[34] *Essex County Standard*, 3 June 1916
[35] *Essex County Standard*, 3 June 1916
[36] *Essex County Standard*, 3 June 1916

The Preparation of the Parish Clergy

Writing in the *Chelmsford Diocesan Chronicle* in March 1916, Watts-Ditchfield emphasised the importance of prayer and preparation amongst the clergy, and he arranged a series of retreats for them between May and July at Warlies, a country house near Waltham Abbey. The clergy were invited according to their years of ordination, in batches of thirty-seven, and two retreats were held per week. By the end of July, every priest in the diocese except four had made a retreat – no mean accomplishment, given the habitual reluctance of the clergy to attend diocesan events.[37]

Colchester ruri-decanal chapter discussed the national mission at each of its five meetings during 1916 and appointed a committee to coordinate activities in the town. In June 1916, the chapter sent a resolution to Watts-Ditchfield assuring him 'of their warm appreciation of the direction and guidance which he had given to them as to the National Mission, and of their readiness to follow his leading in the work which he has set before them'; which was just as well, because the following month he ordered them each to spend an hour in private prayer every day. The Colchester clergy also met on alternate Tuesdays for corporate prayer and preparation.[38]

The Preparation of the Laity

Bishop Watts-Ditchfield had a high expectation of the laity in his diocese. Writing of the national mission in the *Chelmsford Diocesan Chronicle* in July 1916, he said:

> I urge clergy and laity to pray more, to think more, to intercede more. I trust that in every parish, whether large or small, the Communicants have been, or will be, called together to consider how best the spiritual life can be stirred up in their midst ... let all our communicants bind themselves to some definite time every day, for the purpose of getting alone, either in their home, or in the Church, which should always be open to receive them.[39]

---

[37]   Gowing, *Watts-Ditchfield*, pp. 184–5. *St Botolph's Parish Magazine*, August 1916
[38]   ERO, Colchester Ruri-decanal Chapter Minutes, 2 June 1916. *Chelmsford Diocesan Chronicle*, July 1916. *St Mary-at-the-Walls Parish Magazine*, July 1916
[39]   *Chelmsford Diocesan Chronicle*, July 1916

It is interesting to observe that, with the single exception of St Botolph's, the preparation of the laity in Colchester's parishes was generally organised according to sex. This was a continuation of the pre-war practice of holding separate Bible classes for men and women.[40]

Some men viewed the national mission to be a special opportunity to win more men to the Church. Bishop Whitcombe was keen that much use should be made of the Church of England Men's Society in Colchester, and CEMS members played a large role in the practical arrangements for the mission. At St Mary-at-the-Walls, for example, the Rev. Frank Burnett arranged an informal meeting in July to explain the national mission to the CEMS, which resulted in a series of fortnightly meetings in the parish room for instruction and intercession. Other parishes held meetings and open-air services for men. On Sunday 30 July 1916, the chapter arranged a special 'quiet time' in Holy Trinity Church for men from all Colchester's parishes, during which the idea of a retreat for men was mooted, but the response was unfavourable.[41]

Similar arrangements were made for women parishioners throughout the summer of 1916. The chapter planned two quiet days for women at Holy Trinity Church on 25 July and St Martin's Church on 14 September 1916, although only women without jobs would have been free to attend as these were weekdays. Churches made their own arrangements for special meetings and Bible study groups for women parishioners.[42]

Archbishop's Lady Messengers and the Role of Women

As part of the national mission, Archbishop Davidson devised an imaginative plan to send 'Archbishop's Messengers' to preach in every city and

[40]   *St Botolph's Parish Magazine*, August 1916

[41]   *St Botolph's Parish Magazine*, September 1916. *St Mary-at-the-Walls Parish Magazine*, July 1916, August 1916, September 1916. *Holy Trinity Parish Magazine*, September 1916. ERO, Colchester Ruri-decanal Chapter Minutes, 2 June 1916, 15 August 1916. ERO, 'Report of the meeting of the sub-committee of the Chapter National Mission Committee', pasted inside the Ruri-Decanal Chapter minute book. The sub-committee seems to have met in early June, but the report does not bear a date

[42]   ERO, 'Report of the meeting of the sub-committee of the Chapter National Mission Committee,' pasted inside the Ruri-decanal Chapter minute book. *St Mary-at-the-Walls Parish Magazine*, July 1916

large town; the idea was widely welcomed. The same could not be said of his plan also to send 'Archbishop's Lady Messengers', which ignited a storm of controversy over the possibility that women might preach in churches.

Bishop Winnington-Ingram had privately warned Davidson in March 1916 that his plan for female messengers might prove contentious, but to begin with, all was quiet.[43] In July 1916, a controversy was ignited when the central committee of the national mission in London passed a resolution:

> that the aims and ideals of the Women's Movement, apart from the ques-
> tion of its particular political and other claims, are in harmony with the
> teaching of Christ and His Church as to the equality of men and women
> in the sight of God – equality in privilege, equality in calling, equality in
> opportunity of service.[44]

Athelstan Riley, a prominent Anglo-Catholic layman, vice president of the English Church Union and a member of the central committee of the national mission, wrote to Davidson on 14 July 1916, raising an objection to this resolution, and also to a supplementary resolution added by Maude Royden which urged 'upon the Bishops the importance of giving definite directions as to the best ways of using the services and receiving the message of women speakers, whether in church or elsewhere.'[45]

These two resolutions were interpreted in different ways. Watts-Ditchfield, who was a close friend of Riley's despite their very different churchmanships, seems to have envisaged that the archbishop's lady messengers would not speak during church services but would instead simply address small groups of women, and would not do so from the pulpit, lectern or chancel steps.[46] Maude Royden probably hoped for rather more. Riley interpreted the two resolutions as part of a full-blown campaign to allow women to preach from the pulpit, in contravention – as he saw it – of St Paul's teaching in 1 Corinthians 14.34: 'Let your women keep silence

[43]   LPL, Davidson Papers, vol. 195, fol. 269
[44]   LPL, Davidson Papers, vol. 195, fol. 271
[45]   LPL, Davidson Papers, vol. 195, fols 279–83
[46]   *Chelmsford Diocesan Chronicle*, September 1916

in your churches: for it is not permitted unto them to speak; but they are commanded to be under obedience, as also saith the law.'

Riley went on to draw another issue to Davidson's attention: a campaign, which, he claimed, was being planned to introduce the ordination of women priests into the Church of England.[47] Riley had obtained a copy of a letter of 26 March 1914 from Mrs Ursula Roberts of Crick Rectory, Rugby, proposing a conference to discuss the ordination of women, enclosing a summary of the not entirely encouraging answers she had received from the women she had canvassed.[48] In his reply, Davidson did not specifically mention the ordination of women, but he tried to reassure Riley about women preachers, and wrote that he had 'observed with much appreciation what is being done both in England and France by women who have quietly gathered a few girls and children in church and tried to guide their prayers'.[49]

Although the archbishop of Canterbury supported the campaign for women's suffrage, he did not support their ordination. He wrote privately to Riley on 11 August 1916:

> it is difficult to state with logical reasons the grounds for opposition to the Ordination of Women to the Priesthood. It is one of those cases where the sound instinct of the Church has acted in lieu of authoritative direction, and I personally have not the smallest apprehension that this sound instinct will be overridden or that anything that is now happening tends practically to that result.[50]

[47]   LPL, Davidson Papers, vol. 195, fols 279–83
[48]   LPL, Davidson Papers, vol. 195, fols 287–301. Mrs Crick canvassed 144 women: 59 returned no answer, 17 who replied were opposed to the ordination of women, 12 were interested but not convinced, 15 were favourable but would take no action in the matter, 11 were favourable but were not Anglicans, 30 were favourable. Whether a conference was held is uncertain
[49]   LPL, Davidson Papers, vol. 195, fols 279–83. In his war diary kept during a trip to the Western Front in 1916, Davidson noted on 19 May, '[In Fremont] in the Church a Catechism class for girls was being conducted by a lady, no priest being present. We had also seen both at Doullens and at Amiens, little gatherings of women in the Church one of them [sic] leading a group of others in intercessions of a litany sort.' M. Snape, 'Archbishop Davidson's Visit to the Western Front, May 1916', *From the Reformation to the Permissive Society: A Miscellany in Celebration of the 400th Anniversary of Lambeth Palace Library*, ed. M. Barber, S. Taylor and G. Sewell (The Boydell Press, Woodbridge, 2010), p. 485
[50]   LPL, Davidson Papers, vol. 195, fol. 333

Davidson also wrote to Archbishop Lang:

> The number of people who want women to be ordained Priests is negligible. It is like the number of people in the Radical Party who want a Republic. Of course there will always be a few members of any party who go off into extremes.[51]

Riley was not satisfied with Davidson's reassurances and he published some of their correspondence in the *English Church Union Gazette*.[52] The result was a furore which lasted for two months. All over England, resolutions were passed by branches of the English Church Union, opposing women speakers in church and rejecting the claims for women's ordination. Lambeth Palace was deluged with letters.[53] Father Wainwright, the much-revered vicar of St Peter's, London Docks, announced that he would take no part in the national mission unless the proposal to allow women to preach in church was withdrawn, and Percy Dearmer, the vicar of St Mary's, Primrose Hill, clashed with Darwell Stone, the principal of Pusey House, in the columns of the *Guardian* church newspaper.[54]

In August 1916, Davidson sought to end the controversy by advising that women should not give an address in church during the national mission unless it was absolutely necessary.[55] He wrote to Lang:

> When I was in France, there was scarcely a single church without women in little groups praying together, one leading the others, and the Roman Bishop of Southwark, speaking to Burge [Anglican bishop of Southwark] the other day, said 'Your people seem afraid of the very thing we are trying to encourage as much as we can.'[56]

Watts-Ditchfield was irritated by the controversy. He issued a statement in August 1916, in which he claimed that it 'has been the work of the Devil', and added, 'I have therefore decided that during the mission I shall not sanction any woman telling her sisters of the Saviour's love

---

51   LPL, Davidson Papers, vol. 195, fol. 325
52   *English Church Union Gazette*, August 1916
53   LPL, Davidson Papers, vol. 195, fol. 324
54   'Artifex', *Guardian*, 10 August 1916. Wilkinson, *Church of England*, p. 93
55   LPL, Davidson Papers, vol. 195, fol. 327
56   LPL, Davidson Papers, vol. 195, fol. 325

in any church in the diocese of Chelmsford.'[57] In Colchester, Brunwin-Hales applauded the bishop's decision and told the chapter that it would be made plain in the publicity that the archbishop's lady messenger would speak in parish rooms and vicarages, rather than in churches.[58]

The Pilgrimage of Prayer

An altogether happier feature of women's involvement in the national mission was the pilgrimage of prayer. As in other dioceses, this consisted of

> groups of three quite ordinary women, bearing the thought of God to the little villages … they go and tell the people how God loves them, how there is not one soul in the most far-away village in Essex that God does not want to have for His own; and they pray simple prayers in their own words, telling God about the husbands and sons at the front, and telling Him about the sorrow and sin that He alone can cure.[59]

Watts-Ditchfield personally selected the pilgrims: they were mostly middle class, 'from comfortable homes, many not strong, and some no longer in their first youth'.[60]

A retreat was held for the pilgrims in September 1916, and two days later they spent a night at Bishopscourt, Watts-Ditchfield's residence, where their itineraries were arranged and the bishop gave a farewell address, during which he stressed the limited horizons and limited powers of expression of the poor whom they would be encountering. The following morning the pilgrims attended Holy Communion at Chelmsford Cathedral, after which, wearing blue veils and carrying pilgrims' wooden crosses, they knelt at the altar rail and Watts-Ditchfield laid his hands on their heads, saying, 'We send you forth in the name of the Father, and of the Son, and of the Holy Ghost.'[61] None of the pilgrims appears to have visited Colchester, although they may have visited some of the rural

---

[57]   *Chelmsford Diocesan Chronicle*, September 1916
[58]   ERO, Colchester Ruri-decanal Chapter Minutes, 15 August 1916
[59]   *Chelmsford Diocesan Chronicle*, October 1916
[60]   *Chelmsford Diocesan Chronicle*, October 1916
[61]   *Chelmsford Diocesan Chronicle*, October 1916

parishes on the edges of the town. They spent about ten days in each deanery, visiting three or four villages and staying with the cottagers.

Children and the National Mission

There seem to have been no events specifically for children and young people as part of the national mission in Colchester. A few parishes presented their Sunday school children with a somewhat lugubrious prayer:

> O Lord Jesus Christ, who didst become a child for our sakes and lovest all children, bless the Mission to be held in this town. Bring back all who have wandered from Thee, save us from all our sins, teach us to love Thee more and to keep Thy commandments, bless our homes and all whom we love and give us the courage to serve Thee all the days of our life … Authorised by The Lord Bishop of Chelmsford.[62]

Between 1914 and 1918, all the parishes of Colchester had thriving Sunday schools, clubs and organisations for children and young people. It is difficult to explain their omission from the 1916 mission. The national mission preparations and programme in Colchester give the impression of having been very largely directed by the middle aged, to the middle aged.

Prayer and Intercession for the National Mission

In any mission, the months of careful prayer and preparation beforehand are frequently as important to the overall impact as the mission itself. This was understood by Watts-Ditchfield, and he was keen to encourage prayer for the national mission throughout the spring and summer of 1916.[63] He instructed the clergy to preach about the mission during Lent and recommended Lenten books with an evangelistic emphasis.[64]

---

[62]   ERO, 'Colchester Mission Children's Prayer', stuck in St Andrew's, Greenstead, Register of Services, between the pages covering 1916
[63]   *Chelmsford Diocesan Chronicle*, September 1916
[64]   *Chelmsford Diocesan Chronicle*, March 1916

In April 1916, Watts-Ditchfield asked for prayers to be said for the mission daily at noon in every church throughout his diocese, and for Holy Communion with special prayers on Thursdays. He went on:

> I desire that as far as possible, the whole Diocese should be systematically organised for prayer and for intercession … I have allocated one day in each month to each Deanery. I ask that on the day appointed every Church in that deanery should have a special Celebration of the Holy Communion, short services of intercession and a special service in the evening, when an Address may be given.

Colchester's day appointed for special prayer was the twenty-first day in each month. Rural deans were ordered to report to Watts-Ditchfield how their deaneries were responding to his call for prayer. [65]

The parishes of Colchester prepared for the national mission with enthusiasm. At the evangelical St Peter's, the vicar encouraged the congregation to participate in daily prayers at noon, prayer topics were printed in the parish magazine and fortnightly prayer meetings were held in parishioners' houses. At the middle-of-the-road St Botolph's, special open-air evening services were held in the summer, and national mission literature proved popular amongst the congregation. At the Anglo-Catholic St Stephen's, Behr organised four celebrations of Holy Communion with special intention for the national mission each week, two celebrations of Holy Communion, a 'six hours' devotion' and special services at 3.15 p.m. and 8.15 p.m. on the twenty-first day of each month, a complex system of parochial intercessions and the systematic visiting of houses by the laity during the autumn. [66]

On the last Sunday of July 1916, a lengthy pastoral letter from Watts-Ditchfield was read in every church in which he recapitulated the significance of the mission and called for renewed efforts: 'the whole tone of the average Christian life must be raised so that the whole life of the Church may make itself felt in the world. It must mean much to the world when a man or a woman is a Christian.'[67]

---

[65] *Chelmsford Diocesan Chronicle*, April 1916

[66] *St Peter's Parish Magazine*, May 1916, June 1916, July 1916, September 1916. *St Botolph's Parish Magazine*, July 1916, August 1916, October 1916, November 1916

[67] *Chelmsford Diocesan Chronicle*, August 1916

The National Mission in Colchester

There were three distinct parts to the national mission in Colchester. The first of these was the visit of the archbishop's messengers between 16 and 20 September 1916. The second was the official opening service in Colchester on 11 October; the third was the visit of the bishop's messengers to each parish during December.

The Archbishop's Messengers

From a very early stage, it was decided that the preachers sent by the archbishop of Canterbury to the towns and cities of England would be known as 'messengers' rather than 'missioners', and that they would remain anonymous. The same idea was later extended to those sent to parishes by diocesan bishops. We know from his signature in the service register of St Mary-at-the-Walls that the archbishop's messenger was the Rev. William Robins, the vicar of Cirencester. The only clue as to the identity of the lady messenger is that she was 'the sister of an eminent bishop'.[68]

The Colchester federation of the Church of England Men's Society took responsibility for many of the practical arrangements for the visits of archbishop's messengers in September 1916. Robins arrived in Colchester on Saturday 16 September, and the archbishop's lady messenger came three days later. The rural deaneries of Colchester and Dedham combined for their visit, which opened with a special service at All Saints' Church on the evening of Saturday 16 September.

Holy Communion was celebrated at All Saints' at 8.00 a.m. on Sunday 17 September for all members of the CEMS in Colchester. Robins then had a busy morning, preaching at St Mary-at-the-Walls, St Botolph's and St Peter's. He may also have preached at the garrison parade service, although the army had its own separate arrangements for the national

---

[68]   *St Mary-at-the-Walls Parish Magazine*, October 1916. LPL, Davidson Papers, vol. 360, fols 324–5. The Archbishop's Lady Messengers were Mrs Montgomery, Mrs Creighton, Miss Faithfull, Miss Douglass, Alice, Countess of Chichester, Miss Gollock, Adeline, Duchess of Bedford, Mrs Wilberforce, Mrs Gow, Miss E.C. Gregory, Miss Guerney and Mrs H.B. Irving

mission. The theme of Robins's sermon was '"Up to Christ" (Sursum Corda) – Christ Enthroned in the Seat of Majesty and Power', which was described by Brunwin-Hales as 'a remarkable sermon, never to be forgotten'.[69]

Monday 18 September began with Holy Communion at St Leonard's-at-the-Hythe at 7.30 a.m., followed by an afternoon service for members of the Mothers' Union and other mothers at St Nicholas's, and a mass meeting for all church workers at the Moot Hall at 8.15 p.m. On Tuesday 19 September, Holy Communion was celebrated at St Paul's at 7.30 a.m. Robins spent the afternoon at Great Horksley. In the evening he addressed members of the CEMS at St Botolph's, and the lady messenger undertook as her first engagement a meeting for young women and girls at St Giles's parish room. On Wednesday 20 September there was Holy Communion at 8.00 a.m. at Holy Trinity, followed by an intercession service and a conference later in the morning. The lady messenger addressed church people at Great Wigborough rectory in the morning, and members of the Mothers' Union, district visitors and women workers at St Mary-at-the-Walls parish room in the evening. The deanery programme included events to appeal to Anglicans of varying churchmanships, and Holy Communion was celebrated in middle-of-the-road and Anglo-Catholic parishes, but curiously not any evangelical ones. The two messengers' visits were deemed a great success.[70]

The Opening Service

The next stage in the national mission were six services, held in various parts of the diocese over ten days beginning on 2 October 1916, to inaugurate the purely diocesan part of the mission. Watts-Ditchfield ordered that Holy Communion should be celebrated in all churches on 2 October, and that every priest in his diocese should attend one of the opening services. Churchwardens from all churches were encouraged to take part in the processions.[71] The opening service in Colchester was held at St Nicholas's on 11 October. The service began with a procession through

---

[69]   *St Mary-at-the-Walls Parish Magazine*, October 1916
[70]   *St Mary-at-the-Walls Parish Magazine*, October 1916
[71]   *Chelmsford Diocesan Chronicle*, October 1916

Colchester of the parish clergy and churchwardens, accompanied by the mayor and corporation, which was watched by large crowds of people. Watts-Ditchfield preached in St Nicolas's, which was crammed with worshippers, and still more people had to be turned away. There was a good turn-out of clergy – though not quite as many churchwardens as had been expected – on the whole, the opening service seemed to stir up much enthusiasm.[72]

The participation of the mayor and corporation in the opening service is an indication of the support which the social elite of Colchester afforded the national mission. Many prominent local figures, including the deputy mayor, councillors and even a privy councillor, had attended the Bishop Winnington-Ingram's address at the Moot Hall on 27 May.[73] Churchwardens, who were largely drawn from the town's social elite, were visible on the platform at the Moot Hall meeting addressed by the archbishop's messenger on 18 September.[74]

The Bishop's Messengers

The third stage of the national mission was the visits made by the bishop of Chelmsford's messengers to every parish in his diocese between 7 November and 12 December 1916.[75] This was a masterpiece of planning by Watts-Ditchfield and Gowing. The messengers were all diocesan priests. All the clergy at St Botolph's, for example, acted as messengers, and it is probable that other Colchester clergy did too.[76]

There was a flurry of final preparations before the bishop's messengers arrived. Archbishop Davidson issued a special 'Call to the People of the Land' in October, and prayers for the mission were intensified.[77] In October, a letter from Watts-Ditchfield was delivered to every house in the

---

[72] *Essex County Standard*, 14 October 1916. *Chelmsford Diocesan Chronicle*, November 1916. *St Mary-at-the-Walls Parish Magazine*, November 1916

[73] *Essex County Standard*, 3 June 1916

[74] ERO, Colchester Ruri-decanal Chapter Minutes, 15 August 1916

[75] *Chelmsford Diocesan Chronicle*, November 1916

[76] *St Botolph's Parish Magazine*, October 1916

[77] *Holy Trinity Parish Magazine*, October 1916. *St Botolph's Parish Magazine*, November 1916

184 of England and the Home Front, 1914-1918

diocese – a not inconsiderable expense – though its tone might not have been best suited to winning over the lapsed:[78]

> Perhaps, for some reason or other, you are outside the Church? It may be, you have noticed the weakness of the Church rather than her strength; the inconsistencies of some professing Christians rather than the real and saintly lives of thousands of men and women in every walk of life. In this great crisis will you reconsider your attitude to the Church? Our Lord meant His Church (His Own Body) to be the great reforming agency of the world, to be a bond of union among men. Alas! She has not fulfilled Her task. Her Lord endued Her with power which she has never fully used. But She was meant to succeed. Will you join Her? Just as men have joined the Army and died for England, so will you join the Church of Christ and live? This War has shown us that individualism must die. The future must be one of co-operation and unity, but to last it must be in Christ …
>
> Very shortly a Bishop's Messenger will visit your Parish and explain more fully the meaning of this great call back to God. May I ask you, whatever your views may be, to endeavour to be present at the Services? Think of these things, pray about them, examine your own life, ask yourself whether yours is the best kind of life and whether you cannot bring into the common life of the nation and Church that which will strengthen both … 'Choose ye this day whom ye will serve.' 'If the Lord, then follow Him,' but if sin, if the pleasing and apparent satisfaction of the self, then follow these – but remember – 'Whatsoever a man soweth that shall he also reap.'[79]

Watts-Ditchfield's letter at least mentioned corporate sin and the hope of the renewal of society. The same cannot be said for the letters from the bishop's messengers, which were published in church magazines prior to their visits.[80] Without exception, those which survive from Colchester speak of individual conversion, repentance and sanctification, making no mention of the mission's social teaching. It is not unreasonable to assume

---

[78]   *Chelmsford Diocesan Chronicle*, October 1916
[79]   *Holy Trinity Parish Magazine*, November 1916
[80]   *Holy Trinity Parish Magazine*, December 1916. *St Mary-at-the-Walls Parish Magazine* (Christ Church and Berechurch), December 1916. *St Peter's Parish Magazine*, December 1916. St Stephen's (in *St Botolph's Parish Magazine*), October 1916

that many of the bishop's messengers probably also said very little about social teaching in their sermons.

There are several possible explanations for this absence of social teaching. 'Nothing new is put before us,' Watts-Ditchfield had written of the national mission in May 1916, 'the old paths must be trod which led S. Peter and S. Paul to victory after victory, which led Wesley and Whitfield to conquest after conquest; the old methods of faith, of prayer, of devotion and of service.'[81] It may be that many messengers took him at his word and quite simply preached an adaptation of the individualistic message they had been preaching for years.

To be fair, the social aspect of the national mission was not easy to convey in a sermon to a strange congregation; perhaps it was not fully understood or shared by the messengers. It is also possible that the bishop's messengers quickly realised that social teaching was not quite what was needed in November and December 1916: in the face of unparalleled grief and bereavement, many people listening to the messengers probably sought reassurance about God's love and His promise of eternal life for their husbands, sons and brothers killed in the war. The *Essex County Standard* reported that 'inspiring and hopeful' addresses were preached in the parishes of Colchester, and it printed a summary of the messenger's sermon at St Mary-at-the-Walls, which was disappointingly mostly about the Allies.[82]

Some bishop's messengers preached in the open air, and in St James's parish an enterprising messenger addressed people at the war shrines which had been erected in several streets.[83] There was no specified programme for these parochial visits, but in each parish the bishop's messenger and parish priest made their own plans.[84] At All Saints', for example – which was on the catholic side of middle-of-the-road – the messenger was the Rev. Percy Bayne, who began his visit with an address at a special mission service at 7.15 p.m. on Wednesday 6 December. The next day commenced with Holy Communion at 7.15 a.m. celebrated by the vicar, Percival Brinton, followed at 8.00 a.m. by Mattins, which inaugurated a 'chain of prayer' lasting eleven hours. This was punctuated

[81]   *Chelmsford Diocesan Chronicle*, June 1916
[82]   *Essex County Standard*, 16 December 1916
[83]   *Essex County Standard*, 16 December 1916
[84]   *St Botolph's Parish Magazine*, November 1916

with intercessions at 12.15 p.m. and Evensong at 5.30 p.m. At 7.15 p.m. Bayne preached at another mission service. The parish programme was much the same on Friday 8 December, except that Bayne was the celebrant at Holy Communion instead of the vicar, and there was no chain of prayer. The visit ended on Saturday 9 December, when there was Ante-Communion at 7.15 a.m., a 'devotional meeting' between 3 and 5 p.m. and a final mission service at 7.15 p.m.[85]

Follow-up to the National Mission

The departure of the bishop's messengers coincided with the approach of Christmas, and the national mission in Colchester seemed to fizzle out. In October 1916, Whitcombe told the chapter that it was hoped to organise special work amongst sections of churchpeople in 1917 beginning with children, but this failed to materialise.[86] Watts-Ditchfield called a special meeting of the clergy to discuss a follow-up to the mission in January 1917, but this accomplished little and many priests came away feeling confused.[87] It would seem that Watts-Ditchfield had no firm plans, and his hopes for further work in 1917 were overtaken by the intro- duction of national service for the clergy. At the first chapter meeting in Colchester after the national mission in February 1917, it was decided to postpone further discussion until their next meeting 'as the subject so much depended on the National Service proposals'.[88] In the event, the clergy were too stretched by their additional national service work to contemplate continuing the work of the national mission, and the topic was never raised in the chapter again.

The Archbishops' Committees of Inquiry

In the aftermath of the national mission, archbishops Davidson and Lang appointed five committees to examine aspects of the Church of Eng-

[85]   ERO, All Saints', Colchester, Register of Services, 6–9 December 1916
[86]   ERO, Colchester Ruri-decanal Chapter Minutes, 26 October 1916
[87]   *St Mary-at-the-Walls Parish Magazine*, February 1917
[88]   ERO, Colchester Ruri-decanal Chapter Minutes, 9 February 1917

land's life and ministry. Their reports were published in a volume entitled *Reports of the Archbishops' Committees of Inquiry* in 1919.[89]

The report on 'The Teaching Office of the Church' found that the Church of England was out of touch with the bulk of the population and recommended improved clergy training, greater use of the laity, a new catechism and better preparation for confirmation. 'The Worship of the Church' recommended reform of the 1662 Book of Common Prayer and lectionary, the restoration of Holy Communion as the principal act of worship, more congregational music, better liturgical training of the clergy and a more active role for the laity in worship. A majority of the committee recommended more adequate provision of prayers for the departed. 'The Evangelistic Work of the Church' mentioned the difficulties stemming from industrialisation and urbanisation, and from mistrust and misunderstanding of the Church and of its teachings. It recommended tried and tested methods of evangelism, such as missions, visiting, retreats and refresher courses.

The report on 'Administrative Reform and the Church' outlined various abuses in the Church of England and urged, with 'all possible emphasis, that the Church should at the earliest possible moment recover freedom of legislation through its own legislative assemblies'. 'Christianity and Industrial Problems' examined the problems of an industrialised urban society from a Christian perspective and made recommendations concerning wages, working conditions, the unemployed, housing and education, and in an appendix it stressed the need for priests from working-class backgrounds.[90]

The Colchester Federation of the CEMS organised a study of the report on 'The Evangelistic Work of the Church' amongst its parochial branches, and in July 1918 they informed the chapter that they had formed a committee to forward evangelistic work in the town and hoped to recruit a band of men to help. Their offer was warmly welcomed, but it seems to have been short lived, and no further mention of it was made again. At St Mary-at-the-Walls, the report was studied by the Sunday school teachers, and it was decided to form a branch of the Girl Guides to facilitate Christian work amongst girls and young women.[91]

---

[89]   Iremonger, *William Temple*, pp. 215–17. Wilkinson, Church of England, pp. 80–90

[90]   Wilkinson, *Church of England*, pp. 80–8

[91]   ERO, Colchester Ruri-decanal Chapter Minutes, 5 July 1918. *St Mary-at-the-Walls*

An Archbishops' Committee on Church and State had recommended a degree of Church self-government in 1916, and the report on 'The Administrative Reform of the Church' added to the demand for self-government for the Church of England.[92] The pressure was kept up by the 'Life and Liberty' movement, which campaigned for greater self-government for the Church of England, and in 1919 Parliament passed the Enabling Act, which established the Church Assembly and led to parochial church councils in all parishes. The Enabling Act was warmly welcomed by the Colchester clergy, who said the Doxology in thanksgiving for its passing at a chapter meeting.[93]

There is often a sense of anti-climax when a mission comes to an end. It has been preceded by months of prayer, preparation, expense and hard work. The people participating in the mission have been led to expect great things. They may have found themselves stirred and challenged in all sorts of unexpected ways by the preaching and by their overall experience of the mission. Then the mission reaches its conclusion, and the time comes to pack up, pay the bills and go back to the humdrum experiences of daily life. Such feelings were widespread in Colchester when the national mission finally ended in December 1916.[94]

The 1916 national mission was beset by difficulties and problems from its inception. The title 'National Mission of Repentance and Hope' created confusion in some minds, and the wide variety of diocesan programmes did not help.[95] Riley complained to Davidson that the national mission was being used by pressure groups to air their causes – which was probably inevitable in a Church as complex and divided as the Church of England – and the controversy he himself ignited over women preachers did not get the mission off to a good start.[96] This controversy, though, should not be overestimated when assessing the overall effect of the mission. It was a storm in a rather large teacup – Davidson thought it 'an artificial thing'[97] – and it could well be that in the emotionally repressed

Parish Magazine, July 1918, August 1918

92   Iremonger, *William Temple*, pp. 215–81
93   ERO, Colchester Ruri-decanal Chapter Minutes, 17 December 1918
94   *St Mary-at-the-Walls Parish Magazine*, January 1917
95   Wilkinson, *Church of England*, pp. 76–7
96   LPL, Davidson Papers, vol. 195, fols 279–83
97   LPL, Davidson Papers, vol. 195, fol. 340

England of 1916, some Anglicans 'projected' onto this brief controversy their wartime anxieties and sorrows.

The national mission had its fair share of grumblers and critics. The Rev. Conrad Noel, vicar of Thaxted in Essex, nicknamed it the 'Mission of Funk and Despair'.[98] A not-unfriendly critic was W.R. Matthews, later dean of St Paul's Cathedral, who recalled:

> Certainly some excellent material for the Mission was produced, which could have been the basis for a religious revival with a sound theological framework, but when the Mission came most people were busily employed in war work and interested in subjects other than the Mission thought they ought to be interested in. For example, much attention was paid, and justly, to the Christian ideal of society; I think the creation of a 'Christian Sociology' was first attempted in the Mission, but at the time people at large wanted light on matters of individual life and death. Is there a Father in heaven who cares for us his children? Is there life after death? Shall I meet my boy in heaven?
>
> One of the very sound purposes of the Mission was to propagate the conception of collective responsibility; to convince the ordinary man that the guilt of causing the war was not confined to the Kaiser, or to the German General Staff, or to the German people, but that we all had some share in it. Sound doctrine: but difficult to present to congregations without absurd exaggeration. The son of my old vicar, Prebendary Pennefather, told me that he wanted to put a notice in the pulpit for the preacher's eye, 'N.B. This congregation did not start the war.' I knew what he meant. The guilt spread so widely seemed unreal.[99]

It is not uncommon for people to build up unrealistic expectations of what a mission is likely to achieve. This was evident in the Church of England in 1916. It was unrealistic, for example, to hope that the whole diocese of Chelmsford would be ready for a mission at the same moment – even when accompanied by the most careful preparation and ardent prayer – or to expect that a mission, by itself, could bring about some of the hoped-for social changes. Missions are in the business of sowing seeds: the harvest comes later, and not always in the form anticipated.

[98]　Wilkinson, *Church of England*, pp. 77–8
[99]　Matthews, *Memories and Meanings*, p. 88

There was a wide sense of disappointment in late 1916 and early 1917 that the national mission appeared to have had little obvious impact upon non-churchgoers and seemed largely to have attracted those with some church connections. The mission may not have affected many non-churchgoers directly, but it may perhaps have reached rather more indirectly. To take one example from Colchester: soldiers – who were conscripted from all walks of life by late 1916 – were obliged to attend compulsory church parades, which were often held in parish churches, frequently led by the vicar rather than an army chaplain, and sometimes also attended by members of the CEMS and the regular congregation. If the national mission gave a boost to the vicar and congregation – even if it was only an increased sense of confidence in the claims of Christianity, more time spent in prayer and some better sermons from the vicar – some of this may have rubbed off onto the troops. The army in France made its own arrangements for the national mission, with a high degree of support from senior officers, and it is probable that the mission's message reached some troops who in civilian life had not been regular churchgoers.[100]

The 1916 national mission undoubtedly helped existing congregations in Colchester, and it may have deepened the faith of some people on the fringes of church life. Church attendance in Colchester remained at the same level or even increased slightly as the First World War continued, and there was no decline in the numbers of Easter communicants or of confirmations. Rather more important questions – albeit unanswerable – are to what extent the national mission helped the clergy and laity of Colchester to keep going during the tough years of 1917–18, and what fruit did the national mission bear, say, five or ten years later? How many par-ticipants in the well-attended Anglo-Catholic Congresses of the 1920s, to take one example, were there in part as a result of their experiences during the 1916 national mission?

One of the most impressive features of the national mission in Col-chester was the degree of enthusiasm and support it stirred up amongst clergy and parishioners of widely differing churchmanships. The chapter sub-committee, for example, contained priests of all churchmanships,

---

[100] Snape, *God and the British Soldier*, pp. 68–70, 99–100. The army appears to have held its National Mission slightly later than the Church in England, in the closing months of 1916 and the start of 1917

who apparently worked together in harmony.[101] Intercession services for the clergy were arranged at two Anglo-Catholic churches, at one evangelical church and at six middle-of-the-road churches.[102] The willingness of clergy and laity from very varied traditions to sink their differences and cooperate for the wider good is a further indication of the high degree of support enjoyed by the national mission in Colchester.

Iremonger observed that the mission renewed the spiritual life of many parishes, broke down the isolation of some of the clergy and brought them into closer touch with their congregations.[103] The national mission further encouraged lay ministry in the Church of England. The use of special prayers and litanies added to the pressure for liturgical reform. The reports of the Archbishops' Committees of Inquiry, although of varying quality, stimulated discussion and provided a framework for post-war reconstruction.

The 1916 National Mission of Repentance and Hope did not come out of the blue, but was the most ambitious development of an existing tradition. Many of its features were adaptations of established evangelistic practices. With the exception of sacramental confession, the national mission programme at Holy Trinity, Colchester, in 1916 is not very different to that of the mission held at St Paul's, Knightsbridge, in 1869. The difference is one of scale: during the unprecedented conditions of wartime, the Church of England sought to reach the nation as a whole with the challenge and comfort of the Gospel. Nothing of this sort had been tried before, nor has the Church of England had the courage or confidence to attempt it since 1916.

---

[101] ERO, Colchester Ruri-decanal Chapter Minutes, 2 June 1916, 15 August 1916
[102] ERO, Colchester Ruri-decanal Chapter Minutes, note pasted on to p. 186
[103] Iremonger, *William Temple*, p. 214

8

Thought and Attitudes

To return to the England of 1914–18 is to enter a world that is both highly familiar to us a century later, and yet is as remote and strange as the England of Jane Austen. When it comes to understanding the thoughts and attitudes of the Britons who lived through the First World War, we are largely dependent for information upon what they wrote down; and, of course, what passed through their minds, and what they committed to paper, was not necessarily the same thing. In a world before radio, television or the internet, most people's understanding of the First World War was informed by newspapers and letters from soldiers at the front – both of which were censored – and by what troops said whilst home on leave. The historian is always prudent to exercise a degree of caution, and to avoid broad generalisations, when writing about the thoughts and attitudes of previous generations. Attitudes doubtless varied throughout the First World War, depending on news from the front, bereavement, anxiety, hunger and, of course, underlying personal religious and moral convictions.

Later in the twentieth century, the generation of 1914–18 came to be viewed by some writers and commentators with a degree of condescension. They saw them as somehow gulled or benighted, as people who unthinkingly supported a cruel and unnecessary war, which anyone with an ounce of common sense would surely have stopped (without, of course, facing up to how a war might practically have been averted in August 1914, or been stopped once hostilities had commenced). This, however, was to reflect backwards the very different views of the First World War which began to appear in literature half a generation after the Armistice and continued to find currency for much of the rest of the twentieth century. For similar reasons, oral history recordings made later in the twentieth century, although a very valuable resource for the historian, must be treated with a degree of caution: someone's perception of the First World War at the time of the Armistice in 1918, for example, may perhaps have altered by the time of the Depression in the 1930s, or after the Second World War.

However, anyone living in Britain today who is aged over forty has grown up knowing people who lived through the First World War. The Britons of 1914–18 may have had less access to information than we enjoy a century later, but they were still intelligent, reflective and thoughtful people. In the case of the clergy of the Church of England, the vicars and curates of 1914–18 were frequently of higher academic calibre than many of their successors a century later. With this in mind, I propose to examine three aspects of the thoughts and attitudes of Anglicans in Colchester in 1914–18: attitudes towards the war; the ways in which the war narrowed people's outlooks; and the ways in which it broadened them.

Attitudes towards the War

Support for Britain's Cause in the War

Geoffrey Dearmer, a First World War soldier and poet, once said of his father, the Rev. Dr Percy Dearmer, vicar of St Mary's, Primrose Hill, in 1914: 'My father would have been very disappointed if we [Geoffrey and his brother Christopher] hadn't joined up, [though] he took the general view of the tragedy of it all.[1] Percy Dearmer's attitude towards the First World War was the same as that of most of the Anglicans of Colchester. They were not blind to the wicked and destructive character of war, but nonetheless they believed in the righteousness of their country's cause in the face of German aggression.[2]

In 1914, units of the German Army, conquering their way west across Belgium and France – inspired by their own interpretation of the work of the military theorist Carl von Clausewitz, and with the endorsement of senior commanders in the field – employed what they regarded as deterrent terror against the Belgian and French civilian population, in

[1]   Mr Geoffrey Dearmer, interview, 6 October 1984
[2]   See, for example, *St Botolph's Parish Magazine*, September 1914; also the address entitled 'Ethics and the War' given by the Rev. C. Proctor at St Nicholas's on 19 October 1914 to the Colchester Federation of the CEMS, reprinted in the *Essex County Standard* on 24 October 1914

order to secure victory quickly. This involved the wanton destruction of property, and sometimes of entire villages, the harassment and deportation of civilians and the use of civilians as human shields by the advancing German troops. It also led to the murder by German troops of some 6,500 Belgian and French civilians in the first three months of the war: fairly modest by the standards of the Second World War, but deeply shocking to the generation of 1914–18.[3] These German 'barbarities' and 'frightfulness' were reported in the Colchester press.[4]

It has been shown above how Colchester's churches helped to encourage recruiting until the introduction of conscription in 1916, and how they regularly used their liturgy to express their support for Great Britain's cause in the First World War and to pray for victory. Parish magazines were also used from time to time to promote Britain's war effort. In September 1914, for example, Spencer of the middle-of-the-road St Botolph's, used his parish magazine to tell his parishioners that 'the Providence of God has allowed the War to break out, and our Empire to be involved in it. It is incumbent on every member of our Empire to strain every nerve that our cause, which is a just one, shall prevail.'[5] In October 1915, Ward, vicar of the rigorously evangelical St Peter's, described Britain's war with Germany as 'so noble a cause',[6] whilst in July 1916, Monck-Mason of the more moderately evangelical Holy Trinity expressed the hope that the war would lead 'peace and happiness, truth and justice, religion and piety' to be once more established.[7] In January 1918, when parishioners were feeling the effects of bereavement, anxiety, food and fuel shortages and bad winter weather, Brunwin-Hales, of the middle-of-the-road St Mary-at-the-Walls, wrote: 'I wish every loyal member of our Church may have strength given in 1918 sufficient to endure … May we as Churchmen, do our part to bring about a lasting peace through victory.'[8]

Perhaps the clearest Anglican expressions of support for the war were furnished by public meetings held by parishes throughout 1914–18, during which speeches from leading lay and clerical figures were often followed by patriotic resolutions, such as the one passed at St Mary-at-the-Walls

[3]   Horne and Kramer, *German Atrocities 1914*, pp. 161–70, 419, 424
[4]   *Colchester Gazette*, 9 September 1914
[5]   *St Botolph's Parish Magazine*, September 1914
[6]   *St Peter's Parish Magazine*, October 1915
[7]   *Holy Trinity Parish Magazine*, August 1917
[8]   *St Mary-at-the-Walls Parish Magazine*, January 1918

in 1915: 'this meeting records its inflexible determination by God's help to continue the war to a victorious end.' Similar resolutions were also sometimes passed by the Church of England Men's Society in Colchester.[9] In March–April 1918, when it seemed possible that the German spring offensive on the Western Front might lead to a British defeat, Colchester borough council – which contained many prominent Anglican laymen – passed a further resolution of support of Britain's cause and sent copies to Lloyd George, Sir Douglas Haig and Admiral Sir David Beatty.[10] If any clergy or laity in Colchester, whilst generally supporting the war, privately harboured doubts about the policy of trench warfare on the Western Front, they appear to have kept such thoughts to themselves. Thoughts of this nature were not the sort of thing likely to be mentioned by a priest confronted daily by bereaved and anxious parishioners, by wounded soldiers in the military hospitals or by troops in the pews of his church

The Militarisation of the European Mind

The background to this widespread support for the First World War is perhaps what Sir John Keegan termed in his 1998 Reith Lectures 'the militarization of the European mind' during the last quarter of the nineteenth century.[11] Urbanisation, industrialisation, imperialism and conscription on the continent led to military values and traditions impinging upon daily life and thought in much of Europe, to an extent that would have been unthinkable three or four generations earlier. Olive Anderson has shown how popular attitudes towards the army began to change in Great Britain the decade following the Crimean War, with the

> increasing imitation in religious work of military titles, uniforms and accoutrements … the Salvation Army, Church Army and Boys' Brigade were all founded between 1878 and 1883 – and [may be] explained as a reflection of the growing militarism of British society in general.[12]

---

9   *St Mary-at-the-Walls Parish Magazine*, August 1915, September 1915
10   CL, Jarmin Collection, fols 73–6
11   Sir John Keegan, 1998 BBC Reith Lecture. Sir John Keegan, letter to the author, 1 May 1998
12   Anderson, 'The Growth of Christian Militarism in mid-Victorian Britain', 66

In the Church of England, links were developed between county regiments and churches – symbolised by the laying up of old regimental colours in cathedrals and prominent parish churches – after regiments acquired their county titles and affiliations in 1881.[13] The militarisation of the European mind might also be detected in certain well-known Victorian hymns, such as 'Onward Christian Soldiers', 'Fight the Good Fight', 'For All the Saints' and 'Stand up, Stand up for Jesus! Ye Soldiers of the Cross', which, although spiritual in intention, could in wartime take on a more martial or militaristic overtone.

Applications for Exemption from Conscription

In order to test this view of widespread support of the war in Colchester, I have reconstructed details of objections to conscription following the Military Service Act of January 1916.[14] Great Britain was the only European country to introduce both conscription and also a process whereby those liable for conscription might seek exemption. Some 1,800 tribunals were established around the country to adjudicate objections to military service. A Borough of Colchester Tribunal was established in January 1916 and sat weekly or fortnightly in the town hall throughout the rest of the war. The tribunal was composed largely of members of the town's social elite, usually chaired by the deputy mayor, with a military representative.

It is surprising to discover that there were 2,088 objections to conscription in Colchester between 1916 and 1918; that is, by approximately one fifth of the men of military age in the town. Adrian Gregory has suggested that 'the usual response to conscription was not acceptance, but an appeal [to the tribunal] … it must have been a rare individual who did not make a claim for at least temporary exemption.'[15] Gregory has probably overstated his case – I can think of a number of old soldiers I have met who accepted conscription in 1916–18 without demur – but he is

---

[13]   Sir John Keegan, letter to the author, 29 March 2000

[14]   The records of the Borough of Colchester Tribunal have been lost or destroyed. These details have been compiled from the accounts of the proceedings of the tribunal printed in the *Essex County Standard* between 1916 and 1918

[15]   Gregory, *Last Great War*, p. 102

undoubtedly right to point out that tribunals across Britain were kept very busy dealing with applicants. Gregory also notes that some middle-class people believed that working-class men commonly objected to joining the army because they did not wish to forgo the increased wages that the war had brought them, though this may perhaps have been a reflection of middle-class wartime financial anxieties.[16] The bulk of appeals for exemption from conscription in Colchester were for economic or domestic reasons (see Table 4).

Table 4: Appeals for exemption from conscription in Colchester, 1916–18

Year	1916	1917	1918
Grounds for objection			
Economic or domestic	938	682	438
Moral or political	9	7	1
Religious	9	3	2
Total number of applicants	956	692	441
Sittings of the tribunal	40	36	19

Source: Compiled from the proceedings of the Colchester Tribunal printed in the *Essex County Standard*, 1916–18. The records of the Colchester tribunal have been lost or destroyed. In other parts of the country the records of tribunals appear to have been destroyed in 1922.

The Colchester tribunal dealt with most cases very briskly, and full details were printed in the local press, presumably in order to demonstrate that the tribunal was working efficiently, and possibly to deter anyone else thinking of applying for exemption.[17] Although some applications were clearly attempts to avoid the firing line – such as the barber who said he could not be spared because he cut officers' hair – the bulk of objections were on the grounds of the disruption to businesses, or applications for exemption in order to care of elderly or sick relatives. Many firms applied to retain the services of some of their male employees. A few middle-class applicants engaged lawyers to plead their cases before the tribunal,

[16] Gregory, *Last Great War*, pp. 91–2, 102–5
[17] However summarily objectors to conscription were treated in Great Britain, they still fared much better than in France, where pacifists were shot and their relatives sent a curt note that they had 'died as a coward'. Marrin, *Last Crusade*, p. 159

though this did not appear to make much difference to the outcome. The tribunal usually deferred conscription by a month or two, to allow alternative arrangements to be entered into.

One long-running controversy concerned the clerk to the Colchester tribunal and acting town clerk, R.H. Wanklyn, who was the son of a borough councillor. Although a healthy man of military age, Wanklyn's date of conscription was regularly deferred by the Colchester tribunal. The military representatives on the tribunal objected but were told that efforts to find a replacement town clerk in wartime were not proving easy. They retorted that the post was being advertised at such a low salary that it was very unlikely to attract any applicants. Wanklyn junior seems to have made it to the Armistice without being conscripted.[18]

The moral and political applicants for exemption were mostly supporters of the Independent Labour Party, which was opposed to conscription.[19] Of the religious applicants, none belonged to the Church of England: one applicant was a member of the Plymouth Brethren, a few were Quakers, but the bulk were members of the Headgate Congregational Church, where they were actively supported in their Pacifism by the minister, the Rev. Roderick Dunkelly. These statistics support the impression that for the most part the war received widespread support amongst Anglican laity in Colchester, though they also suggest that this was frequently at a high economic and domestic cost.

Attitudes towards the Germans

In his book *The Last Crusade: the Church of England in the First World War* (1974), Albert Marrin claims that many in the Church of England did not merely believe in the righteousness of Britain's involvement in the First World War, but came to regard it as a holy crusade against a demonised foe: 'It was almost as if everyone born between the Rhine and the Polish frontier had been tainted with a double dose of original sin. The Germans were so evil as to be incapable of understanding anything but force and responding to any emotion save fear.'[20]

---

[18]   *Essex County Standard*, 20 September 1917
[19]   Marrin, *Last Crusade*, p. 181. Lloyd George, *War Memoirs*, p. 437
[20]   Marrin, *Last Crusade*, p. 174

Martial metaphor and imagery are to be found in the Bible and are as old as Christianity itself; it is hardly surprising that some British Christians of all denominations, when confronted with German brutalities in Belgium and France, the use of asphyxiating gas, the sinking of the *Lusitania*, and so on, employed such martial words and concepts. Yet, Marrin's assertion needs to be qualified. After careful examination of the surviving archival material from Colchester, I have discovered no evidence that Anglicans of any churchmanship in the town regarded the war as akin to a holy crusade. They firmly believed that Great Britain had been right to declare war on Germany in 1914, but their attitude to the conflict was very sober. On the whole, they may be said to have viewed the war with Germany as a sad necessity which had to be seen through to a victorious conclusion.

If some Britons greeted the outbreak of war in August 1914 with displays of patriotism, or by seeking to make themselves useful, others experienced shock or were gripped by a sense of crisis or foreboding. Most people probably experienced a jumbled mixture of emotions. Several Essex clergymen preached fiercely anti-German sermons in the late summer of 1914 and continued to do so from time to time throughout the war, especially after incidents such as the German torpedoing of the *Lusitania* in 1915.[21] These should not be ignored, but neither should they be exaggerated. It should also be admitted that the Church of England has long provided a refuge for a rich variety of clerical eccentrics, as well as for priests who are plainly a bit odd. It may simply be that some of the clergy who demonised the Germans in their sermons had been preaching unbalanced or peculiar sermons about all sorts of other things prior to 1914, and that the coming of war just gave them further scope. Other preachers of anti-German sermons may have been motivated by personal fearfulness, seeking an easy popularity or uncritically reflecting the mood of those around them.

It would be unwise to claim that no sermons demonising the Germans were preached in Colchester during the First World War; but if they were, they were not noted at the time, and their texts have not survived. It would be surprising if all twenty-six priests – shocked by German atrocities, hungry, exhausted, anxious or sometimes grieving the loss of a son – always managed to avoid saying something from

---

[21] Rusiecki, *The Impact of Catastrophe*, p. 42

the pulpit that demonised the enemy, especially if their sermons were extempore, when one is sometimes apt to get carried away. But, as far as one can gather, any such anti-German preaching appears to have been very rare, and undoubtedly was the exception rather than the rule in Colchester.

Wilson Marriage, the mayor of Colchester, evinced a balanced approach towards the enemy when he wrote to the *Colchester Gazette* in September 1914, urging the townsfolk to protect naturalised British subjects, including Germans.[22] The anti-German hysteria which gripped many towns and cities in 1915 following the sinking of the *Lusitania* appears not to have arisen in Colchester. The worst that can be discovered is that an elderly German couple, Mr and Mrs Gröne, who ran a private school in Wellesley Road, had to leave Colchester because many of the townsfolk shunned them, and no parents would send their sons to be educated there. An Austrian subject, Tommie Rehberger, who was married to the daughter of Councillor Jarmin, seems to have spent the First World War with his wife under a not too uncomfortable house-arrest in Colchester.[23] There were a few references to 'the Hun' in parish magazines, alongside suggestions that the German troops would stoop to depths to which the British would not, particularly with regard to killing civilians, but that is apparently as bad as it got.

Kaiser Wilhelm II became a hated and sometimes demonised figure during the war. Preaching in Chelmsford Cathedral on 2 January 1916, Bishop Watts-Ditchfield said: 'The civilized nations must either abolish Capital Punishment or hang the Kaiser. I mean it. If this war is as we think it is, then we must make for all time a dramatic example.'[24] There is little evidence, however, of such demonisation of the Kaiser in Colchester. The single example that I have found was a lecture delivered by the Rev. Dr E.P. Drew of Massachusetts at the Moot Hall in October 1918, entitled 'America's Answer to the Challenge to Civilisation'. Drew described the Kaiser – fairly mildly when compared with some of the other things said about him – as 'this awful criminal … this monstrous transgressor against the rights of civilised people, this horrible assassin'. It is likely that Drew

[22]   *Colchester Gazette*, 16 September 1914. Rusiecki, *The Impact of Catastrophe*, pp. 58–9

[23]   Albert Sloman Library, University of Essex, sound recording 2130, interview between Mr David Phillips and Mrs Emma Rehberger (née Jarmin), 30 May 1989

[24]   ERO, Watts-Ditchfield diaries, 2 January 1916

was an American Congregationalist rather than an Episcopalian, and his talk was probably part of a government-sponsored propaganda tour.[25] Colchester's Anglican clergy seem to have remained silent in public about the German emperor.

Elsewhere in the diocese of Chelmsford, the *Chelmsford Diocesan Chronicle* printed anti-German articles on three occasions in 1915–16 – possibly to help promote enlistment – and Bishop Watts-Ditchfield once denounced the Prussian militaristic spirit in 1917.[26]

Bishop Arthur Foley Winnington-Ingram

No account of Anglican attitudes during the First World War can avoid mentioning Bishop Winnington-Ingram, who has been portrayed by some historians and makers of television programmes over the past half-century as a bloodthirsty warmonger, if not as a bit of an episcopal buffoon. This depiction is not easy to reconcile with what we know of the pastoral side of his character. Winnington-Ingram was the bishop of London between 1901 and 1939. He combined insightfulness with naivety, and kindliness with a breezy, optimistic enthusiasm. Winnington-Ingram was not the brightest bishop on the episcopal bench, but neither was he stupid. One of his contemporaries, Dom Anselm Hughes OSB, wrote of him: 'He was known by practically all the clergy of his diocese, as well as by countless others throughout England, with affection, or exasperation or with both, as "Uncle Arthur".'[27] London, because of its size and diversity, was not an easy diocese of which to be bishop, and Winnington-Ingram was sometimes criticised for being a lacklustre administrator, around whom some of his naughtier priests ran rings.[28] His strength lay as a pastor, and when he retired in 1939, aged eighty-one, 12,000 clergy

---

[25] CL, Jarmin Collection, fol. 119. The lecture was attended by the Rev. K. Lloyd Parry, minister of Lion Walk Congregational Church, who seconded a motion of thanks afterwards. None of the Anglican clergy is listed as having been present

[26] *Chelmsford Diocesan Chronicle*, October 1915, January 1916, February 1916. *Essex County Standard*, 22 September 1917

[27] Hughes, *The Rivers of the Flood*, p. 71

[28] Hughes, *The Rivers of the Flood*, p. 72. Hughes asserts in a footnote that the criticism was exaggerated

and laity crammed into the Albert Hall to bid him an affectionate farewell.[29]

Winnington-Ingram was highly patriotic and was an imperialist.[30] He was no stranger to martial imagery: preaching at the consecration of a bishop in 1895, he remarked that the Church had been called 'the oldest fighting regiment in Europe'.[31] Whilst addressing a meeting in Colchester in 1916, he told his audience that the choice that faced them was between 'the nailed hand and the mailed fist'.[32]

During the First World War Winnington-Ingram appears to have been utterly convinced of the rightness of Great Britain's cause; if he privately harboured any doubts about the conflict or about trench warfare, he failed to express them publicly. Like many other Anglican clergy and laity, Winnington-Ingram threw himself into promoting enlistment, and into supporting men once they had joined up, visiting the Western Front and the Royal Navy. He did not hesitate to employ martial language about the war. In 1915, the *Guardian* church newspaper asked Winnington-Ingram for a sentence summing up his views about the Church and the war. He replied:

> I think the Church can best help the Nation first of all by making it realise that it is engaged in a Holy War, and not be afraid of saying so. Christ died on Good Friday for Freedom, Honour and Chivalry, and our boys are dying for the same things. Having once realised that everything worth having in the world is at stake, the nation will not hesitate to allow itself to be mobilised. You ask for my advice in a sentence as to what the Church is to do. I answer mobilise the nation for a holy war.[33]

On Advent Sunday 1915, Winnington-Ingram preached a sermon about the war in Westminster Abbey. Taking as his text Isaiah's vision of peace, he said:

> 'They shall not hurt nor destroy in all My holy mountain,' and we see Belgium stabbed in the back and ravaged; then Poland, then Servia, then

[29]   S.C. Carpenter, *Winnington-Ingram* (Hodder and Stoughton, London, 1949), p. 317

[30]   Carpenter, *Winnington-Ingram*, p. 279

[31]   *Guardian*, 24 April 1895

[32]   *Essex County Standard*, 3 June 1916

[33]   *Church Times*, 1 October 1915, quoted by Marrin, *Last Crusade*, p. 139

the Armenian nation wiped out – 500,000 as a moderate computation actually killed. Then as a necessary consequence, to save the freedom of the world, to save liberty, to save the honour of women and the innocence of children, everyone who loves freedom and honour, everyone who puts principle before ease and life itself beyond mere living, is banded in a great crusade – we cannot deny it – to kill Germans, to kill them not for the sake of killing, but to save the world, to kill the good as well as the bad, to kill the young men as well as the old, to kill those who have shown kindness to our wounded as well as those fiends who crucified the Canadian sergeant, who superintended the Armenian massacres, who sank the *Lusitania*, and who turned the machine-guns on the civilians of Aerschott and Louvain; and to kill them lest the civilisation of the world itself be killed.[34]

Winnington-Ingram went on to say he did not intend to stir up un-Christian hatred of the German race. He spoke of individual Germans who repudiated the Prussian militaristic spirit – and mentioned a last letter sent by a soldier who had died in a German hospital, testifying to the kindness he had received there – but went on to claim that he sought to protect Christianity, alleging that there was a spirit of anti-Christ abroad in Germany.

Parts of Winnington-Ingram's Advent 1915 sermon have frequently been used against him, and his posthumous reputation has suffered in consequence. The Rev. Stuart Bell, a Methodist historian of the First World War, has recently re-examined Winnington-Ingram's wartime preaching and has successfully challenged the predominantly blood-thirsty view of him.[35] Bell has shown that Winnington-Ingram's Advent 1915 sermon was edited by George Bedborough, a secularist and free-thinker, for inclusion in his book *Arms and the Clergy (1914–1918)*, which was published by the Secular Society in 1934. Bedborough printed Winnington-Ingram's 'kill Germans' passage and omitted much of the rest of his sermon, concluding with his words, 'As I have said a thousand

---

[34] A.F. Winnington-Ingram, 'A Word of Cheer', *Christian World Pulpit*, 8 December 1915. Winnington-Ingram included a slightly amended version of this sermon, entitled 'Missionary Work the Only Final Cure for War', in a collection of sermons, *The Potter and the Clay* (The Young Churchman Co., Milwaukee, 1917)

[35] S. Bell, 'Malign or Maligned? – Arthur Winnington-Ingram, Bishop of London, in the First World War', *Journal for the History of Modern Theology/Zeitschrift für Neuere Theologiegeschichte* 20/1 (November 2013), 117–33

times, I look upon it as a war for purity, I look upon everyone who dies in it as a martyr.'[36] Winnington-Ingram's words were further edited in 1938 by Lyall Wilkes for his book *Would I Fight?*, in which he merged the two separate quotations reproduced by Bedborough into one single text.

Professor Roland Bainton used Wilkes's twice-altered and partial version of Winnington-Ingram's sermon in his 1960 book *Christian Attitudes Toward War and Peace*, in which he said the bishop:

> with brutal candour exhorted young England to do that which in war had to be done: 'Kill Germans – to kill them, not for the sake of killing, but to save the world, to kill the good as well as the bad, to kill the young as well as the old, to kill those who have shown kindness to our wounded as well as to those who crucified the Canadian sergeant. As I have said a thousand times, I look upon it as a war for purity. I look upon everyone who dies in it as a martyr.'[37]

In 1971 Professor Bainton wrote to the journal *Theology*, to say that at the request of one who had known Winnington-Ingram, he had re-examined the words from the bishop's 1915 Advent sermon and had revised his opinion. He now believed that what Winnington-Ingram had been saying was that:

> whereas a distinction can be drawn between a combatant and a non-combatant, none can be drawn between a good combatant and a bad combatant. To win the war, the good, unhappily, will have to be killed as well as the bad. This statement is what I call 'brutally candid' ... In a revision of my book I would delete 'with brutal candour exhorted young England' and substitute 'regretfully but candidly called upon'.[38]

Bainton's revised interpretation went largely unnoticed, and, until Stuart Bell's recent research, the malign view of Winnington-Ingram was

[36] Bell, 'Malign or Maligned?', 129
[37] R.H. Bainton, *Christian Attitudes Toward War and Peace: A Historical Survey and Critical Re-Evaluation* (Abingdon Press, Nashville, 1960), p. 207, quoted by Stuart Bell, 'Malign or Maligned?', 127
[38] R.H. Bainton, 'Bishop A.F. Winnington-Ingram', *Theology* 74 (1971), 32–3, quoted in Bell, 'Malign or Maligned?', 127–8

believed and repeated by many historians and writers.[39] Winnington-Ingram could certainly be accused of not choosing his words with enough care on Advent Sunday 1915, but he has not deserved all of the opprobrium which has been levelled at him since the publication of Bainton's book in 1960. In truth, it should be recognised that Winnington-Ingram's overall view of the Germans was rather more nuanced than might at first appear. He was also clear that war itself was a very dubious medium. At the start of the war, Winnington-Ingram had appealed to the British people to treat Germans in Great Britain kindly.[40] In June 1917, he preached at the mass burial of sixteen children killed by a German bomb which fell on Upper North Street School, Poplar, and spoke out strongly against the agitation for reprisals, saying that he did not think the mourners wanted sixteen dead German children to avenge the sixteen London children, but deterrent naval and military action and punishment for the perpetrators.[41] Winnington-Ingram's biographer, S.C. Carpenter, commented:

> he knew well enough that modern war means smashed faces, crushed and mangled limbs, stomachs ripped and torn with shells. He knew, none better, of the sorrow that war brings to innumerable homes and of the crippling for years afterwards of the national life. So he said that war was damnable, but he also said that, as it had been forced upon us, we must see it through.[42]

Edith Cavell

One curious omission from Colchester parish magazines from 1915 concerns Edith Cavell. The daughter of an Anglican priest from Norfolk, Cavell embarked upon a nursing career and was working as the director of a training school for nurses in Brussels in 1914. She was on holiday with her family in Norfolk in late July 1914 when war broke out in Europe and deliberately chose to return to Brussels on 2 August 1914, remaining

---

[39] This view of Winnington-Ingram was repeated by Jeremy Paxman in an interview with Michael Snape on *The Big Questions*, BBC1, 18 May 2014

[40] Wilkinson, *Church of England*, p. 217

[41] R. Taylor and C. Lloyd, *A Century of the East End: Events, People and Places over the Last 100 Years* (Sutton Publishing, Stroud, 1999), pp. 34, 35, 101

[42] Carpenter, *Winnington-Ingram*, p. 281

there when the city was captured by the Germans. Whilst nursing German as well as Belgian patients, Cavell helped organise an escape line, which assisted some 200 Allied soldiers and others to escape into the neutral Netherlands, and thence sometimes to England. Arrested by the Germans, she was imprisoned for ten weeks in St Gilles prison, Brussels, before being shot on 12 October 1915, aged forty-nine. The night before her execution, Cavell told the Rev. Stirling Gahan, the Anglican chaplain from Brussels who had been allowed to give her Holy Communion before her death, 'Standing as I do in view of God and Eternity: I realize that patriotism is not enough, I must have no hatred or bitterness towards anyone.' According to the German Lutheran prison chaplain, Paul Le Seur, Cavell's final words before execution were '*Ma conscience est tranquille. Je meurs pour Dieu et ma patrie.*'[43]

The absence of any reference to Edith Cavell in parish magazines from Colchester in 1915 is puzzling: King George V and Queen Mary attended a memorial service for Edith Cavell in St Paul's Cathedral on 29 October 1915, and one would have thought that the execution of a devout Anglican nurse from a clerical family would have made good 'copy'. Cavell may have been mentioned in sermons preached in Colchester in October 1915, but if so, these were not reprinted or mentioned in parish magazines. The people of Colchester are unlikely to have missed the special train carrying Cavell's body for burial outside Norwich Cathedral, following her state funeral in Westminster Abbey, when it passed through the town after the war on 15 May 1919. In all likelihood, the news of Cavell's death on 12 October 1915 – which took place during the Allied Artois–Loos offensive on the Western Front – was one of many competing news items that autumn, and the significance of her execution by the Germans grew afterwards, aided by British propagandists.

Reprisals

In 1916 and again in early 1917, the British press agitated for air reprisals against Germany in response to Zeppelin raids and the torpedoing of British liners. In 1917 British and French aeroplanes bombed Freiburg

[43]   D. Souhami, *Edith Cavell* (Quercus, London, 2011), pp. 372, 377

in reprisal for the German bombing of two British hospital ships.[44] Archbishop Davidson was deeply concerned about reprisals and warned Convocation in 1916: 'let us take care that at an early stage of the wrong doing we stand across the path and warn people that there are ethical as well as military considerations which attach to action such as is now being suggested.'[45] Not everyone shared his scruples. The leading modernist theologian H.D.A. Major wrote in *The Modern Churchman*:

> The strongest moral argument against reprisals is that some are punished who are not actually guilty ... If the innocent cannot be separated from the guilty, ought the guilty therefore to be spared and allowed to continue unpunished their evil ways? It is not for the good of humanity that the guilty should be spared, even though the innocent should suffer with them ... If the only way to protect adequately an English babe is to kill a German babe, then it is the duty of the authorities, however repugnant, to do it. More particularly is this so when we reflect that the innocent German babe will in all probability grow up to be the killer of babes himself, or at least an enthusiastic advocate of that horrible policy of frightfulness of which the killing of babes is one of the features.[46]

This controversy over reprisals does not seem to have made a great impact in Colchester. The *Colchester Gazette* argued in an editorial on 9 February 1916 that retaliations were 'the only way that is sure to have effect and to give pause to this wild policy of "frightfulness" that obsesses the foe'.[47] The *Essex County Standard* claimed three days later that the likelihood of reprisals against the Germans would receive approbation in Britain and would result in 'discomfort to our conscienceless adversaries'.[48] Both newspapers, however, chose to reprint a letter to *The Times* from Field Marshal Sir Evelyn Wood, the son of an Essex clergyman, who was living in retirement at Harlow, in which he denounced reprisals as 'always useless'; though they accompanied this with the suggestion that, aged

---

[44]   Wilkinson, *Church of England*, pp. 98–100
[45]   Wilkinson, *Church of England*, pp. 98–100
[46]   H.D.A. Major, 'Sentimentalists and Casuist', *The Modern Churchman*, August 1917, 212–13, quoted by Marrin, *Last Crusade*, pp. 173–4
[47]   *Colchester Gazette*, 9 February 1916
[48]   *Essex County Standard*, 12 February 1916

seventy-eight, the field marshal was out of touch.[49] A stronger response
was not long in coming from the Rev. W.E. Spencer, vicar of St Botolph's,
Colchester, who roundly denounced reprisals in a sermon on 20 February
1916:

> [Germany] is doing evil in deliberately making war on non-combatants.
> And then comes a cry from certain people for reprisals: 'Germany has killed
> our women and children; let us go off and kill theirs; that may stop them.'
> We must ask ourselves, Can the England that we love and honour be guilty
> of such a thing as this? Some of our newspapers are reviling the Baby-
> killers of the Huns. Shall we make things better by organising bands of
> British Baby-killers against them? It seems to me plain to any sane person
> that every bomb we have to drop should be dropped on German soldiers
> and warstuff, for it is by such operations only that an end can be found to
> the war. It would seem to me abhorrent to every Englishman deliberately
> to make non-combatants, women and children, an object of our arms. It
> would seem to me that in entering upon reprisals we shall be beaten at that
> game, simply because we are English and they are Germans and will do
> things which we English cannot and will not do.[50]

This sermon was printed verbatim in the *Essex County Standard*, after
which there were no further references to reprisals. It is revealing that,
whilst we find condemnation of the enemy and their methods, no Anglican priests or laity in Colchester – a town which had suffered many
German air raids – appear to have advocated bombing German civilians
in retaliation.

How is the absence from Colchester of demonising views of the Germans, and of belief that the war was a holy crusade, to be understood?
There are several possible explanations. Firstly, Albert Marrin has most
probably overstated his case. Anti-German feeling, and the belief that
the war was a sort of crusade, evidently did exist amongst some sections

[49]   *Essex County Standard*, 12 February 1916; *Colchester Gazette*, 16 February 1916. The
Colchester Gazette also published an anonymous letter from a soldier attacking conscientious objectors and Field Marshal Wood – without naming him – on 23 February
1916
[50]   *Essex County Standard*, 26 February 1916

of the population, but it is important to recognise that a lot of the people Marrin quoted were part of Britain's social elite. Their judgement may have been swayed by an excess of patriotism, or by concern over the war's outcome. One should also remember that the British government employed censorship and propaganda during the war.[51] The people do not always believe what their leaders would wish them to believe, and perhaps, at a grass-roots level, although support for the prosecution of war to a victorious conclusion remained high, more Anglicans simply retained a sense of proportion about the Germans than Marrin expected or allowed for.

A second possible explanation in Colchester may be the influence of the garrison. The army, on the whole, had a respect for the German troops which it did not always feel for its French allies.[52] British troops did not usually regard their German adversaries as demons and sometimes found it difficult to believe the tales of German atrocities – if anything, their attitude was 'poor old Fritz' – and this view probably communicated itself to the townsfolk of Colchester.[53] In her 1931 book *Society at War*, Caroline Playne told the wartime tale of a clergyman who entered a railway carriage full of troops returning to France. He exclaimed with some enthusiasm, 'So you are going to fight God's war.' When this elicited no response, he repeated his statement, which again was greeted with silence. The clergyman then asked the troops, 'Don't you believe this is God's war?' After a short silence, one of the soldiers replied, 'Sir, hadn't you better keep your poor Friend out of this bloody mess?'[54] With their churches

---

[51] Munson, *Echoes of the Great War*, diary entries for 4 January 1916, 12 August 1916. Wilkinson, *Church of England*, p. 215

[52] Munson, *Echoes of the Great War*, diary entry for 2 July 1917. The Rev. V.J. Allard told the author (3 January 2000) that his father, H.G. Allard, who had served in the trenches in a fusilier regiment, used to say that he would have preferred the Germans on his right flank and the French in the trenches on the opposite side of no-man's land. Such remarks are not uncommon. British soldiers, for example, were sometimes horrified by the lack of care shown by the French cavalry towards their horses

[53] Wilkinson, *Church of England*, pp. 209–13

[54] Quoted by Wilkinson, *Church of England*, pp. 230–1. It ought to be borne in mind that Caroline Playne had once helped the Church of England Peace League, and she included this tale in a chapter entitled 'The Failure of the Clerics' in her *Society at War, 1914–1916* (Allen and Unwin, London, 1931), and so she probably had her own agenda. The tale may perhaps have grown slightly in the telling, but there is no reason to doubt its essential veracity. Of course, another clergyman, of more tactful or sensitive disposition, in another carriage full of soldiers, might have elicited a different response

full of soldiers, the Colchester clergy were probably aware of the attitudes to be found amongst the troops and were accordingly more circumspect when preaching or writing about the war in their parish magazines.

There may possibly also have been lingering folk memories in Colchester of the British German Legion, who were recruited from the various kingdoms of pre-unified Germany to fight for Great Britain during the Crimean War and were based in the town in 1856. Marriage registers show that there were a very large number of weddings between soldiers of the British German Legion and Colchester girls; indeed, these appear to have been actively encouraged as part of a government scheme to resettle some of the German soldiers in the Eastern Cape, South Africa. A number of people in Colchester in 1914–18 may thus have had German fathers or grandfathers, as well as relatives in Germany; this may have ameliorated their perception of the enemy.

Narrowed Outlooks

In August 1914 Parliament passed three Defence of the Realm Acts (DORA), giving the government sweeping powers in wartime, including censorship.[55] The local press in Colchester printed details and sometimes photographs of townsfolk who had been killed or wounded in the war, but nevertheless still managed on the whole to strike a bright and optimistic note throughout the war. Military and naval setbacks were reported in the newspapers, but were generally played down, whilst modest advances on the Western Front tended to be portrayed as significant gains. For those who could not afford a newspaper, official government bulletins were regularly posted in post offices across the country. These bulletins were heavily censored and, as we would say today, 'spun': an example is that of 2 July 1916, the day after the beginning of the battle of the Somme: 'British Official. Attack launched 7.30 am north of Somme combined with French. British broken into German forward system on 16 mile front. French attack equally satisfactory. Remainder front successful British raiding parties.'[56]

---

[55] Lloyd George, *War Memoirs*, p. 106. Marrin, Last Crusade, p. 177
[56] Munson, *Echoes of the Great War*, diary entry for 2 July 1916

Rumours and gossip thrived in wartime, and anxious individuals started imaging German spies busying themselves throughout East Anglia.[57] In Colchester, the Rev. G.M. Behr of St Stephen's found himself the object of great suspicion because of his Germanic surname. He wrote in his parish magazine in September 1914:

I have been put to some inconvenience, and not only I, but my mother and sister also, because some 'busy people' have set going a story that we are Germans, and not that only, but 'German spies.' I believe even our two col-lie dogs – according to the story – have been trained for no good purpose! … In reply to these statements that have been given out as facts, may I just say – that I am not a German – I was born in England and have never set foot on German soil, not even for a holiday; that the same may be said of my sister; that my mother is English born and bred. My father was indeed of German nationality, but was naturalised on coming to England some-where as far back as the 'sixties.' That our collie dogs are quite harmless.[58]

Chief Constable J.A. Unett recorded that the Essex Police had had to deal with many reports of strange lights, which people imagined were 'signalling to the enemy'. The authorities feared that German sympathis-ers would cause damage in Essex, and special constables were recruited in large numbers to prevent this.[59] Fear of a German landing at Harwich was widespread in Colchester, and there were several invasion scares in parts of Essex. On one occasion, the troops in Braintree were turned out and the population prepared to flee.[60]

The Great Russian Myth and the Angels of Mons

One of the strangest rumours of the Great War was the 'great Russian myth', according to which a large Russian army was reported to have landed in Scotland in 1914 and believed to have travelled by train to the

[57] D.E. Johnson, 'The Essex Spy who Got Away', *Essex Countryside*, October 1973
[58] *St Botolph's Parish Magazine*, September 1914
[59] ERO, J.A. Unett, 'Orders, Reports and Letters relating to Essex Special Constabulary, Colchester Division, during the Great War', November 1930, p. x
[60] Mr Jack Ashton, interview, 10 February 1998. Munson, *Echoes of the Great War*, diary entries for 19 March 1916, 31 March 1916, 27 April 1916

south coast, to embark for France. It was freely reported in Colchester that several trains full of Russian soldiers had passed through the North Station, and that the black horses of the Russian cavalry had been plainly seen.[61]

A comparable wartime myth is that of the Angels of Mons. For about a year after the battle of Mons (23–24 August 1914), stories circulated of how the sorely pressed British soldiers had been aided by angels.[62] This story may perhaps have originated in hallucinations of exhausted British troops during the retreat from Mons, but in all probability it was started by a short fictional story, 'The Bowmen', published by Arthur Machen in the *Evening News* on 29 September 1914, which soon began to circulate as fact. Angels, of course, are important figures in both Old and New Testament literature, where their role might be summed up as being God's messengers and policemen.

Later in 1915 the Rev. Alexander Boddy – the vicar of All Saints', Monkwearmouth, and significantly, well-known as one of the founders of Pentecostalism in Britain – published a book called *The Real Angels of Mons*, which presented the story as fact and quoted 'eyewitnesses'. The imprimatur of the official censor was displayed on the book, which doubtless led many readers to credit its veracity.[63] For the next few months, the story of the Angels of Mons took on a life of its own, and spread throughout the country in several different forms. One version appeared in *St Mary-at-the-Walls Parish Magazine* in July 1915:

> All Saints' Clifton, Parish Magazine publishes the following remarkable story headed 'The Angelic Guard at Mons.' The magazine says it is a well authenticated account which has been handed them by a friend.
>
> > Last Sunday I met Miss M., the daughter of the well known Canon M., and she told me she knew two officers both of whom had themselves seen the angels which saved our left wing from the Germans when they came right upon them during the retreat from Mons. They expected annihilation, as they were almost helpless, when, to their amazement, they stood like dazed men, never so much touched their guns, nor stirred till we had turned round and escaped by some cross roads.

[61]   Hunt, *Souvenir*, p. 67
[62]   Marrin, *Last Crusade*, p. 137
[63]   Wilkinson, *Church of England*, pp. 194–5

One of Miss M.'s friends, who was not a religious man, told her that he saw a troop of angels between us and the enemy. He has been a changed man ever since.

The other man she met in London. She asked him if he had heard the wonderful stories of angels. He said he had seen them himself under the following circumstances:–

When he and his company were retreating, they heard the German cavalry tearing after them. They saw a place where they thought a stand might be made, with sure hope of safety; but before they could reach it the German cavalry were upon them.

They, therefore, turned round and faced the enemy, expecting nothing but instant death, when, to their wonder, they saw between them and the enemy, a whole troop of angels. The German horses turned round terrified, and regularly stampeded. The men tugged at their bridles, while the poor beasts tore away in every direction from our men.

This officer swore he saw the angels, which the horses saw plainly enough. This gave them time to reach the little fort, or whatever it was, and save themselves.[64]

The remarkable thing about this story is that Canon Brunwin-Hales, a well-educated and level-headed man, permitted it to be published in his parish magazine. Like many others of his generation, Brunwin-Hales had doubtless been brought up to believe in Progress, and yet he circulated what might pass for a medieval myth amongst his parishioners. The explanation is most likely to be found in the psychological shock and strain of the war, and the craving of many people in a world turned upside down to discover a sign that God was on their side, especially in 1915, when the British public began to perceive that the war would be long and drawn out. It is not impossible that British government propagandists, spotting a good thing, may have lent the Angels of Mons a helping hand.

One might imagine that the myth of the Angels of Mons would have found especial credence amongst Anglo-Catholics, with their penchant for saints and the miraculous, but it was believed in by evangelicals and middle-of-the-road Anglicans too. Some clergy seem to have given the

---

[64] J. Hayward, *Myths and Legends of the First World War* (The History Press, Stroud, 2010), p. 53, identifies 'Miss M' as Sarah Marrable, the daughter of Canon Marrable, of All Saints, Clifton

war an apocalyptic interpretation, particularly during 1914–15, though there is no evidence of this in Colchester. Stories of the miraculous circulated widely: tales of an altar destroyed, whilst the tabernacle containing the Blessed Sacrament remained unharmed, and of crucifixes and statues of the Virgin and Child standing, whilst all around them had been destroyed. The most famous statue was that of the Golden Virgin on the tower of the basilica of Notre-Dame de Brebières at Albert. This had been knocked horizontal by a German shell, and it was widely believed that so long as it hung precariously from the basilica, the Allies would not lose the war. Whilst German gunner tried to hit the statue, the Royal Engineers strengthened it with chains by night. The Golden Virgin statue eventually fell down in April 1918, during the German spring offensive.[65]

Such stories from the front were reported home in letters, such as that from 'An Officer' and ex-worshipper at St Mary-at-the-Walls, who wrote: 'There is a wayside crucifix at a cross roads a hundred yards behind our trench, in what was once a small hamlet, the houses all around are in ruins but the crucifix has not been touched. The houses are so close that it could not be a question of good shooting.'[66] Many soldiers carried lucky talismans, and the inventor of a lucky charm for soldiers claimed to have sold a million and a quarter by August 1915.[67]

One possible explanation of this may be that many people often hold a rather eclectic collection of beliefs: a man or woman may have a perfectly orthodox Christian faith as far as credal doctrine is concerned, and yet also hold superstitious ideas about not walking under a ladder, or throwing a pinch of spilt salt over one's shoulder.[68] It would appear that although many people maintained and practised Christian faith during the First World War, belief in legends, supernatural happenings and lucky charms also grew under the unparalleled pressure of wartime anxiety and bereavement, in a way that would have seemed unthinkable before 1914, and which does not seem to have occurred during the Second World War.[69] It would be fascinating to know if there were similar phenomena in France, Germany and Austria-Hungary in 1914–18.

---

[65]   Marrin, *Last Crusade*, p. 137. Wilkinson, *Church of England*, pp. 194–5
[66]   *St Mary-at-the-Walls Parish Magazine*, March 1915
[67]   Wilkinson, *Church of England*, p. 195
[68]   A fuller treatment of this theme will be found in S. Williams, *Religious Belief and Popular Culture in Southwark, 1880–1939* (Oxford University Press, Oxford, 1999)
[69]   Snape, *God and the British Soldier*, pp. 28–46

Broadened Horizons

Russia and the Orthodox Church

Before August 1914, Colchester's newspapers, the *Essex County Standard*, the *Colchester Gazette*, and the *Essex County Telegraph*, concentrated mainly on local and national news. The First World War led to an expansion of interest in events overseas, especially amongst Britain's allies. Collections were held in Colchester for the Italian and French Red Cross associations, and an interest arose in all things to do with Britain's ally Russia. Interest grew amongst Anglicans in the Russian Orthodox Church. The *Chelmsford Diocesan Chronicle*, for example, printed an article in September 1915 on 'The Russian Church' by the Rev. G.B.H. Bishop. In October 1915, the 'missionary study band' at St Mary-at-the-Walls decided to study the Russian Orthodox Church, and they subsequently worked their way through Davey Biggs's book *Russia and Reunion*.[70] St Mary-at-the-Walls also regularly used a Russian Orthodox litany during its weekly intercession services between 1915 and 1917.[71] Interest in Russian Orthodoxy extended to evangelical parishes: Ward of St Peter's urged his congregation to attend two lectures given by Bishop Bury, the Anglican bishop for North and Central Europe, in the Moot Hall on 20 March 1916.[72] The lectures attracted big audiences, and a collection raised the large sum of £32.0.6 – the equivalent of nearly a year's wages for an agricultural labourer – which was sent to Bishop Bury to assist Anglican chaplains who had had to flee enemy countries in Europe.[73]

Two months later, in May 1916, thirteen members of the Council of the Russian Empire and of the Imperial Duma, led by the vice president of the Duma, Alexander Protopopov, visited Colchester. They were greeted by the mayor in his robes, schoolchildren singing 'God Save the Tsar' and a guard of honour of Boy Scouts. A luncheon was held in their honour in the Moot Hall, followed by a military review on the Abbey Fields, commanded by Major General Blomfield.[74] Interest in all things Russian

---

[70] *St Mary-at-the-Walls Parish Magazine*, November 1914
[71] ERO, St Mary-at-the-Walls Registers of Services, 1915–17
[72] *St Peter's Parish Magazine*, March 1916
[73] *St Mary-at-the-Walls Parish Magazine*, April 1916, March 1916
[74] *Essex County Standard*, 13 May 1916. Protopopov was starting to show signs of mental

26 Visit to Colchester of members of the Russian Imperial Duma, May 1916

quickly faded after the 1917 revolutions: following the treaty of Brest-Litovsk between Russia and Germany in March 1918, Brunwin-Hales removed the Russian flag from amongst the flags of the Allies hanging in his church, adding in his parish magazine, 'The flag of Russia is conspicuous by its absence on the north side, but it would be a joy to be able to replace it as a symbol of Russia alive again in the struggle for justice and liberty.'[75]

Jerusalem

Another land which attracted the interest of many Anglicans in Colchester was Palestine.[76] As the war spread across the Holy Land, a widespread famine arose, and two public meetings were held in Colchester in 1917 in support of the Syria and Palestine Famine Relief Fund. During the evening meeting on 10 December 1917, the speaker from the fund, Miss F.E. Newton, interrupted her address to announce the news, 'Jerusalem has been taken by our troops. Jerusalem, the cradle of our faith is once more under Christian government.' The audience rose to their feet, and sang 'God Save the King', followed by the Doxology. General Allenby had been a popular garrison commander in Colchester before the war, and his capture of Jerusalem was celebrated with great enthusiasm in the town: St George's flag was flown from Colchester town hall, from St Peter's and St Mary-at-the-Walls, and the bells of St Peter's and St Nicholas's were rung for an hour.[77] Bishop Watts-Ditchfield suggested that the Te Deum might be sung in churches to celebrate Jerusalem being back in Christian hands for the first time since the Crusades.[78]

---

instability: one or two figures in the Russian government may have been only too happy to pack him off to England for a few weeks

[75] *St Mary-at-the-Walls Parish Magazine*, June 1918

[76] At St Peter's, for example, the Holy Land was mentioned in the parish magazine in October and December 1917, and also in June, August, September and November 1918, when the magazine reported the return of two missionaries, Miss Tiffin and Miss Beard, to the English Hospital in Jaffa

[77] CL, Jarmin Collection, fol. 16

[78] *Colchester Gazette*, 28 November 1917

Attitudes towards the British Army

One curious change effected by the First World War concerned attitudes towards the British Army. Before 1914, soldiers – who were mostly drawn from the unskilled working classes – were often regarded by the public with a degree of disdain, as potential causes of drunkenness and disorder.[79] By 1918, although British soldiers were still drunken and disorderly from time to time, the army had come to be perceived by many people in Britain as an organisation that – apart from its primary business of killing people – was more or less fair towards its troops and tried hard to care for them. This change in civilian attitude towards soldiers is discernible from at least the middle years of the war. To take three small but revealing examples, Adrian Gregory points out that there was an increasingly angry demand from 1916 that private 'squares' in the wealthy residential districts of London be opened for the recreational use of wounded soldiers. Secondly, there was also a demand that wounded soldiers be given priority in first-class seating on commuter trains (presumably despite having only paid a third-class fare). Thirdly, King George V frequently opened the gardens of Buckingham Palace during the war for afternoon parties for wounded soldiers, something that did not occur before 1914.[80] The king would probably have had a number of motives for doing so, but, by the middle of the war, one of them would surely have been the recognition that his armies were for the most part composed of civilians-in-uniform, who were drawn from all social classes and backgrounds and were frequently of higher educational and social calibre than their pre-war predecessors in the regular army. Great Britain mobilised some 8,375,000 men during the First World War, of whom 5,704,416 served in the army. Of these, 673,375 soldiers were killed or were presumed dead, and a further 1,643,469 were

---

[79]   Inspector William Drane, 'Twenty-Eight Years Policing in Colchester: When Saturday Night was a Terror', *Colchester Gazette*, 3 October 1934. Soldiers appear to have perpetually caused trouble in the streets of Colchester in the early twentieth century, prior to the outbreak of war in 1914. Vineyard Street was a regular trouble spot, and at times – for example, when troops were shortly to be sent overseas – police constables had to patrol areas of Colchester in twos for mutual protection, because of drunken and obstreperous soldiers in the streets. Inspector Drane said that things were much quieter in the 1920s and 1930s, and he ascribed this change in part to the effect of better education and the impact of the cinema

[80]   Gregory, *Last Great War*, pp. 135–6

wounded; 39,527 men serving in the Royal Navy and in the Royal Flying Corps or Royal Air Force were killed or were presumed dead, and another 16,862 were wounded.[81] Prior to 1914, most people in Britain had only very limited direct experience of the army; by 1918, the majority of people had some relative, however distant, serving in the war, and this would doubtless have broadened and changed their view of the army.

As far as the troops themselves were concerned, the British Army – unlike the French, Russian or Italian armies – went to very great and somewhat paternalistic lengths to care for its troops. British soldiers knew that if they were wounded, there was a reasonably efficient system to evacuate from the front to hospital, where they would receive proper medical care. The British Army on the Western Front – unlike the French Army – allotted regular periods of leave, and rotated its troops, so that spells in the front trenches were alternated with longer periods behind the lines. The army tried to ensure that its soldiers had baths when practicable, a reasonable good diet (certainly better than the wartime diet of their families in Britain) and regularly received their letters and parcels from home. The first experience many working-class recruits had of using a toothbrush was when they were issued with one by the army. British officers were schooled to care for their men – even to the extent of inspecting their feet for signs of 'trench foot' – and regularly organised sports, lectures and concert parties. The Army Chaplains' Department underwent a large expansion during the war, to cater for the troops' spiritual needs. It is surely significant that, apart from a few days' disturbance at Étaples in 1917 and some minor disorders in late 1918, the British Army experienced no mutinies during the First World War, unlike the French, Russian, Italian, German and Austro-Hungarian armies.[82]

None of this, of course, should obscure the suffering of the troops during the First World War, the awfulness of trench warfare and of having to go 'over the top', and the appallingly high physical and psychological casualties. Nevertheless, in 1914–18, the British Army came to be viewed in a more positive light by many civilians at home as well as by many of

[81] Corrigan, *Mud , Blood and Poppycock*, pp. 54–5. Figures from 'The Long, Long Trail, The British Army in the Great War of 1914–1918' website, www.1914-1918.net (accessed 3 March 2015)

[82] Many of the myths about life in the British Army during the First World War are exploded with great relish by Gordon Corrigan in his very readable book, *Mud, Blood, and Poppycock*

the men who served in it. This change was reflected in the pride that many ex-soldiers took in their former regiments after 1918, and the burgeoning post-war membership of regimental associations and organisations such as the British Legion.

In 1914 Francis Foljambe was a second lieutenant serving with the 120th Battery, Royal Field Artillery. He went to France with the British Expeditionary Force in August 1914 and kept a war diary until July 1917, when, after a period of ill-health, he was transferred to the Ministry of Munitions in London, where he remained until the Armistice. On 7 July 1917, before returning to London, he made his last entry in his diary:

> Spent my last night at the Observation Post and returned to the battery at daybreak, when I said goodbye and rode back to the wagon line. Thence to Arras station and so home. The end of a most enjoyable three years.[83]

Making some notes after re-reading his wartime diary in 1965, Foljambe wondered how in 1917 he could possibly have described his time on the Western Front as 'enjoyable'. Looking back over half a century, he wrote that he now believed the First World War had witnessed

> the tragic elimination of a large proportion of a generation, including the best of the young men at that time, [which had] undoubtedly resulted in the poor leadership by lesser men from which this country has since suffered and which led it into a Second World War.[84]

Foljambe did, however, admit that if 'enjoyed' was not exactly the word he would wish to use in 1965, his time on the Western Front had certainly afforded him many privileges and unique experiences.[85]

The truth is that although the passage of time may have helped Foljambe see his wartime experiences in context, the views about the war which he expressed in 1965 were not the views he had held in 1917: he was – consciously or unconsciously – reinterpreting them in 1965 in the

---

[83]   J. Jackson, *Family at War: The Foljambe Family and the Great War* (Haynes Publishing, Sparkford, 2010), pp. 230–1

[84]   Jackson, *Family at War*, p. 11

[85]   Jackson, *Family at War*, p. 12

light of subsequent events and cultural shifts. Foljambe wrote two years after Joan Littlewood's anti-war musical play *Oh, What a Lovely War!* was first performed in London, and a year after the screening of the BBC's television series *The Great War*.

Foljambe's experiences in 1917 and 1965 are symbolic of the way in which the First World War has been perceived in different ways at different times. Looking at thoughts and attitudes of clergy and laity in Colchester during the war, what emerges is rather different from what was widely believed and taught as historical 'orthodoxy' by many historians and writers later in the twentieth century. The people of Colchester, like many civilians elsewhere in Britain, had a much better and more detailed grasp of what was happening in France than has long been believed. The same point could be made of many of the men who volunteered or were later conscripted to serve in the army.[86] They did not think they were somehow benighted or foolish. Most people in Colchester – and indeed elsewhere in the country – believed that it was entirely just and right for Great Britain to go to war in 1914 to help the people of Belgium and France, and to prevent the establishment of a militaristic German hegemony in Europe.

One of the frustrations of writing about Colchester in 1914–18 is that very few personal letters and papers have survived. An associated – and equally frustrating – consequence is that it is not easy to chart much in the way of development of thoughts and attitudes during the course of the First World War. What one can affirm, with a high degree of certainty, is that there was a strong level of support in Colchester for Britain's participation in the war throughout the whole of the First World War, and a determination to continue to a victorious conclusion. The cost to individuals and families was very high, but I have found no evidence of defeatist views, and indeed, quite the reverse: during the German spring offensive in March 1918, when there was a possibility that Britain might be defeated, there was a renewal of patriotic endeavour and determination in the town.

If the men and women of Colchester's churches believed in the war in a way that sometimes seemed strange or unlikely to later generations of writers, it is equally noteworthy that they remained so level-headed about the enemy. Although German outrages in Belgium and France were

---

[86]   Gregory, *Last Great War*, pp. 133–6

deplored, there was very little serious demonisation of the German Army or people, and no support for retaliation, for example, by aerial bombing of civilians. This is especially interesting, given that Colchester was regularly subject to German air raids and was fully prepared for evacuation in the event of an enemy landing on the east coast.

If the First World War led to a temporary increase in belief in myths, superstitions and what we might term 'edginess' born out of anxiety, it also led to a broadening of horizons. The conclusion is inescapable that, whilst firmly supporting the nation's war effort – and in spite of a multitude of hardships, scares, personal sorrows and the efforts of British government propagandists – the clergy and laity of Colchester's parish churches, on the whole, seem to have continued to think carefully for themselves and managed to retain a sense of proportion, throughout the First World War.

9

Armistice, Remembrance and Aftermath

It was something of an historical accident that the First World War ended at 11.00 a.m. on Monday 11 November, 1918. Lloyd George had instructed Admiral Sir Rosslyn Wemyss, the British representative at the Armistice negotiations at Compiègne, to arrange that the Armistice should commence at 2.30 p.m. in order that he might announce it in the House of Commons between 2.45 p.m. and 3.00 p.m., and presumably make political capital of the news.

Admiral Wemyss exceeded his orders: he felt that more lives might be lost if the war dragged on for even a few hours longer than was absolutely necessary; and the poetry of hostilities coming to a close at the eleventh hour of the eleventh day of the eleventh month appealed strongly to him. The French and the Germans agreed to Wemyss's suggestion of 11.00 a.m., and the Armistice was signed at 5.10 a.m. The French agreed to transmit the news to the Allied front line. Wemyss hurried back to Paris, and, fearing Lloyd George's reaction to his initiative, he bypassed the prime minister and managed to telephone George V at Buckingham Palace. The king and his staff spent the next few hours telephoning the news of the Armistice to the government and military and naval authorities. Wemyss's anxiety about the reaction of Lloyd George was well founded: when he reported to the prime minister and cabinet on 19 November, he was shocked to find them ungrateful and vindictive. Wemyss did not receive the £100,000 grant awarded by the government to other service chiefs, such as Admiral Beatty. He also had to wait a year longer for his peerage than the other senior officers honoured at the end of the war, and he was only made a baron (Baron Wester Wemyss) rather than an earl, like the others.[1]

---

[1]   Lord Neidpath, letter to the author, 27 May 1999. Admiral Wemyss discreetly omitted

The Armistice in Colchester

The news of the Armistice reached Colchester during the morning of 11 November 1918. Jack Ashton recalled seeing a bugler march to the centre of the square at Goojerat Barracks and stand to attention. On the stroke of 11.00 a.m., he sounded his bugle.[2] The town council was meeting when the news was received. They all rose and sang 'God Save the King'. The mayor, George Wright, and the councillors hurriedly donned their robes, three buglers were found to sound a fanfare, and, surrounded by the councillors and army and navy officers, the mayor announced the Armistice from the balcony of the town hall to the crowds in the high street:

> Fellow citizens, rejoice with me this day – the greatest day in the world's history. An Armistice has been signed (Loud cheers). Congratulate your-selves on this marvellous victory. The fighting is over (Loud cheers). Thank God for the victory. May we have a world's peace, and may all those waiting for their dear loved ones have them soon returned to their homes. (Cheers). I am proud to be your mayor this day. I am prouder still to give you this message. God bless you all.[3]

The crowds outside the town hall sang the national anthem, followed by loud cheers for the king. An open-topped lorry was found and filled with wounded troops in their blue uniforms, who were then driven around Colchester, accompanied by the cheers of the crowds on the pavement. The mayor decided to ignore wartime anti-aircraft regulations and to illuminate the town hall during the evening. The band of the 6th Battalion of the Essex Regiment marched up and down the High Street playing patriotic airs, soldiers appeared in fancy dress, and the bells of St Peter's and St Nicholas's rang out. In the suburbs, impromptu street parties were held for the children. The crowds were well behaved and there was not a

---

this information from his own account of some of these transactions, and it was not mentioned in the *Life and Letters of Lord Wester Wemyss* published by Lady Wester Wemyss in 1935. The details were recalled by Admiral Wemyss's daughter, Alice, a very good historian

2 Mr Jack Ashton, interview, 10 February 1998

3 CL, Jarmin Collection, fol. 119

FOR THE HONOUR of COLCHESTER
FEED the GUNS.
OUR GUN WEEK IS NOV. 25ᵗʰ ᴛᴏ NOV. 30ᵗʰ?

27 The mayor of Colchester announcing the Armistice from the town hall,
11 November 1918

single case of drunkenness or misbehaviour at the magistrates' court the following morning (perhaps the Colchester Police turned a blind eye).[4]

Services of Thanksgiving

There was a widespread desire in Colchester to go to church after the Armistice to give thanks for victory and the end of the war. Several parishes, such as St Nicholas's and St Paul's, hurriedly arranged thanksgiving services for the evening of 11 November.

The town's main act of thanksgiving was held in St Peter's on Tuesday 12 November, attended by the mayor and corporation in state, and a large congregation. Every seat in the church was taken, 2,000 people

[4]   ERO, J.M. Harris, 'S. Nicholas and S. Runwald Record of the Great War 1914–1918'. 12 November 1918

were turned away, and an overflow service was held at Lion Walk Congregational Church. Both services were surprisingly interdenominational. Thirty Anglican clergy, military chaplains and Nonconformist ministers attended St Peter's. The sermon was delivered by the Rev. K.L. Parry of Lion Walk Congregational Church, who told the congregation that it felt 'as though we were slowly awakening from a night of restless sleep, disturbed by a hideous dream', and exhorted them in the future to lead lives worthy of those who had been killed.[5] This was the first time a Nonconformist minister had ever preached in an Anglican church in Colchester. In return, the service at Lion Walk Congregational Church was conducted by the Rev. J.M. Harris of St Nicholas's, and the preacher curiously was the Rev. Frank Burnett of St Mary-at-the-Walls, a former Nonconformist who had joined the Church of England.

St Mary-at-the-Walls held a service of thanksgiving on Wednesday 13 November, and Berechurch on Friday 15 November.[6] Other parishes held thanksgiving services the following Sunday, 17 November. All attracted very large congregations: at Berechurch one of the clergy noted in the service register 'practically the whole of the parish present'.[7] The large attendance at all the services of thanksgiving in Colchester is revealing: although the town's social elite were present, so, it should be noted, were working-class Anglicans in very considerable numbers.

Remembrance

There was a gradual return to normality in Colchester in the weeks after the Armistice. The borough tribunal did not meet again, and the troops slowly began to be demobilised. The Borough of Colchester Social Club for the Troops carried on until June 1919, when it too was 'demobilised' at a garden party held by Mrs Coats Hutton at Lexden Manor.[8] Gostwyke and Hamilton Road hospitals were wound down, although soldiers were still dying of wounds in the military hospital in the summer of 1919.

---

5   CL, Jarmin Collection, fol. 120
6   ERO, J.M. Harris, 'S. Nicholas and S. Runwald Record of the Great War 1914–1918', 12
     November 1918. St Paul's Register of Services, 11 November 1918. *St Mary-at-the-Walls
     Parish Magazine*, December 1918
7   ERO, Berechurch Register of Services, 15 November 1918
8   *East Anglian Daily Times*, 13 June 1919

28 Peace Day in Colchester, 19 July 1919: saluting the 'Glorious Dead'

The war did not officially end until the treaty of Versailles was signed on 28 June 1919, five years to the day after the assassination of Archduke Franz Ferdinand which had precipitated the conflict. In the meantime, the parishes were concerned with the troops returning from France or from hospital. At St Mary-at-the-Walls and Berechurch, 'welcome home' committees were formed and district visitors were asked to report on the welfare of demobilised soldiers.[9] On 16 July 1919, the parish held a special service at St Mary-at-the-Walls for returned troops and their families, after which they walked past a guard of honour of infant school children to the rectory, where 300 people sat down to afternoon tea and a promenade concert, followed by dancing until midnight (all of which left Brunwin-Hales and his congregation with the not-inconsiderable deficit of £25 to make good). Similar entertainments were held elsewhere for the wounded.[10]

[9]   *St Mary-at-the-Walls Parish Magazine*, January 1919
[10] Hunt, *Souvenir*, p. 74

On 9 July 1919, a service of thanksgiving was held in Castle Park for the 'celebration of the peace'. Once again, the mayor and corporation, the borough magistrates and officials attended in state, to give thanks for the nation's deliverance and to pray for the future. Ten days later, Colchester celebrated 'Peace Day' with a parade of demobilised soldiers in the High Street. The mayor addressed them from the town hall balcony and warmly thanked them on behalf of the borough 'for all their heroic efforts that have enabled us to meet to-day to celebrate so great and successful victory'.[11]

War Memorials

Honouring the dead of the First World War took two forms in the years after the Armistice: the erection of war memorials, and the evolution of rituals of remembrance. During the war, churches had displayed rolls of honour bearing the names of parishioners serving in the forces, and lists of those who had been killed. Similar street shrines commemorating those killed were also erected in various parts of Colchester. These later evolved into permanent memorials to the dead. The first parish in Colchester to erect a memorial was St Leonard's, Lexden, where a memorial cross was dedicated as early as December 1918. War memorials were usually one of the first subjects to be debated in 1919 by the newly formed parochial church councils, and many churches formed special sub-committees. Memorials sometimes took the form of external crosses or monuments, such as those at St Botolph's or All Saints', Stanway, but most memorials were memorial plaques erected inside churches. At St Mary-at-the-Walls, a special 'Warriors' Chapel' was constructed. Parish magazines and local newspapers throughout the early 1920s contain detailed descriptions of the inauguration of war memorials, which were usually unveiled by a senior military officer and dedicated by the incumbent or by a bishop.

Colchester borough council decided to erect a town war memorial, and a committee was established to look into the subject. One member advocated the establishment of a borough art gallery as a war memorial, but in the end the committee decided upon a monument, which was erected beside Colchester Castle through the generosity of Lord Cowdray. A

---

[11]   Hunt, *Souvenir*, p. 40

29 The dedication of Colchester War Memorial in 1924

30 Colchester War Memorial surrounded by crowds of emotional townsfolk who had surged forward after it was unveiled

rather self-congratulatory little volume, *The Colchester War Memorial Souvenir*, was published and the memorial was dedicated in 1924.

Photographs of the dedication of Colchester's war memorial show that, after the formal unveiling ceremony, the crowds burst through the ranks of soldiers and civic and ecclesiastical dignitaries, and crowded around the base of the war memorial. It was clearly a highly emotional occasion, and here lies a clue to the importance of war memorials: for many people who could not afford to visit military cemeteries overseas, or whose loved ones had no known resting place, the war memorial became a surrogate grave and place where grief and loss could be focused and expressed.[12]

Two Minutes' Silence

Rituals of remembrance were another way in which grief could be addressed and channelled. The observance of two minutes' silence on the first Armistice Day on 11 November 1919 was a last-minute decision which proved immensely moving and popular. There was no official act of remembrance in 1919 at the Cenotaph in Whitehall, which was still a temporary wooden memorial erected for the peace celebrations in July that year. Armistice Day grew in the popular mind after 1920, when George V unveiled the permanent stone Cenotaph and the Unknown Warrior was buried in Westminster Abbey.[13] Within a week, somewhere between 500,000 and a million people had paid homage at the tomb in

---

[12]   This subject is treated in detail by Alex King in *Memorials of the Great War in Britain*

[13]   Roger T. Stearn, in his entry for 'Unknown Warrior, the (d. 1914?)' in the *Oxford Dictionary of National Biography* (2004), writes: 'The Curzon committee [charged with making the arrangements for the burial of the Unknown Warrior] apparently intended that a corpse from 1914 should be exhumed, and the chosen one was probably a regular army soldier of the original 'contemptible' British expeditionary force, and therefore a young unmarried man in his twenties or possibly an older married reservist recalled from civilian life to the colours. He might have been a Territorial, since the London Scottish and other Territorial units were at the western front from September 1914.' If Stearn is right in his supposition about the Unknown Warrior dying in 1914 – and if the Unknown Warrior was not killed before 26 August 1914, when troops from Colchester saw action for the first time in the Great War at the battle of Le Cateau – one may speculate that there is a slim but real possibility that the Unknown Warrior who was buried in Westminster Abbey in 1920 may have been a regular soldier from the pre-war Colchester garrison, or may have been an army reservist who reported to Colchester barracks when he was recalled in 1914

Westminster Abbey, and 100,000 wreaths were laid at the Cenotaph.[14] In 1921, George V participated in an act of remembrance at the Cenotaph for the first time, and a pattern was established which has continued, with minor changes, until today.

In Colchester, Armistice Day grew in significance as the years passed. In 1919 it seems to have caught people by surprise, and many churches still had not erected their war memorials. In 1920, Behr at St Stephen's encouraged his parishioners to observe Armistice Day, and later reported that 'the Memorial in Church was covered with wreaths and flowers in memory of our "Bravely Dead",' which had been left by a large congregation.[15] Following the unveiling of the town war memorial, the mayor and corporation began attending Armistice Day commemorations, in much the same way that they had participated in Declaration Day services during the war.[16]

In many towns and cities in the early 1920s, special gala dinners and dances were held on the evening of Armistice Day, and in the Albert Hall there was an annual Victory Ball. Such events were seen by those who participated in them as celebrations of victory, or continuations of the revels of Armistice night in 1918. As the years passed, such events became highly controversial: it seemed unfair that former officers with money should dance the night away, whilst impoverished ex-officers and former ordinary soldiers and sailors struggled to make ends meet. Such celebrations also seemed insensitive to civilians trying to come to terms with painful bereavements.[17] At the last moment in 1925, the Victory Ball was deferred by twenty-four hours, and the Albert Hall was made available on Armistice night to Canon Dick Sheppard, who improvised a service of Remembrance. From this point dinners and dances on Armistice night quickly faded away, and in 1927 the *Daily Express* sponsored the first British Legion 'Festival of Remembrance' at the Albert Hall, which was attended by the Prince of Wales and relayed by radio all over the British Empire.[18]

---

[14] Gregory, *Silence of Memory*, pp. 8–33
[15] *St Botolph's Parish Magazine*, November 1920, December 1920
[16] Colchester War Memorial was a focus of grief following the death in 1997 of Diana, Princess of Wales, when it was covered in floral tributes: an interesting indication – albeit in a different context – of its continued significance for later generations
[17] Gregory, *Silence of Memory*, pp. 61–80
[18] *Manchester Guardian*, 12 November 1937, quoted by Gregory, *Silence of Memory*, p. 84

Interestingly, dinners, dances or other celebrations do not appear to have been held in Colchester on Armistice night. Perhaps the wounds of war were too fresh. To this day, one senses that in Colchester, as in many other military and naval towns, Remembrance Sunday is observed with a special degree of seriousness.

10

The Church of England and the First World War

It is commonly claimed that the Church of England had a 'bad' First World War, and a rather 'better' Second World War. Adrian Hastings, for example, wrote in *A History of English Christianity 1920–2000*:

> There was no genuine religious revival during the [First World] war nor after the war, nor was there a pastoral or theological revival – though these things were sought for, and even claimed to be coming, at the time. The war unleashed bewilderment and hate, and the churches had done very little to help with either. By the end of the war many were sorry enough for the simplistic clerical bellicosity of the early months. What in retrospect did it really matter? Christianity already appeared to have lost the intellectual battle well before the First World War began. What the war did was to shatter its social and political role as well: to unveil the truth to high and low alike of ecclesiastical near-irrelevance.[1]

The First World War historian Michael Snape has observed:

> The war that spawned in the national psyche the sense of a lost generation, an abiding anger at the supposed incompetence of the chateau generals and an ultimate vision of the suffering and futility of war, has also inspired a distinctly negative perception of Anglican army chaplaincy. This perception holds that, while the Church of England acted as a cheerleader for the war, and was thus complicit in wholesale slaughter, the influence of its chaplains on those in uniform was woefully slight … These perceptions, like so much

---

[1]   Hastings, *History of English Christianity*, pp. 47–8

of the popular memory of the First World War, owe far more to literary contrivance than they do to fact.[2]

If it were possible to return to Colchester on the evening of 11 November 1918, and to tell the Anglican clergy and laity – and the tens of thousands of troops who had passed through their churches and parish clubs between 1914–18, or to whom they had ministered in the town's hospitals – that the Church of England had experienced a 'bad' First World War and had become a near-irrelevance, they would have had great difficulty reconciling that claim with their own experience and would simply not have believed it.

How did the idea of the Church of England's 'bad' First World War arise? The Church was not unmindful that the war had laid bare many of its problems and shortcomings, as is evidenced by the *Reports of the Archbishops' Committees of Inquiry* published in 1919. The same year also saw the publication of another report, *The Army and Religion*, which had its origins in a questionnaire submitted to chaplains on the Western Front in 1917. Although *The Army and Religion* contained much interesting research, it was sombre in tone and claimed that 80 per cent of troops were untouched by the Church of England's ministry or teaching.[3]

Any vicar or curate worth his salts in 1918 would already have known that large segments of the English population rarely if ever entered his parish church, or only paid lip service to Christianity; but in truth – and without seeking to deny or minimise the Church of England's considerable failures and mistakes – the situation was less bleak in 1918 than these reports might lead one to imagine. If large sections of the working-class population did not go to church on a regular basis, many other working-class people did. As we have seen in Colchester, church attendance kept up during the war, and the vast majority of people in the pews were working class.

The Reports of the Archbishops' Committees of Inquiry and *The Army and Religion* also neglected to pay sufficient attention to a fundamental

---

[2]   M. Snape, 'Church of England Army Chaplains in the First World War: Goodbye to "Goodbye to All That"', *Journal of Ecclesiastical History* 62/2 (April 2011), 318–45, 318–19

[3]   Alan Wilkinson looks at *The Army and Religion* in detail and examines the flaws in its methodology in his *Church of England*, pp. 160–5

consideration: namely, that no one is born a Christian (let alone, born a member of a particular Church or denomination): Christian faith is a pilgrimage, involving choice, perseverance, suffering and change; and one has to start one's pilgrimage from somewhere. If one has a model of the Church and society in which it is normative for the bulk of the population to be believers and regular churchgoers, the reality is going to fall somewhat short. Such a model of Church and society will inevitably ultimately fail, because it does not take sufficient account of the problems and paradoxes of human life and behaviour, as well as the untidiness (one might even say, messiness) of much Church life, and is predicated upon an over-simplistic understanding of Christianity.

The Anglican clergy and laity of Colchester in 1914–18 were all too aware that lots of their fellow townsfolk were not deeply affected by Christianity, and they sought to do something about it – hence, for instance, the elaborate system of district visitors in the parishes – but this did not mean that they felt themselves to be failures, or believed that their Church was thereby rendered irrelevant.

Post-war Reaction

In the 1920s, most people seem to have wanted to put the First World War behind them and get on with living life.[4] Although the war left hundreds of thousands of ex-soldiers physically or psychologically damaged for life, the majority of men readjusted remarkably well and picked up the threads of civilian life.[5] There was probably a greater continuity with pre-war patterns of daily life than later generations believed.[6] I have shown, for instance, that there appears to have been a return to pre-war sexual morality in Colchester. The same was true of church life. If one looks at parish magazines of the 1920s, they are almost indistinguishable from those of the decade before 1914. Much the same may be said of registers of services from parish churches. It seems probable that men

---

[4] I can recall such views being expressed by my grandparents, and great-aunts and great-uncles, who had participated in, or lived through, the First World War

[5] Gregory, *Silence of Memory*, pp. 51–2

[6] A.J.P. Taylor, *English History, 1914–1945* (Oxford University Press, Oxford, 1992), p. 259, writes about changes in attitude and most probably overstates his case

returning from the war and families coping with bereavement did not want lots of change but craved continuity with what was familiar from the past.

Yet, a country and its people could not endure something as traumatic as the First World War, and simply take up the reins of pre-war life, without undergoing some sort of reaction. There were small signs of a reaction in literature published in the 1920s, and this grew apace from around 1928, when the tenth anniversary of the Armistice led some people to reflect upon the war in the light of their subsequent post-war experiences.

Reaction to the First World War took two principal forms. In the 1920s there arose a widespread, disillusioned, anti-war sentiment; from this evolved pacifism and, later, following the rise of Nazism, support for appeasement. As the anger over Germany's role in starting the war and German wartime atrocities slowly started to fade – and it became known that some (though certainly not all) of the stories of wartime German atrocities in France and Belgium had been invented by Allied propagandists – the public increasingly focused its attention not upon Germany, but upon the war's casualties.[7] The men and women, who, in the 1920s and 1930s looked back to 1914–18 and said, 'Never again', tended sometimes also to look askance at the Church of England, which they saw as having offered uncritical support for the war, and felt was to some extent thereby tainted by association.

War Books

This change in perception was aided by the appearance of a plethora of war books of various sorts. It is a truth of publishing that a book has to sell, and it is in the interests of neither the author nor the publisher to produce one that fails to grip the reader's attention. Just as bad news is said to sell more newspapers, so, unpleasant or highly dramatic accounts and novels of the First World War were believed by writers and publishers to be more likely to sell more copies than even-handed or positive histories and novels. Ian Hay, a soldier from the Western Front-turned-author, complained in a letter to the *Methodist Times* in February 1930:

---

[7]   Gregory, *Last Great War*, p. 270

We are being submerged by a flood of so-called war books which depict the men who fought for us in the last war for the most part as brutes and beasts, living like pigs, and dying like dogs. Some of these books are conceived in dirt and published for the profit dirt will bring. Nobody seems to be able to write on this subject without yielding to this tendency, and even if it is not the intention, it is so interpreted.[8]

Hay may have been led to write his letter by Robert Graves's recent book, *Goodbye to All That*, which was published in November 1929. Graves later freely admitted that he had deliberately 'mixed in all the ingredients that I know are mixed into other popular books', including suicides, murders, ghosts, battles, love affairs, poets, Lawrence of Arabia and the Prince of Wales.[9] Graves's publisher was seeking to capitalise on the success of the German Erich Maria Remarque's very successful novel *All Quiet on the Western Front*, which had appeared earlier in 1929. Graves's motive was similar: he needed to make 'a lump of money' quickly.

Graves is responsible in *Goodbye to All That* for being the first author to claim that Church of England chaplains on the Western Front skulked in safety behind the front line, whilst Roman Catholic chaplains by contrast bravely ministered to the troops in the trenches. This notion was effectively demolished by Michael Snape in an article in the *Journal of Ecclesiastical History* in 2011, in which he suggested that Graves had an animus against the Church of England. By his own account, Graves had begun the First World War as an evangelical Anglican, and ended it 'a complete agnostic'. He later married Nancy Nicholson, a staunch feminist and convinced atheist, and developed an anti-clerical streak.[10] The Church of England and the Army Chaplains' Department took no effective steps to refute Graves's inaccurate assertions, which went on to be widely read and believed to be true.

Another persistent canard, which seems to date from this period, is the claim that Church of England bishops and priests (probably army chaplains) blessed rifles, tanks and artillery. In 1965, for example, A.J.P. Taylor

8   *Methodist Times*, 6 February 1930, quoted by Snape, 'Church of England Army Chaplains', 320
9   Snape, 'Church of England Army Chaplains', 329
10   Robert Graves, *Goodbye to All That*, 2nd edition, pp. 45, 207, 221, 223, and Robert Graves, *But it Still Goes on*, p. 145; quoted by Snape, 'Church of England Army Chaplains', 331

wrote in *English History 1914–1945* – without citing any sources – that 'the sight of priests and bishops blessing guns or tanks during the Great War was not a good advertisement for the gospel of the Prince of Peace', and this story was publicly repeated as recently as 2012 by Dr Susan Williams of the University of London in the Blakeway/Channel 4 television programme *Edward VIII: The Plot to Topple a King*.[11] David Blake, curator of the Museum of Army Chaplaincy, has researched this legend and denies that the blessing of rifles, artillery and tanks ever took place: the nearest thing he could find was a reference to the chaplain general, Bishop John Taylor Smith, pronouncing a blessing during a ceremony to 'christen' a Sopwith Camel aeroplane by Princess Patricia of Connaught in 1918.[12] Of course, one can never state with entire certainty that no chaplain ever said a blessing or made the sign of the Cross over a tank or gun at some point during the war, but it seems pretty unlikely – bishops and chaplains were more likely to bless ambulances or hospitals – and there was certainly no official army provision for blessing guns. Mr Blake speculates that someone may have seen a photograph of a Russian Orthodox bishop blessing some of Tsar Nicholas II's troops during the First World War and muddled this up with the Church of England. What is significant, though, is that this myth was repeated and believed.

Two important background factors need to be borne in mind. First, the appearance of large numbers of wartime books and Graves's remarks about chaplains coincided with a time during the late 1920s and early 1930s when the Church of England was experiencing a period of unpopularity. The Commons' rejection of the 1927 and 1928 Revised Prayer Books had undermined the confidence of many in the Church of England and seen a great deal of Anglican dirty linen washed in public. There was lingering resentment – amongst both Labour and Conservative voters – concerning the role played (or rather, not played) by the Church of England in the 1926 General Strike. The early 1930s saw rural anti-tithe demonstrations, during one of which Archbishop Cosmo Gordon Lang of Canterbury was burnt in effigy. Lastly, the tragi-comic tale of the 1932 conviction and unfrocking of the Rev. Harold Davidson, rector of Stiffkey in Norfolk, for consorting with prostitutes, and his subsequent death in

---

[11]   Taylor, *English History, 1914–1945*, pp. 168–9. Blakeway/Channel 4, *Edward VIII: The Plot to Topple a King*, 9 May 2012
[12]   David Blake to the author, 10 May 2013

1937 from mauling by a circus lion, resulted in a great deal of adverse comment and publicity for the Church of England.

Second, the late 1920s and early 1930s saw the deaths of many people who had occupied important positions during the First World War. Field Marshal Haig died in 1928, widely mourned, with his reputation still intact. In Essex, Bishop Whitcombe died in 1922, Bishop Watts-Ditchfield in 1923 and Canon Brunwin-Hales in 1932. Many laypeople who had been churchwardens in Colchester, or had occupied positions that gave them special knowledge of the Church's wartime role, died around this time. This meant that, by the time that errors, misunderstandings and sometimes falsifications were starting to spread about the Church of England in the First World War, many of the people who might have taken steps to counteract them were either dead or too old to do very much. By the 1930s, positions of authority and influence in Church and state were starting to be occupied by people who had been young during the First World War, and who, for the most part, wanted to look forward to the future, and not back to the sad years of 1914–18.

The Second World War

Attitudes to the First World War and the role played in it by the Church of England evolved further as a result of the Second World War. British public consciousness has proved somewhat fickle in what it remembers about both world wars. The British disasters from 1914–18 – the Somme, Passchendaele and Gallipoli – are well known. The British successes, and not least the final hundred days of the war in 1918, leading to the defeat of the German Army on the Western Front, are much less familiar.

By contrast, Britain's heroic moments from the Second World War – notably Dunkirk, El Alamein and D-Day – are all remembered. In the popular mind, these – together with the Allied ultimate victory – have to some extent overshadowed Britain's wartime disasters: Norway, France, the Western Desert, Greece, Crete, Hong Kong, Burma, Dieppe, Tobruk, Singapore, parts of the Italian and Normandy campaigns, some of the Bomber Offensive and Arnhem.[13] In retrospect, the Second World War came to be seen as a 'good' war, and thus a contrast with the 'bad' First

---

[13] Gregory, *Last Great War*, p. 4

World War. This, of course, is largely because there was not the same high level of British military casualties in the Second World War (though the Second World War was much worse for civilians than the 1914–18 war), but also because the discovery by the Allies in 1945 of Hitler's extermination camps exposed beyond doubt the wickedness of the Nazi regime.[14]

Insofar as the Church of England may be said to have had a 'better' Second World War, it was a more mature Church by 1939, having learnt lessons from 1914–18 (in October 1939, for instance, Archbishop Lang cautioned against bloodthirsty 'patriotic' sermons); conscription from the beginning meant that the Church did not have to help promote the recruitment of volunteers; in Cosmo Gordon Lang and William Temple, the Church of England had two experienced and wise archbishops of Canterbury and York who had lived through the First World War; Bishop Winnington-Ingram had retired in 1939 and there were no bishops like him during the Second World War; and lastly, the feeling that the Second World War had been a 'good' war which overcame an evil Nazi regime that had gassed 6 million Jews (although that was not why

---

[14] One may speculate about other causes of this popular 'Dunkirk and D-Day' perception of the Second World War in late twentieth- and early twenty-first-century Britain. I would suggest that factors included a sense of gratitude in the years immediately after 1945 that Hitler's regime had been vanquished; the exigencies of post-war reconstruction; the Cold War; decolonisation and the social and cultural changes of the 1960s. The impact of cinema and television should not be underestimated, nor the effect of the Americanisation of English-speaking culture: the viewing in Britain of American films set in the Second World War may have led to a slightly different 'take' on the conflict. Scratch the surface, however, and a very different and much sadder British narrative of the Second World War emerges. I can think of two old soldiers I knew well who had served in the Second World War. One had been a prisoner of war of the Japanese, whilst the other had fought at Arnhem. Both were devout Christians and had managed to forgive their former enemies (though they could be pretty scathing about the British 'top brass'), and yet both would quietly weep whenever they spoke about their wartime experiences. Again, there was much disquiet amongst British ex-servicemen that it took until 2013 for a campaign medal to be awarded to those who took part in the Arctic convoys, whilst some survivors of Bomber Command were irritated that they were fobbed-off, as they saw it, with a clasp, rather than a specific medal and felt that this was a slur. I have sometimes encountered elderly parishioners who have been troubled in old age by long-buried memories of the Blitz and other painful wartime experiences. It will be interesting to observe how the popular perception of the Second World War changes over the coming decades. I hope that by the centenary of the Second World War, a more rounded and accurate understanding may have emerged – just as I hope for a more rounded and accurate understanding of the First World War

Britain went to war in 1939) seems somehow in the post-war years to have shed a certain lustre over the Church of England, which had supported Britain's involvement in that war. A mythologised and distorted version of the Second World War may thus be said to have triumphed over a mythologised and distorted version of the First World War.

Post-1945 Interpretations

This vision of a 'good' Second World War and a 'bad' First World War was quite often reflected by writers and television programme makers in the 1960s, whose histories frequently – though not always – viewed the First World War in a negative light: one well-known example was Alan Clark's 1961 book *The Donkeys* (he later revealed that he had invented a conversation between the German generals Hindenberg and Ludendorff, in which Ludendorff was supposed to have described the British troops as 'lions led by donkeys'[15]). The 1964 BBC television series *The Great War*, although it interviewed many survivors of the First World War, was largely made and edited by people who had grown up between the wars, and it reflected the attitudes of that era, rather than those of 1914–18 (not that I should grumble: watching a repeat of *The Great War* with my grandfather, a survivor of 1914–18, first kindled my interest in the First World War). Nearer our own time, a very one-sided and inaccurate view of the war was portrayed in the popular 1989 BBC drama series, *Blackadder Goes Forth*, which is now being used in schools to 'teach' the First World War to a new generation of children.

As far as the Church of England is concerned, it too, has suffered from myths and legends. The 1969 film *Oh! What a Lovely War* contained a scene in which an ineffectual army padre – played by Gerald Sim, who made something of a speciality of playing comic clergymen – conducted a church parade during which parodies of well-known Christian hymns were sung. It was good, entertaining stuff, but it reinforced the Gravesian image of inadequate chaplains, far from the front line, unable to say anything very meaningful to the troops.

[15] I. Trewin, *Alan Clark: The Biography* (Weidenfeld and Nicolson, London, 2009), pp. 182–9

Alan Wilkinson's 1978 book *The Church of England and the First World War* has been criticised by some historians and writers for being too negative about chaplains and the Church of England.[16] Similarly, the 1996 Channel 4 television series *Canterbury Tales*[17] tended for the most part to ignore the Church of England at home – apart from references to recruiting, reprisals and a quotation from Bishop Winnington-Ingram's Advent 1915 sermon (wrongly said to have been preached at a 'mass rally') – and concentrated on chaplains ministering on the Western Front. 'To men who knew the realities of trench warfare,' the programme asserted, 'the comfortable certainties of Edwardian Anglicanism now rang hollow.' One longs to ask what the makers of *Canterbury Tales* thought those certainties were: large stipends, an assured social position and commodious rectories, or belief in the Crucifixion, Resurrection and Atonement? The army chaplains – with the exception of 'Woodbine Willie', the Rev. Geoffrey Studdert Kennedy – were depicted as mostly having nothing in common with the troops to whom they ministered, and tales of them staying in safety behind the front lines, at least for the first part of the war, were once more repeated.

'Pure' History?

As I have studied the impact of the First World War in Colchester and reflected on the way in which we have understood it over the past century, my mind has turned to the quest for the historical Jesus. At various times since the eighteenth century, scholars such as Hermann Reimarus (1694–1768), Ernest Renan (1823–92) and Albert Schweitzer (1875–1965) have sought to write the life of Jesus as though he were an ordinary biographical subject. Scholars engaging in this quest for the historical Jesus – whom they frequently contrast with the Christ of faith – have been impelled by a variety of motives, ranging from an interest in the texts of the New Testament, to a dislike of the miraculous in Christianity and of various elements of religious doctrine and practice. They have usually brought rather a lot of intellectual or emotional 'baggage' with them, and the quest for the historical Jesus has ultimately proved unsuccessful.

[16] Snape, 'Church of England Army Chaplains', 343
[17] Twenty-Twenty Television, *Canterbury Tales*, Channel 4, 19 September 1996

Fascinating though it would be to know more about Jesus the Carpenter from Nazareth, our primary texts, the Epistles and Gospels, were written by Christians who looked back and interpreted events through the lens of their Easter experience of the Risen Lord, and it is impossible to recreate events without that experience.

Like the scholars seeking the historical Jesus, I have similarly wondered whether it might possible to cut through the multiple layers of legend, myth, distortion and misunderstanding, to create a 'pure', objective and over-arching history of the First World War. My conclusion is that, for the most part, it is not.

As the First World War was being fought, it inevitably proved to be highly controversial. Differing contemporary and post-war interpretations of events resulted in differing histories of the war. So, for example, Irishmen from the north and south of Ireland fought alongside one another in the First World War, but came to write very different histories of it afterwards, as a result of the post-war history of Ireland. Or again, the Gallipoli campaign has come to have a particular resonance in Australia and New Zealand – because of its place in the history and development of those countries – despite the fact that more British and French troops were killed or wounded in the Dardanelles than ANZAC forces. We must frankly recognise that there are many different and distinct histories of the First World War, which come together at some points and part company at others. This is nothing to be irritated or confused about: it is, rather, an admission that the First World War is simply too big and complex for a single, objective history of it. 'Pure' history, I must remind myself, is the prerogative of Heaven.

Having said that, there are certainly some areas of our First World War history which might be 'purer' and more objective than they sometimes are. No historian comes to the task of writing history free from inclinations or prejudices, and the best we can do is to try to be aware of them. I, for example, would freely admit to not finding Bishop Watts-Ditchfield of Chelmsford a very congenial character. Conversely, I find myself warming to Canon Brunwin-Hales, who comes across from all that I have read, and heard about him from elderly parishioners who knew him, as a very kind and pastorally effective rector of St Mary-at-the-Walls. In these instances, I must try to avoid depicting Watts-Ditchfield in the worst possible light and bathing Brunwin-Hales in an unnecessarily rosy hue.

The writer of history is also dependent upon sources. I am all too aware that very few letters and diaries from Colchester in 1914–18 have survived, and that in looking at the primary material available to me I see largely only what Mayor Jarmin, Alderman Hunt, Father Behr, Mrs Coats Hutton and others have left behind, and thus to some extent their 'take' on the war. The historian must beware of the danger of filling in the gaps with speculation, although there is nothing wrong with an intelligent guess, so long as you say that is what it is. Of course, the advantage that the writer of history has over Mayor Jarmin, Alderman Hunt, Father Behr or Mrs Coats Hutton is that one has access to a great deal more information than they had at the time. This means that one can see events in their wider context, in a way that was denied to them. It also means that, with a bit of perseverance, reflection and common sense, one can unpick some of the myths, legends, distortions and misrepresentations that have arisen around parts of First World War history, and see what lies behind them. If what emerges is not exactly the 'pure' truth, it is likely to be a lot more accurate than much of what has been repeated and believed, largely without question, over the past century.

The Church of England's 'Mixed' First World War

There undoubtedly were parish clergy and army chaplains who preached bellicose 'patriotic' sermons from time to time during the war, but these were never the majority. Some parish clergy and chaplains failed to cope very well with wartime stress, provided ineffectual leadership, took refuge in drink, or even lost their faith. A few priests – of whom Geoffrey Studdert Kennedy is the most well known – came to exercise very effective wartime ministries. The majority of parish priests and chaplains fell somewhere in the middle, experiencing successes and failures, sharing the sufferings of their people and shouldering their own pains and losses. For the most part, their ministry appears to have been more effective than has long been recognised. In 1970, looking back to his time as a chaplain on the Western Front in 1916–18, Bishop Russell Barry wrote:

> As a senior chaplain I got used to hearing, 'Of course all padres are wash-outs, but we are very fortunate in ours, and I don't know how we could get

on without him.' When that had been said to one in every unit, one began to wonder just who were the washouts.'[18]

In concentrating on chaplains and clergy, many histories of the First World War have neglected the important role of the laity. This book has shown that in Colchester, the laity responded to wartime needs with resourcefulness, imagination and self-sacrifice. There was little sense of Christianity or adherence to the Church of England leaching away during the war; if anything, the opposite was true, with parish churches providing pastoral care and structures which could successfully be adapted to meet wartime needs and circumstances. The picture that emerges from Colchester is of the Church of England having neither a good, nor a bad First World War, but a mixed war.

Never the Same after 1918?

One of the popular myths about the Church of England and the First World War is that things were never the same after 1918. The evidence from Colchester does not support this view. The war undoubtedly did lead to changes in the Church of England, such as the 1919 Enabling Act, the establishment of the Church Assembly, compulsory parochial church councils, and liturgical changes, but perhaps only the latter affected ordinary Anglicans. In most churches in Colchester, patterns of parish worship – with Mattins and a sermon as the principal Sunday liturgical expression of Anglicanism – remained largely unchanged for a further forty or fifty years.

From the perspective of the early twenty-first century, the last half-century appears to have been one of growing secularisation in English society; though secularisation itself is the subject of much debate and controversy amongst scholars and writers. The causes of secularisation are many, complex and varied; one's view of secularisation depends upon what one expects the normative expression of religion to be. Common sense suggests that the First World War must have played a part in secularisation, but it is not exactly easy to pin down what it was. It may be that, over the years, the retrospective perception of the war may have been

[18]   F.R. Barry, *Period of my Life* (Hodder and Stoughton, London, 1970), pp. 60–1

as powerful as the reality of the war: if you think the Church of England was complicit in a cruel and unnecessary war, you may find it hard to take it seriously when the same Church seeks to preach the Gospel to you.

As I have said, the Church of England was faced with many serious problems by the time of the Armistice in 1918, but the situation was far from bleak. Although the parochial clergy and many laity were exhausted, they were not broken. Some people lost their faith during the war, but others came to faith, or deepened their belief.[19] Rituals of remembrance after the war came to provide an important link between many people and the Church. A large number of officers and soldiers developed vocations to ordination: by November 1918, over 2,700 names of service ordination candidates had been sent to the Chaplains' Department, and shortly after the Armistice a School of Instruction for 250 ordination candidates was established at Le Touquet and another in 1919 at Knutsford.[20] The number of Easter communicants continued to rise after the Armistice, peaking in 1927.

Looking at the example of Colchester – and bearing in mind that the situation was possibly different elsewhere – it may reasonably be concluded that the role played by the First World War in secularisation was not so much the impact of the war upon the Church as its impact upon the wider society in which that Church was located. Colchester's society in 1914 was very class conscious and hierarchical. The Church of England was woven into the very fabric of this society. Colchester's social elite supported the parish churches in many ways; for example, by frequently providing the churchwardens. The clergy were part of the social elite, but ministered to everyone. Parish churches attracted congregations from all strata of the town's society and provided an important environment where all classes might meet and cooperate in a common purpose and Christian faith. Following pre-war precedent, church work in wartime to help the troops or further the war effort was generally led by the social elite and supported by the rest of the parishioners; it proved to be quite successful.

One impact of the First World War was the dissolution of this hierarchical and class-bound society. At first this change was gradual:

---

[19] Van Emden and Humphries, *All Quiet on the Home Front*, pp. 110–11
[20] Wilkinson, *Church of England*, pp. 277–8. During the next three years 675 service candidates trained at Knutsford, of whom 435 proceeded to ordination

Colchester in the 1920s and 1930s was still a class conscious town, though not to the same extent as prior to 1914. The dissolution of Colchester's class-conscious society accelerated after the Second World War, and in particular after the 1960s. After 1945, Colchester's social elite no longer had the money – assuming they still had the sense of noblesse oblige – to aid the poor, and the nation now thought of itself as a 'Welfare State'. Colchester also grew in size.

What seems to have happened is that, as the fabric of Colchester's close-knit, inter-dependent society came apart, the Church of England was separated and came to occupy a peripheral position, instead of being an element woven amongst the strands as hitherto. Henceforth, one would have to take more of a conscious decision to opt into parish life than had been the case for previous generations.

The aim of this book has been to reconstruct and to understand the impact of the First World War upon the parish churches of Colchester, and to examine how those churches responded to the unparalleled circumstances of the world crisis of 1914–18. Parish life in many ways reflects and is moulded by the nature of the society in which a church is set. The parish churches of Colchester in 1914–18 were part of a stable and cohesive society with an existing tradition of charitable works, organised along class lines, which proved capable of being adapted to meet wartime needs and conditions. Crucially, the population was large enough to contain a wide variety of human resources and also small enough to make anonymity difficult. Members of the social elite felt obliged to take the lead in wartime good works and could not get away – had they wanted to – with the sort of licentious behaviour which was so noticeable amongst the 'leisured classes' in the West End of London during the First World War.[21] By 1914 compulsory elementary education meant that the bulk of the town's population were better equipped to follow the example of wartime good works set by the town's social elite. Parish life was also centred to a very great extent on parochial branches of national organisations such as the CEMS, and these provided structures which could be well adapted to support the war effort and to meet pastoral needs.

The thread running through much of the wartime experience of Colchester's parishes was the presence of the army in the shape of

---

[21]   Marwick, *The Deluge*, pp. 240ff

hundreds of thousands of troops in training, many thousands of wounded soldiers in the military hospitals, and a high proportion of families with relatives at the front. This affected the wartime work and experience of clergy and laity alike. It also seems to have had a bearing upon thoughts and attitudes, most notably concerning the enemy and reprisals.

The one area where the presence of the garrison did not have much of an overt impact was the 1916 National Mission of Repentance and Hope because separate arrangements were made for the troops. The national mission was a remarkable and not unsuccessful attempt by clergy and laity from all parishes, under the very difficult circumstances of the war, to work together to bring the comfort and challenge of the Gospel to the town's population. The national mission is also symbolic of another feature of parish life in Colchester in 1914–18: namely, that differences of Anglican churchmanship were apparently not a serious problem. Admittedly, there was not such a broad range of liturgical or doctrinal diversity as was to arise in the Church of England later in the twentieth century, but the ritualistic controversies of previous generations were no longer of such significance. The pre-war pattern of the clergy not interfering or criticising their neighbours continued, and the existing tradition of common action for certain purposes was intensified by the war, which greatly expanded the scope for mutual cooperation.

Later generations might question the support afforded to the war by the clergy and parishioners of 1914–18, and they might wonder why the people did not do more to challenge the policy of trench warfare, but such questions stem from hindsight and are perhaps not entirely fair. In conclusion, the parish churches of Colchester may be said to have responded to the crisis of 1914–18 with resourcefulness, compassion and hard work. At a parochial level, the Church of England fared significantly better during the First World War than has been understood or acknowledged for much of the past century.

Although many memorials to the dead of the First World War were erected throughout Colchester in the years after the Armistice, no monuments were set up to record the unique wartime work of the twenty-six priests and thousands of laymen and laywomen of Colchester's Anglican parishes. The sole exception is a very simple plaque at the bottom of the war memorial in Holy Trinity Church, which quietly bears witness to the daily outpouring of prayer, hope, grief and pain that occurred in that church throughout the war:

> No day passed from August 1914 to November 1918
> but Intercessions were offered up in this Church,
> and the fact is here placed on record.

Bibliography

Unpublished Primary Sources

Balliol College, Oxford

Correspondence concerning patronage in Colchester, 1893–1947 (10 volumes)

Mrs Sarah Bradley

Papers of the Right Reverend Dr R.H. Whitcombe, Bishop of Colchester, 1909–22

Colchester Cemetery and Crematorium

Borough of Colchester Burial Registers, 1914–18

Colchester Library, Local Studies Department (CL)

E.Col.1.920: Collection of local material compiled by A.M. Jarmin during his mayoralty of Colchester, 1917–18
E.Col.1.940.3: Two boxes of local material, labelled 'World War 1'
Box 1
E.Col.1.940.3: Colchester Emergency Committee, 'Instructions to Inhabitants, 1915'
E.Col.1.940.3: Letters from Mayor of Colchester and Ministry of National Service, 1918
E.Col.1.940.3: Food Control Campaign, 1917
E.Col.1.940.3: Air Raids, Notices, 1917
E.Col.1.940.3: Registration Forms and Cards, 1915–1917
Box 2
E.Col.1.940.3: Accounts, War Kitchen, St Mary Magdalen Parish Hall
E.Col.1.940.3: Order of Service. 'The Fourth Anniversary of the War. Colchester Citizens' Commemorative Service', 4 August 1918

E.Col.1.940.3: Colchester Food Economy Committee posters, December 1917
E.Col.1.264: Order of Service. 'War Memorial. Unveiling and Dedication of the Monument, etc.', 24 May 1923
E.Col.1.940.3: 'Order of Service for the Celebration of Peace', 6 July 1919
E.Col.1.940.3: Colchester Ration Books Belonging to the Blaxhill Family, 1918–19
E.Col.1.940.3: Colchester Emergency Committee, 'General Instructions to the Inhabitants of Colchester in Case of Invasion' (revised instructions)

Essex Record Office, Chelmsford (ERO)

All Saints', Colchester
D/P 200/8/6: Vestry Minutes, 1910–21
D/P 200/1/29: Register of Services, 1905–15
D/P 200/1/30: Register of Services, 1919–24

St Barnabas's
Acc. C817 (uncat.): Register of Services, 1904–28

St Botolph's
D/P 203/1/33: Register of Services, 1908–15
D/P 203/8/5: Minutes of Easter Vestries and Annual Parochial Church Meetings, 1855–1985

St Giles's
D/P 324/8/2: Vestry Minutes, 1867–1936

Holy Trinity
D/P 323/8/2: Vestry Minutes, 1859–1951

St James's
D/P 138/1/31: Register of Services, 1917–25, including newspaper cutting re. funeral of the Rev. C.C. Naters
D/P 138/1/46: Service sheet for the deposition of the Roll of Honour for those who fell during the Great War, 1925

St Leonard-at-the-Hythe
D/P 245/1/36: Register of Services, 1911–15
D/P 245/1/37: Register of Services, 1915–20
D/P 245/29/1: Minutes of Vestry Meetings, 1881–1945, and of Parochial Church Council Meetings and Annual Parochial Meetings, 1920–45

St Martin's
D/P 325/8/3: Vestry Minutes, 1895–1952

St Mary-at-the-Walls

D/P 246/1/52: Register of Services, 1907–17
D/P 246/1/53: Register of Services, 1917–28
D/P 246/6/18: Faculty for the adaptation of chapel on S. side of church for use as a war memorial (the Warriors' Chapel), 1921

St Nicholas's

D/P 176/1/19: Official Parochial Register and Register of Services, 1908–23
D/P 176/3/2: Accounts of fees and other income, etc., 1913–28, including War Service, 1917–18; prisoner in Germany, 1916–18
D/P 176/28/3: S. Nicholas and S. Runwald Record of the Great War 1914–18
D/P 176/28/4: Minutes of Parochial Church Council, 1920–29

St Peter's

D/P 178/1/35: Register of Services, 1906–18
D/P 178/1/36: Register of Services, 1918–28
D/P 178/8/2: Vestry Minutes, 1837–1917
D/P 178/29/1 Minutes of Parochial Church Council

Berechurch, St Michael's

D/P 199/1/13: Register of Services, 1913–51
D/P 199/29/1: Vestry Minutes, 1914–37

St Leonard's, Lexden

D/P 273/1/26: Register of Services, 1906–29
D/P 272/8/2: Vestry Minutes, 1856–1947

St Andrew's, Greenstead-juxta-Colchester

D/P 399/1/24: Register of Services, 1911–28

St Michael's, Mile End

D/P 410/1/24: Register of Services, 1916–26
D/P 410/8/4: Vestry Minutes, 1892–1922
D/P 410/28/26: Postcard receipts for food parcels despatched by Essex Regiment Prisoners of War Fund
D/P 410/28/27: England's Heroes from Mile End. *c.*1920

St John the Evangelist

D/P 525/1/7: Register of Services, 1911–18
D/P 525/8/1: Vestry Minutes, 1878–1917

All Saints', Stanway (Shrub End)

D/P 548/1/13: Register of Services, 1899–1917
D/P 548/1/14: Register of Services, 1917–27

St Paul's

D/P 551/1/13: Register of Services, 1909–16

D/P 551/1/14: Register of Services, 1916–25

D/P 551 8/2: Easter Vestry and Annual Church Meeting Minutes, 1912–48

D/P 551/28/2: Parish copies of incumbent's annual 'Statistical Return of Parochial Work', 1906–7 and 1916–17

D/P 551/29/1: Minutes of Church Council, 1913–54

Chelmsford Diocesan Archives

D/CAf 1/1,2: Diocesan Board of Finance, minutes and reports, 1912–21

D/CAf 1/11–14: Diocesan Board of Finance, Letter Books, 1914–22

D/CAf 2/1,2: Finance and General Purposes Committee, minutes, 1913–22

D/CAf 3/1: Maintenance Committee, minutes, 1914–39

D/CAf 4/1: Church Building Committee, minutes, 1914–36

D/CAf 7/1: Deanery ledger, 1914–18

D/CAf 8: Cash Book, 1914–26

D/CAf 10/1–10: Annual Summaries of Church Work and Finance in the Diocese of St Albans and of Chelmsford, 1912–21

D/CV 2/2: Episcopal Visitation of Colchester Archdeaconry, 1911

D/CV 3/2: Episcopal Visitation of Colchester Archdeaconry, 1920

Acc. A8009(pt): Scrap book, 1911–26

Acc. A7632 Boxes 54–6: Muniment Books, 1914–

Acc. A7632 Box 59 (pt): St Albans and Chelmsford Church Trust Committee Minutes, 1913–

Postcard Collection

Col. Gen. 12: Air raid on Colchester, bomb craters, officers' inspection of debris, wrecked sheds, 1915

Miscellaneous

C4: Colchester Borough Council newscuttings collection, vols 1913–16, 1916–18

D/Z 77/1-2: Unett, J.A., Essex Special Constabulary, Colchester Division orders, reports and letters

Acc. C4 (pt): Colchester Borough Council Emergency Committee minutes, 1914–15

D/Du 689/15: Printed circulars including instruction for evacuation of Colchester, blackout, air raids, etc., 1915–18

D/E 4/3: Colchester Deanery Chapter Minutes, 1886–1933

Acc. C948: Annual Reports and Committee Minutes, Borough of Colchester Social Club for the Troops

Acc. C246 Box 1: Annual Reports, Colchester Borough Medical Officer of Health, 1913–20

Acc. C4 (part): Borough and Port Health Committee Minutes, 1914–18

Acc. C4: Borough of Colchester Council-in-Committee Minutes, 1890–1923 (4 vols)

C32 AMS 31: Annual Reports of the Colchester Clerical Society, 1914–19

Acc. A13528: Diaries of the Right Rev. J.E. Watts-Ditchfield, 1897–1917

Imperial War Museums, London (IWM)

08/87/1: Papers of W. Deasy

02/43/1: Papers of G.R. Wilkinson

08/36/1: Papers of E.W.S. Bailey

Lambeth Palace Library, London (LPL)

Davidson Papers

Lang Papers

National Army Museum, London (NAM)

1996-12-9-3: Papers of Lieutenant Perry Vaughan Morgan

2004-08-84-17: Correspondence of Driver R. Burdett

1982-10-23-1: Papers of RQMS George Kendall

1978-08-80-1: Memoirs of Bandsman Victor Shawyer

1977-04-61-2: Photograph collection of Captain Thomas Haworth Preston

The Royal Archives, Windsor (RA)

GV/PRIV/GVD: Diaries of King George V

PS/P50/PS/WAR/QQ5/4191/22.6.1916: Inspection on the Clacton Peninsula, 22 June 1916

PS/PSO/GV/PS/WAR/QQ5/4191/NARRATIVE: Narrative of events during inspection by H.M. The King in Essex

PS/PSO/GV/PS/WAR/QQ5/5117/DECORATIONS: 66th (East Lancashire) Division. List of Decorations awarded to Officers and Other Ranks not yet presented. 19 February 1917

PS/PSO/GV/PS/WAR/QQ5/5117/20.2.17: Special Order No. 2, 20 February 1917

PS/PSO/GV/PS/WAR/QQ5/5117/22.2.17 Memo from Lord Wigram to the Master of the Household, 22 February, 1917

Published Primary Sources

Government Reports

General Register Office, *Report of the Registrar General*, 1913–1919 (HMSO, London, 1915–20)
—— *Registrar General's Statistical Review of England and Wales*, 1920 and 1921 (HMSO, London, 1922 and 1923)
Office of Population Censuses and Surveys, *Birth Statistics, Historical Series FM1, No. 13* (HMSO, London, 1987)

Newspapers and Periodicals

The Church Union
The English Church Union Gazette, 1916

Colchester Library, Local Studies Department (CL)
Essex County Standard newspaper, 1913–21
Colchester Gazette newspaper, 1914–19
Essex County Telegraph newspaper, 1917 (part)
Holy Trinity Parish Magazine, 1911–20
Benham's Almanack and Directory of Colchester, 1912–19 (8 vols)
Cullingford's Annual, 1914

Chelmsford Cathedral, Knightsbridge Library
Chelmsford Diocesan Chronicle, 1915–20

Essex Archaeological Society Library, Holly Trees House Museum, Colchester
St Mary-at-the-Walls Parish Magazine, 1917

Essex Record Office (ERO)
D/P 246/28/31: St Mary-at-the-Walls monthly parish magazine bound with copies of the monthly periodicals *The Kingdom* and *The Living Church*, 1914
D/P 246/28/32–6: St Mary-at-the-Walls monthly parish magazine bound with copies of the monthly periodical *The Sign*, 1915, 1916, 1918, 1919, 1920

Lambeth Palace Library, London (LPL)
Crockford's Clerical Directory, 1914–20
English Church Union, *Religious Ministrations in the Army, Report of the Proceedings of a Meeting of the English Church Union held in the Hoare Memorial Hall at the Church House, Westminster, on Wednesday, February 23rd, 1916* (English Church Union, London, 1916)

The Reverend Canon Robin Wilson
St Peter's Parish Magazine, 1913–20

The Reverend Kevan Tailby
St Botolph's Colchester Parish Magazine, 1914–1921

Miss Betty Nicholls
Lexden Parish Magazine, April 1917, January 1918

Diaries, Memoirs and Addresses

Barry, F.R., *Period of My Life* (Hodder and Stoughton, London, 1970)

Bickersteth, J., ed., *The Bickersteth Diaries* (Leo Cooper, London, 1996)

Close, F. *The Restoration of the Churches is the Restoration of Popery: Proved and Illustrated from the Authenticated Publications of the 'Cambridge Camden Society': A Sermon Preached in the Parish Church, Cheltenham, on Tuesday, 5 November, 1844* (J. Hatchard and Son, London, 1844)

—— *The Roman Anti-Christ, a 'Lying Spirit': Being the Substance of a Sermon Preached in the Parish Church, Cheltenham, November the 5th, 1845* (J. Hatchard and Son, London, 1845)

—— *Semper Idem; or Popery Everywhere and Always the Same: A Sermon Preached in the Parish Church, Cheltenham, November 5th, 1851* (J. Hatchard and Son, London, 1851)

—— *'The Catholic Revival', or, Ritualism and Romanism in the Church of England* (Hatchard and Co, London, 1866)

Cowan, R., ed., *War Diaries, A Nurse at the Front: The First World War Diaries of Sister Edith Appleton* (Simon and Schuster, London, 2012)

Hankey, D., *A Student in Arms* (Andrew Melrose, London, 1916)

Lloyd George, D., *War Memoirs of David Lloyd George* (Odhams Press, London, 1936)

Matthews, W.R., *Memories and Meanings* (Hodder and Stoughton, London, 1969)

Mason, A.J., *Memoir of George Howard Wilkinson, Bishop of St Andrews* (Longmans and Co., London, 1909)

Munson, J., ed., *Echoes of the Great War: The Diary of the Reverend Andrew Clark, 1914–1919* (Oxford University Press, Oxford, 1985)

Sheffield, G. and J. Bourne, *Douglas Haig: War Diaries and Letters 1914–1918* (Weidenfeld and Nicolson, London, 2005)

Snape, M., ed., *The Back Parts of War: The YMCA Memoirs and Letters of Barclay Baron, 1915–1919* (The Boydell Press, Woodbridge, 2009)

Watts-Ditchfield, J.E., *Reservation: Addresses by the Bishop of Oxford, the Right Rev. Charles Gore, DD, and the Bishop of the Diocese, the Right Rev. J.E.*

Watts-Ditchfield, DD, to the Clergy of the Diocese of Chelmsford, together with a Series of Questions and Answers (Robert Scott, London, 1917)

Winnington-Ingram, A.F., *Good Shepherds* (Wells Gardner, Darton and Co., London, 1904)

—— *The Potter and the Clay* (The Young Churchman Co., Milwaukee, 1917)

Secondary Sources

Published Books and Articles

Anderson, O., 'The Growth of Christian Militarism in Mid-Victorian Britain', *English Historical Review* 86 (January 1971), 46–72

Anson, P.F., *The Call of the Cloister: Religious Communities and Kindred Bodies in the Anglican Communion* (SPCK, London, 1955)

Arthur, M., *Forgotten Voices of the Great War* (Ebury Press, London, 2002)

Bainton, R.H., *Christian Attitudes Toward War and Peace: A Historical Survey and Critical Re-Evaluation* (Abingdon Press, Nashville, 1960)

—— 'Bishop A.F. Winnington-Ingram', *Theology* 74 (1971), 32–3

Baynes, J., *Far from a Donkey: The Life of General Sir Ivor Maxse* (Brassey's, London, 1995)

Beaken, R.W.F., *Reverence My Sanctuary* (Taverner Publications, East Harling, 2007)

—— *God's Gifts for God's People: Reservation of the Blessed Sacrament* (The Fitzwalter Press, East Harling, 2009)

—— *Cosmo Lang: Archbishop in War and Crisis* (Tauris, London, 2012)

Beeson, T., *The Bishops* (SCM Press, London, 2002)

Bell, G.K.A., *Randall Davidson, Archbishop of Canterbury* (Oxford University Press, Oxford, 1935)

Bell, S., 'The Church and the First World War', *God and War: The Church of England and Armed Conflict in the Twentieth Century*, ed. S.G. Parker and T. Lawson (Ashgate, Farnham, 2012), pp. 33–60

—— 'Malign or Maligned? – Arthur Winnington-Ingram, Bishop of London, in the First World War', *Journal for the History of Modern Theology/Zeitschrift für Neuere Theologiegeschichte* 20/1 (November 2013), 117–33

Bicknell, E.J., *A Theological Introduction to the Thirty-Nine Articles of the Church of England* (Longmans, Green, London, 1955)

Brown, A., *Colchester, 1815–1914* (Essex Record Office, Chelmsford, 1980)

Carpenter, S.C., *Winnington-Ingram* (Hodder and Stoughton, London, 1949)

Chadwick, O., *The Victorian Church, Part Two, 1860–1901* (SCM Press, London, 1987)

Church of England Board of Education, *All Are Called: Towards a Theology of the Laity* (Church Information Office, London, 1985)

Cockerill, C. and D. Woodhead, *Colchester as a Military Centre* (Essex County Council, Chelmsford, 1978)

Corrigan, G., *Mud, Blood and Poppycock* (Cassell, London, 2003)

Cox, J., *The English Churches in a Secular Society, Lambeth 1870–1930* (Oxford University Press, Oxford, 1992)

Crofton, E., *Angels of Mercy: A Women's Hospital on the Western Front 1914–1918* (Birlinn, Edinburgh, 2013)

Davey Biggs, C.R., *Russia and Reunion: A Translation of Wilbois' 'L'Avenir de l'Eglise Russe'* (A.R. Mowbray and Co., London, 1908)

Davies, H., *Worship and Theology in England: From Newman to Martineau* (Oxford University Press, Oxford, 1962)

—— *The Ecumenical Century, from 1900 to the Present* (Erdmans, Michigan, 1996)

Davis, C.M., *Orthodox London: Or, Phases of Religious Life in the Church of England* (Tinsley Brothers, London, 1876)

Van Emden, R. and S. Humphries, *All Quiet on the Home Front: An Oral History of Life in Britain during the First World War* (Headline, London, 2003)

Elrington, C.R., ed., *The Victoria County History of Essex, Volume 9* (Oxford University Press, Oxford, 1994)

Foley, M., *Essex in the First World War* (The History Press, Stroud, 2009)

Foster, J., *Alumni Oxonienses, 1715–1886* (Parker and Co., Oxford, 1888)

Gilbert, M., *First World War* (HarperCollins, London, 1994)

Gore, J., *The Life of Mary Maxse* (Rolls House, London, 1949)

Gowing, E.N., *John Edwin Watts-Ditchfield, First Bishop of Chelmsford* (Hodder and Stoughton, London, 1926)

Gray, D., *Earth and Altar* (Canterbury Press, Norwich, 1986)

Gregory, A., *The Last Great War: British Society and the First World War* (Cambridge University Press, Cambridge, 2008)

—— *The Silence of Memory: Armistice Day, 1919–1946* (Berg, Oxford, 1994)

Greenwood, R., *Transforming Priesthood: A New Theology of Mission and Ministry* (SPCK, London, 1995)

De Groot, G.J., *Blighty: British Society in the Era of the Great War* (Longmans, London, 1996)

Harris, C., 'The Communion of the Sick', *Liturgy and Worship: A Companion to the Prayer Books of the Anglican Communion*, ed. W.K. Lowther Clarke and C. Harris (SPCK, London, 1936), pp. 541–615

Hart, P., *1918, A Very British Victory* (Phoenix, London, 2009)

Hastings, A., *A History of English Christianity, 1920–2000* (SCM Press, London, 2001)

Hawker, R., *Four Sermons on Particular Occasions* (T. Williams, London, 1804)

Hayward, J., *Myths and Legends of the First World War* (The History Press, Stroud, 2010)

Hewitt, G., *A History of the Diocese of Chelmsford* (Diocese of Chelmsford, Chelmsford, 1984)

Horne, J. and A. Kramer, *German Atrocities 1914: A History of Denial* (Yale University Press, New Haven, CT, and London, 2001)

Hughes, A., *The Rivers of the Flood: A Personal Account of the Catholic Revival in England in the Twentieth Century* (Faith Press, London, 1961)

Hunt, E.A., ed., *Colchester War Memorial Souvenir* (Essex Telegraph, Colchester, 1923)

Iremonger, F.A., *William Temple, Archbishop of Canterbury* (Oxford University Press, Oxford, 1949)

Jackson, J., *Family at War: The Foljambe Family and the Great War* (Haynes Publishing, Sparkford, 2010)

Johnson, D.E., 'The Essex Spy who Got Away', *Essex Countryside* 201 (October 1973), 39

Kent, J., *Holding the Fort: Studies in Victorian Revivalism* (Epworth Press, London, 1978)

King, A., *Memorials of the Great War in Britain: The Symbolism and Politics of Remembrance* (Berg, Oxford, 1998)

Lang, C.G., *The Opportunity of the Church of England: Lectures Delivered in the Divinity School of the University of Cambridge in 1904* (Longmans, Green, London, 1905)

Lloyd, R., *The Church of England, 1900–1965* (SCM Press, London, 1966)

Lockhart, J.G., *Cosmo Gordon Lang* (Hodder and Stoughton, London, 1949)

Lomax, S., *The Home Front: Sheffield in the First World War* (Pen and Sword Books, Barnsley, 2014)

MacCulloch, D., 'The Myth of the English Reformation', *Journal of British Studies* 30 (1991), 1–19.

McMillan, J., 'War', *Political Violence in Twentieth Century Europe*, ed. D. Bloxham and R. Gerwarth (Cambridge University Press, Cambridge, 2011), pp. 40–86

Madigan, E., *Faith under Fire: Anglican Army Chaplains and the Great War* (Palgrave Macmillan, Basingstoke, 2011)

Marrin, A., *The Last Crusade: The Church of England and the First World War* (Duke University Press, Durham, NC, 1974)

Martin, G., *The Story of Colchester from Roman Times to the Present Day* (Benham Newspapers, Colchester, 1959)

Marwick, A., *The Deluge: British Society and the First World War* (Macmillan, London, 1991)

Massie, R.K., *Dreadnought: Britain, Germany, and the Coming of the Great War* (Random House, New York, 1991)

Mears, N., A. Raffe, S. Taylor, P. Williamson and L. Bates, eds, *National Prayers: Special Worship since the Reformation, Volume 1* (Church of England Record Society, The Boydell Press, Woodbridge, 2013)

Moorhouse, G., *Hell's Foundations: A Town, its Myths and Gallipoli* (Hodder and Stoughton, London, 1992)

Moorman, J.R.H., *The Anglican Spiritual Tradition* (Darton, Longman and Todd, London 1983)

Morris, J., *Religion and Urban Change: Croydon 1840–1914* (Royal History Society, London, 1992)

Neil, C. and J.M. Willoughby, eds, *The Tutorial Prayer Book, for the Teacher, the Student, and the General Reader* (Harrison Trust, London, 1912)

Neillands, R., *The Great War Generals on the Western Front 1914–1918* (Robinson Publishing, London, 1999)

Nockles, P.B., *The Oxford Movement in Context* (Cambridge University Press, Cambridge, 1994)

Paul, L., *The Deployment and Payment of the Clergy* (Church Information Office, London, 1964)

Penfold, J.B., *The History of the Essex County Hospital, Colchester (formerly the Essex and Colchester Hospital), 1820–1945* (Lavenham Press, Lavenham, 1984)

Phillips, A., *Colchester: A History* (Phillimore, Stroud, 2004)

—— *Colchester in Old Photographs* (Alan Sutton Publishing, Stroud, 1996)

—— 'Four Colchester Elections', in *An Essex Tribute*, ed. K. Neale (Leopard's Head Press, London, 1987), pp. 199–227

Pinnington, J., *Anglicans and Orthodox, Unity and Subversion, 1559–1725* (Gracewing, Leominster, 2003)

Playne, C.E., *Society at War, 1914–1916* (Allen and Unwin, London, 1931)

Pullan, L., 'Prayer Book Revision: The Absurdities and Dangers of the Convocation Proposals', *All Saints' Margaret Street Church and Parish Paper*, 25/329 (March 1911), 53–57

Randolph, B.W., ed., *Spiritual Letters of Edward King, DD, Late Lord Bishop of Lincoln* (A.R. Mowbray and Co. Ltd, London, 1910)

Reynolds, D., *The Long Shadow: The Great War and the Twentieth Century* (Simon and Schuster, London, 2013)

Rimell, R.L., *Zeppelin! A Battle for Air Supremacy in World War 1* (Conway, London, 1984)

Robbins, K., *England, Ireland, Scotland and Wales: The Christian Church 1900–2000* (Oxford University Press, Oxford, 2008)

Rusiecki, P., *The Impact of Catastrophe: The People of Essex and the First World War (1914–1920)* (Essex Record Office, Chelmsford, 2008)

Sadler, J. and R. Serdiville, *Tommy at War, 1914–1918: The Soldiers' own Stories* (The Robson Press, London, 2013)

Sheffield, G., *The Chief: Douglas Haig and the British Army* (Aurum Press, London, 2011)

—— *The Great War, 1914–1918: The Story of the Western Front* (SevenOaks, London, 2014)

Shipley, O., *The Church and the World* (Longmans, Green, Reader and Dyer, London, 1867 and 1868)

Snape, M., *God and the British Soldier: Religion and the British Army in the First and Second World Wars* (Routledge, London, 2005)

—— 'Archbishop Davidson's Visit to the Western Front, May 1916', *From the Reformation to the Permissive Society: A Miscellany in Celebration of the 400th Anniversary of Lambeth Palace Library*, ed. M. Barber, S. Taylor and G. Sewell (The Boydell Press, Woodbridge, 2010)

—— 'Church of England Army Chaplains in the First World War: Goodbye to "Goodbye to All That"', *Journal of Ecclesiastical History* 62/2 (April 2011), 318–45

Snape, M. and E. Madigan, eds, *The Clergy in Khaki: New Perspectives on British Army Chaplaincy in the First World War* (Ashgate, Farnham, 2013)

Souhami, D., *Edith Cavell* (Quercus, London, 2011)

Stallion, M.R., *Our Duty Has Been Done: A Record of Colchester Borough Police 1836–1947* (published privately by M.R. Stallion, Braintree, 2012)

Stearn, R.T., 'Unknown Warrior, the (d. 1914?)', *The Oxford Dictionary of National Biography* (Oxford University Press, Oxford, 2004)

Stone, J., 'Colchester', *Garrison: Ten British Military Towns*, ed. P. Dietz (Brassey's, London, 1986), pp. 3–22

Taylor, A.J.P., *English History, 1914–1945* (Oxford University Press, Oxford, 1992)

Taylor, R., and Lloyd, C., *A Century of the East End: Events, People and Places over the Last 100 Years* (Sutton Publishing, Stroud, 1999)

Terraine, J., *Impacts of War, 1914 and 1918* (Hutchinson, London, 1970)

Thompson, D.M., 'War, the Nation, and the Kingdom of God: The Origins of the National Mission of Repentance and Hope, 1915–16', *The Church and War*, ed. W.J. Shiels, Studies in Church History 20 (Ecclesiastical History Society, London, 1983), pp. 337–50

Tombs, R.. and E. Chabal, *Britain and France in Two World Wars: Truth, Myth and Memory* (Bloomsbury, London, 2013)

Trewin, I., *Alan Clark: The Biography* (Weidenfeld and Nicolson, London, 2009)

Venn, J.A., *Alumni Cantabrigienses, 1752–1900* (Cambridge University Press, Cambridge, 1951)

Voll, D., *Catholic Evangelicalism* (Faith Press, London, 1963)

Weber, E., *Peasants into Frenchmen* (Stanford University Press, Stanford, CA, 1976)

Wilkinson, A., 'Searching for Meaning in Time of War: Theological Themes in First World War Literature,' *The Modern Churchman* 2 (1985), 13–21

—— 'Christ in No-Man's Land', *Church Times*, 4 November 1988

—— *The Community of the Resurrection* (SCM Press, London, 1992)

—— *The Church of England and the First World War* (SCM Press, London, 1996)

—— 'Changing English Attitudes to Death in the Two World Wars', *The Changing Face of Death, Historical Accounts of Death and Disposal*, ed. P.C. Jupp and G. Howarth (Macmillan, London, 1997)

Williams, S., *Religious Belief and Popular Culture in Southwark, 1880–1939* (Oxford University Press, Oxford, 1999)

Williamson, P., 'National Days of Prayer: The Churches, the State and Public Worship in Britain, 1899–1957', *English Historical Review*, 128/531 (April 2013), 323–66

Winter, J.M., *The Great War and the British People* (Macmillan, London, 1987)

Wolfe, J., *God and Greater Britain: Religion and National Life in Britain and Ireland 1843–1945* (Routledge, London, 1994)

Interviews

The Rev. Victor Allard, Shepshed, 3 January 2000

Mr Jack Ashton, Copford, 10 February 1998

Miss Mary Beattie, Colchester, 1 February 1999

The Rev. Paul Davis, Colchester, 20 December 1998

Mr Geoffrey Dearmer, London, 6 October 1984

Mrs Alice Hicks, Colchester, 18 March 1998

Mr Andrew Phillips, Colchester, 18 May 2000

Mrs Dolly Thimblethorpe, Colchester, 7 January 1998, 16 March 1998

The Rev. Canon Robin Wilson, Colchester, 17 December 1998

Sound Recordings

Albert Sloman Library, University of Essex

2130: Mrs Emma Rehberger (née Jarmin)

Imperial War Museums, London (IWM)

7376: Mrs Parker Bird, VAD Nurse at Colchester Military Hospital

563: Joseph Price, NCO, 12th Battalion, the Middlesex Regiment

National Army Museum, London (NAM)

1989-12-47-1: Trooper John Brett

Theses

Fielden, K.C., 'The Church of England in the First World War' (East Tennessee State University MA thesis, 2005)

Mews, S., 'Religion and English Society in the First World War' (Cambridge University PhD thesis, 1973)

Broadcast Sources

BBC, *The Big Question*, BBC1, 18 May 2014

Blakeway/Channel 4, *Edward VIII: The Plot to Topple a King*, Channel 4, 9 May 2012

Twenty-Twenty Television, *Canterbury Tales*, Channel 4, 19 September 1996

Index

Note: page numbers in *italics* refer to illustrations; those in **bold** to tables. References to footnotes are indicated by n. and the footnote number after the page reference.